Swing,
That
Modern Sound

Swing, *That* Modern Sound

Kenneth J. Bindas

University Press of Mississippi
Jackson

www.upress.state.ms.us

Copyright © 2001 by University Press of Mississippi

All rights reserved

Manufactured in the United States of America

09 08 07 06 05 04 03 02 01   4 3 2 1

∞

All Martin advertisements appear courtesy of The Martin
Company. All Buescher, Vincent Bach, Bundy, and Selmer
advertisements appear courtesy of The Selmer Company. The
illustration from "SWING—What Is It?" appears courtesy of
Musical America Archives. All Conn and King advertisements
appear courtesy of United Musical Instruments U.S.A., Inc. The
two cartoons entitled "For Musicians Only," the photo of Anita
O'Day, and the front cover of *Downbeat* appear courtesy of Maher
Publications, Inc.

Library of Congress Cataloging-in-Publication Data

Bindas, Kenneth J.

Swing, that modern sound / Kenneth J. Bindas.

p.   cm.

Includes bibliographical references and index.

ISBN 1-57806-382-5 (cloth : alk. paper)—ISBN 1-57806-383-3
(paper : alk. paper)

1. Swing (Music)—History and criticism.   I. Title.

ML3518.B56   2001

781.65'4—dc21   2001024068

British Library Cataloging-in-Publication Data available

To Jean-Anne

Contents

Acknowledgments

This project reflects the contributions of many people. When I first began reading and gathering research information and working out initial outlines and theoretical models, the late Edward Pessen, Kathy Ogren, and Burt Peretti provided direction and critical comment. Later, as the monograph began to take on a clearer patina, William Kenney provided musical and historical insight and critique. I presented several papers concerning this topic at a variety of conferences and research colloquia and the questions raised and the conversations afterward helped clarify specific aspects of the text and sharpened the argument. I received research grants, from the State University of West Georgia and Kent State University, which allowed me to do research at Rutgers University's Jazz Oral History Project collection and the Hogan Jazz Archive at Tulane University. At both of these facilities I was given open access, and Bruce Raeburn and Tad Hershorn helped locate materials and aided in the acquisition of much of the primary source material. Lori Lester took much of the raw data and entered it into SPSS (Statistical Package for Flexsocial Sciences) so that it might yield information not obvious at first glance. Seetha Srinivasan, University Press of Mississippi's director, provided regular encouragement; and the editorial staff has worked hard to guide this monograph to its publication. All of these folks, and many more, helped me find the voice to write this book. While I am responsible for its flaws, they deserve a share in any of its praises.

None of this could have been done without the assistance and support of my family. My sons, Zachary and Colin, have grown into fine young men during the duration of this project and have shown themselves to be coura- geous, loving, and helpful. My daughter, Savannah, was born near the final stages and has provided hours of laughter, joy, and love. Without the love of my partner, and our almost nightly discussions, this book might not have ever been finished. She gave me the support I needed to trust myself to finish what I had begun. It is to Jean-Anne Sutherland-Bindas that I dedicate this book.

Introduction

Swing music has experienced a revival of sorts over the last few years. Scan the entertainment sections of the nation's newspapers and see the advertisements for bands with swing-like names and clubs announcing swing dance lessons. Going to one of these events, you notice what these people—who obviously weren't around in the 1930s or 1940s—have appropriated regarding swing. They are not authentic swing bands, nor are the songs they play swing by musical definition. Yet the people in these clubs are stylistically connected to the swing era. Many of them dress in period clothes, use language from the era, and mimic dance styles such as the Lindy Hop.

It is their selection of symbols of the swing era that concerns this study. They are attracted to the style of swing, from the hard streamlines of their jackets, pants, and dresses, to the symmetry of their fedoras and pillboxes, to their fascination with the precision required of the dances they try to learn. Their appropriation of swing's more symbolic appearances does not suggest an inauthentic response, for during its era many saw the music as less modern and innovative than the jazz that came before it or the bebop that would follow. In fact, one of the characteristics of swing was its commercial appeal, which many critics, and even musicians, associated with a certain watering-down of the creative aspects of jazz, as though its success made it less authentic. When the kids screamed and swayed and called out for hot solos during a show, some found it too *popular*, as if by their visible and vocal demands *they* were running the show and not the bandleader or musician. When *Downbeat* published its *Yearbook of Swing* in 1939, the editors included a disclaimer, written by Fletcher Henderson, that reminded its readers that the salvation of the music would come with the help of a few informed persons. The popularity of swing would, with their assistance, lead to "the evolution of an even finer jazz." To some, swing was an interloper in the development of an American art music. The trade-off that came with popularity meant that the swing bands catered to the audiences who validated them and who, through their support, provided them with the economic means to create authentic swing music. Certainly, this music was different from the jazz that came before it and the bebop that would follow, but it was authentic because it fit its generation's needs and desires.[1]

This perception that swing was more style than substance is at the core of the swing phenomena and this monograph. How and why did swing achieve its audience? How did its success help to define and redefine its generation? What accounted for its ability to unify disparate peoples? How and why did it decline? The recent revival of swing seems only fitting, as the cultural and social context that will answer these questions identifies the major themes of the twentieth century and defines the lives of its people. These new swing kids are paying final homage to that *modern* century.

Swing, That Modern Sound explores the cultural context that allowed for this unique modern music to emerge and achieve popularity. The key ingredient to this process was its embrace of modernity. This meant more than just an attraction to machine-produced and machine-inspired goods, it suggested a new way of being for the American people. Oftentimes, our understandings of modernity, modernism, and modernization overlap one another, for each informs the other. Modernization is the most obvious manifestation of modern society, as it reflects the rise of industry and technology and the systemization of these processes. Modernism, as a cultural manifestation, rose up to challenge the loss of individuality resulting from modernization and challenged the ideals and practices of the generation that preceded it. It is within this lens of modernism that swing is most often placed, but only as a stage between early jazz and bebop. Modern artists in music, literature, and art explored innovation at the expense of the past while sampling liberally from the experiences of the past. Because of this, they were closely connected to the avant-garde ideal of experimentation.

These modern artists viewed with disdain the commercial aspects of their art and worked on the fringes of American society.[2]

Modernity is the acceptance, appropriation, and dissemination of things modern, both technological and cultural. In essence, modernity makes modernism and modernization part of the daily fabric, no longer strange to its people and fitting within the larger construct of the social mores under which the people live. As Henri Lefebvre reminds us, there are "two sides to the picture of Modernity": (1) the adaptation and use of technological ideals and principles which streamline social relations and create new understandings of progress and society and (2) the alienation and isolation which result from the increased efficiency of the society. These factors leave those within modern society accepting new ways of being while at the same time not quite understanding how and why they are changing. They accept change as a part of modern life, yet mourn the loss of the past; they utilize new means of technology to better participate in the modern society, while recognizing that using the technology means a degradation of their skills and an increased reliance on the machine. As a whole, there is a general increase in the "average cultural level," but the sheer volume of information available through the myriad of media makes acquisition nearly impossible. In essence, modern people are "neutralized" by the volume of information.[3]

During the Great Depression era it seemed as though most things were undergoing this modern shift. Economically, the United States moved away from the emphasis on production and toward consumption. Politically, the New Deal's activities signaled an acceptance of increased government planning on social as well as economic matters. Socially, the American people found that the experiences of the stock-market crash allowed them to come together for the common good, replacing age-old animosities and prejudices with collective action. This could be seen in union and civil rights activities during the era, as well as in the increased presence of women in key governmental positions. America also experienced a cultural revival, where things that identified the people and their history were held up as valid representations of this collective identity. Long dependent on European validation, Americans in the 1930s saw the emergence of an American culture—music, film, painting, dance, and photography—that would claim its independence and become a major industry for the country. All of these were constructed with the assistance of the ideology of modernity, for at the core of each was an attention to organization, efficiency, and mass acceptance based on the newness of its image. The depression era brought forth a new America, and swing came to exemplify these modern times.

Many have already examined swing from a variety of perspectives, for there are many ways to view swing. Some, such as George Simon and Gene Fernett, have placed it within their own personal context and describe the music and its musicians with little critical analysis.[4] The same can be said of the numerous swing autobiographies, which are helpful in their descriptions of the time and place of swing to those who were part of the music, but sometimes lack a critical and historical lens.[5] The most frequent analysis of swing has come from those able to understand its musical lineage. These studies, from people such as Martin Williams, Andre Hodier, Bob Yurochko, Gunther Schuller, Ted Gioia, Mark Gridley, and Scott DeVaux, place the swing moment within the larger musicological development of swing as an American art music and within the jazz canonical outline.[6] Others, such as Neil Leonard and Marshall Stearns, pioneered the study of jazz and swing history and have encouraged further investigations from James Lincoln Collier, Burton Peretti, David Stowe, Louis Erenberg, and others. These contributors to the swing discourse place the music within the larger historical context of American society from 1930 to 1950: Collier focusing on Benny Goodman's role and significance; Peretti, on the racial and urban dimensions of the creation of jazz leading to the swing moment; Stowe, on the similarities and connections to the ideologies of the New Deal and American business; and Erenberg focusing on the populist nature of this democratic youth movement.[7] Each of these in their own way contributes to our understanding of swing and has played a formative role in the creation of *Swing, That Modern Sound.* Each tells a story and describes a time and place in America's musical and social history from a unique perspective. This work draws upon these approaches but seeks to place the music within the larger cultural, historical context.

Swing, That Modern Sound examines the music and its time within its modernist connection to the Great Depression and World War II eras. Using Raymond Williams's theory that to understand intellectual or cultural products one must also understand the context in which the item was produced allows us to see swing from vantage points not necessarily connected to the music but to the social structures that encouraged its creation, acceptance, and popularity. *Swing, That Modern Sound* uses this "cultural formation" concept to explore the social and cultural concerns that identified and informed the music. This means less focus on the vividly descriptive time-place method and more on trying to locate swing within the cultural experience of America in the twentieth century. By casting a larger net over the social context of the swing era, this study will attempt to explore the consciousness that allowed for the rise, acceptance, and, finally, the demise of swing. To do this involves exploring the place of swing in regard to its generational qualities and its identity in relation to class, race, ethnicity, and gender, and the society in which these situations operated, namely, modern capitalism.[8]

To unpack these ideologies and identities, I had to first come to some understanding of those who created the music. This meant researching their stories, experiences, and values through interviews, biographies, autobiographies, and the collections of oral histories at Rutgers University (Jazz Oral History Project) and Tulane University (Hogan Jazz Archive). I hoped that by examining their words and understandings I could open up a new lens to discover what they experienced while growing up, what encouraged their move to music, and how that choice affected their understanding of themselves and their larger world. The limitations of utilizing this type of primary source information, and some of the problems associated with its ability to convey accurately historical information, have been discussed by several scholars, including Ronald J. Grele, Paul Thompson, Michael Frisch, Burton Peretti, and Douglas Henry Daniels. This monograph is less concerned about the accuracy of their historical memories regarding jazz, recording sessions, or daily activities and more concerned with memories of childhood in relation to work, family, and race. In discussing these, whether from an autobiography or an oral history, one gets a better sense of identity and emotion, and an authentic read on their place within the construct of their experience. In essence, oral histories can tell us better who they were and what experiences defined this consciousness.[9]

To place these into their cultural context, *Swing, That Modern Sound* uses modernity as one core lens, as it affected nearly all aspects of the American experience in the first half of the twentieth century. Modernity promised that old divisions would be replaced with new unity, that Victorian values would give way to modern ones, that superstition would stand aside for the science of possibilities—all to create a new, modern way of being. Swing, the product of modernism and modernization, became the embodiment of modernity as it accepted the pragmatic logic of technological innovation, broke and challenged its generational past, and experienced the alienation, isolation, and ambivalence of modern life. The formation and ideology of the bands reflected the "newness" of the music. Swing did more than simply remarket and whiten jazz for new and emerging markets, it created a new music that built its foundation on jazz and reflected its own authentic response to the society in which it existed. The white bands who popularized swing did so with organizations that reflected the diverse ethnicity and culture of America in the 1930s; they were full of Protestants, Jews, Catholics, Italians, Irish, Anglos, French, Slavs, Russians, Poles, and even a smattering of African Americans. The popularity of swing came through its utilization of radio and records; this meant fewer jobs, greater competition, and an increased reliance on technology and the marketplace. These swing experiences created the outline for the emergence of modern America.

To fully explore these complex modern relationships, *Swing, That Modern Sound* examines first the perception of swing within its generational cohort. Since the music was set in a specific time and place, chapter 1 begins by examining what characterized the generation of swing. The economic uncertainty of the 1930s had social and generational ramifications, as some young people delayed marriage plans and educational goals, or found themselves with a limited professional or occupational future. Within this crisis of diminished opportunities came a renewed sense of Americanism. The New Deal played an active part in this reinvention process, whether it be through the CCC (Civilian Conservation Corps), TVA (Tennessee Valley Authority), WPA (Works Progressive Administration), Social Security, or the Wagner Act. Young people in search of meaning called out for cultural manifestations that spoke to and for them. They understood their role in the new and changing world and celebrated those things that separated them from their elders. Swing became one such generational identification. Young people saw in the swing bands representatives of their neighborhoods, with bands made up of people named Rollini, James, Arshawski, Fazola, Goodman, Basie, or Wilson. The audiences reacted to the music not as an extension of jazz—it did not matter that Duke Ellington or others had em-

ployed the big band style before Goodman—but as music for their generation.

The appropriation of the music by this generational cohort is as much a
part of their identity as their lived experiences. In order to understand why
they saw the music as part of their consciousness we need to see what social
and cultural ideologies were informing their choices. In chapter 2, swing as
the musical extension of modernity—where the machine becomes both a
means of production and an organizational ideal—is explored. Swing promoters, bandleaders, and their record companies utilized modern methods
to reach and sell to audiences, to create systems to maximize studio time
and production, to streamline distribution, and to create market tests to
better determine future sales. Radio played a major role in this process, both
as a disseminator and controller of swing. The modern approach also aided
the reemergence of the record and phonograph industries, stimulating sales
in record and appliance stores and affecting the production of other, more
raw material–based industries. Also, since the musicians themselves became
celebrities, many of their younger fans sought to dress, talk, or act like their
musical heroes.

Magazines, advertisements, and Hollywood catered to this swing generation. As businesses began to advertise their wares in the magazines, they
used techniques designed to appeal to the young swing enthusiast, tapping
into their cultural understanding of modernity. Chapter 3 examines many
of the ads for musical instruments and their employment of modern symbols
and language to encourage consumption. Trumpets and trombones flying
through the air, with copy emphasizing the machine precision and perfect
lines, appealed to young and emerging musicians. Ads sometimes included
an endorsement from the likes of Goodman, Webb, Dorsey, and many others. All of the industries that benefited from swing wanted the potential
consumer to know that the most modern sounds, clothing, instruments,
phonographs, hats, or shoes were available to them. The advertising stressed
the need for the consumer to keep in tune with the times by favoring their
business, shop, or product. The text of the ads alluded to the better wages
and improved lifestyle that came with playing the right instrument, wearing
the right clothes, or having the right demeanor.

Chapters 1 through 3 construct the cultural perception of swing by set-
ting it in its time and place. To better understand the social construction,

or what factors informed this perception, an investigation into the lived experiences of those who made the music is necessary. The cohort who came of age during this time period, roughly those born between 1905 and 1920, had grown up watching their parents toil in factories or offices in the often cutthroat marketplace. Many swing fans, like the musicians, grew up in situations broadly labeled "working class," and chapter 4 examines class identification among the musicians and discusses what effect it had on their career choices and the societal acceptance of their music. For the musicians and their fans, swing became both a reward and an escape. The musicians found they could make a good living doing what they enjoyed, and the fans saw the music as an authentic means of escape from their work or life situations.

Working-class membership in America was made up of a variety of ethnicities, racial groups, and both genders. So, too, was swing. Chapter 5 analyzes the intersection of ethnicity, race, and gender among the musicians to better understand how they oftentimes negotiated generational fear and racism in order to create swing. Shortly after Goodman was crowned King of Swing (fronting a band made up of a variety of ethnicities), he integrated his band by forming a trio with Teddy Wilson, later adding Lionel Hampton. By 1937 they were full-fledged members of the band, and soon other bandleaders added black members to their orchestras. By 1940 it was not that unusual to see whites and blacks playing either on the same stage or within the same band. African American musicians traveling with white bands oftentimes stayed in separate hotels and, in the South, faced constant hostility. But swing did not turn from its heritage and recognized the important contributions that African Americans made to the music. Swing tried to open the forum to all who could play, as many of the musicians believed that color mattered less than one's ability to play. Gender, however, did matter, as women found it difficult to gain entrance into the musician's world. Many found it easier to perform in all-women bands, such as those led by Rita Rio or Ina Hutton or the International Sweethearts of Rhythm (even though these were formed or managed by men). Occasionally, someone such as Mary Lou Williams or Lil Hardin Armstrong would play with the male bands, and during World War II several bands hired women instrumentalists. Generally, women musicians operated in an industry and society unwilling to accept them as equals.

The dynamic relationships—ideology, economics, politics, technology, ethnicity, race, gender, and class—that allowed swing to resonate within its generation and create its cultural understanding were organic. The era that gave birth to swing was informed by specific social and cultural identities which by the mid- to late 1940s had begun to change. The combined effect of World War II and the emerging cold war sounded the end of the era, and chapter 6 makes plain the reasons for this decline. Problems within the American Federation of Musicians and the industry pitted workers against each other, and with the challenge of new popular musics and technologies, swing found itself hard pressed to remain relevant. By the latter part of the 1940s its sound was no longer uniquely identified as the music of the generation but was part of a larger and more competitive industry vying to capture the American consumer. Eventually, swing lost out to both country and rock and roll, both of which owe a great debt to the swing phenomenon.

Taken separately, each of these chapters reveals aspects of a social and cultural moment in America's modern history. Combining them exposes the complex yet simple patterns of the Great Depression and World War II eras, where the ideals of modernity, reform, and capitalism were employed to create a new vision of the American dream. In the new America, which would be tested during World War II and defined by the ideals of the cold war consensus, the country would appear open to a wider variety of peoples and cultures, albeit restricted by the fear of others. The swing generation and the musicians who were part of that world help us to understand the impact and effect of modernity on America's history and provide an excellent window into the exploration of this era of transition. Swing as music did not have the lasting power to continue in the postwar, for reasons that include commerce and ideology, but it did identify and inform a generation of people attempting to survive the worst crises in the nation's history while trying to redefine the ideals of America. The swing generation is the introduction of modern America.

Swing,
That
Modern Sound

The Swing Generation

What Is Swing and How Is It the Music of Its Era?

During the spring and summer of 1935, popular memory has told us, swing was born when Benny Goodman and his band won the approval of the audience at the Palomar Ballroom in Los Angeles after a grueling tour that began in New York City. The band's performances in Pittsburgh and Milwaukee met with lukewarm audience response and continued through Denver, Salt Lake City, and San Francisco. The tour had not gone well and the Goodman band found itself back against the wall in Los Angeles for an extended gig at the Palomar. As the band set up to play in this venue, with its noisy food and bar service and large dance floor, they worried that this might be their last performance together. The show began with the band playing its more "soft," standard songs with little reaction from the crowd. Recognizing he had little to lose, Goodman decided to take some musical risks. He pulled out Fletcher Henderson's best arrangements and decided that since it might be their "last night together" they would play the "hard" jazz songs, or as Helen Ward called them, "killer dillers." The result was pandemonium and acceptance, and, as Marshall Stearns has written, "the Swing Era was born on the night of 21 August, 1935."[1]

After their success in Los Angeles the band began its triumphant return

3

to the East, stopping off for several months to play in Chicago's Congress Room. They finally arrived in New York City as popular phenoms with an extended gig in the Hotel Pennsylvania's Madhattan Room. Success had seemingly come overnight for Goodman's swing band.[2]

After Goodman's breakthrough, the market opened up for many other artists who had been playing in a similar style for some time, as well as for musicians playing in other bands. The popularity and success of Goodman meant that many of these musicians could leave their old jobs and join or form swing bands. Included were now familiar names such as Basie, Ellington, Shaw, the Dorseys, Henderson, Webb, Hines, Lunceford, Miller, and others. Perhaps the influence this new music had over the young but seasoned vaudevillian Buddy Rich can help explain its appeal. Rich had worked as a novelty drummer in vaudeville since he was eighteen months old, but by 1935 he was caught up in the decline of that once popular art form. He wanted to become a jazz drummer, but his father thought playing in a band would be a waste of the teenager's talent. However, Rich, like many of the nation's youth, found something appealing in the sounds of swing and, with Goodman's success and the subsequent outpouring of swing bands in 1936, became a committed swing kid. Rich believed his father was still "living in the past."[3]

If 1935 saw the birth of swing, then it was Goodman's three-week stay at the Paramount in New York City in March 1937 that solidified its popularity. Throngs of young people waited hours to see the Goodman band, which played five shows a day beginning at 10:30 A.M. and ending about 10:30 P.M. After the evening shows the band raced to the Madhattan Room, where they played until 2:30 A.M. In between, they found time for recording and radio work. Popularity meant work, but it also meant money. The stint at the Paramount grossed nearly $50,000 a week, and the publicity generated by these crowds and the media covering the events made swing not only popular, but also viable and profitable.[4]

Indeed, the entire entertainment industry reaped the rewards of Goodman's success. The 1929 economic collapse had leveled the recording industry; sales had fallen by 39 percent in 1930 from the $75.1 million of a year earlier. Profits continued to slide, and by 1932 the industry tallied only $11 million in profit. Even though Franklin Roosevelt's election and early administration brought a temporary increase in sales to the beleaguered industry, afterward sales continued to plummet until Goodman's 1935 breakthrough.

There had been attempts previous to Goodman to stimulate record sales. RCA Victor, for example, beginning in 1934, introduced a low-price record player which attached to existing radio units to give better sound. Other phonograph companies followed suit with the hope that these devices would become popular with the younger record buyers and stimulate sales. But the innovation had little effect until swing began to attract large audiences, especially in the 40 percent youth market. Sales skyrocketed to $30 million in 1936, nearly seven times the 1932 level. Swing made an immediate impact in the music business: sales in the coin-machine, or jukebox, trade increased by 25 percent by 1937 and by 1940 grew to a $20 million a year industry with over one hundred thousand employees; RCA Victor, Goodman's label, experienced a 300 percent sales increase from 1935 through 1936; and Andy Kirk's song *The Real Thing* suddenly took off, selling over one hundred thousand copies. The industry saw the light. Swing-produced profits meant that by 1937 and 1938 most record companies were boasting profits that recalled the halcyon days of 1929. By 1939 swing made up 85 percent of all record sales, and the dance-band business boasted profits of $90 million to $100 million and was employing between thirty thousand and forty thousand musicians.[5]

Goodman and swing's influence also had a dramatic impact in terms of employment. The *International Musician*, the periodical of the American Federation of Musicians, told its membership that the most significant aspect of swing was its ability to create and sustain jobs. The union reported 1936 to be the best year for musicians since 1927, as employment increased nearly 30 percent. In early 1938, *Downbeat* added to this optimistic outlook by reporting that in 1937 over four hundred thousand full or part-time swing musicians brought in more than $80 million through live shows. Furthermore, the growing profitability of the music and the increased "use of the word Swing as a 'catch phrase,'" meant that booking agencies like the Music Corporation of America and Rockwell-O'Keefe made greater profits. The addition of these larger agencies meant increased opportunities for the bands, as their proven track record to bring in crowds and cash made them viable and attractive promotional items.[6]

Benny Goodman and his band obviously struck a popular chord with their generation. But was he the father of swing, or was this King of Swing, as he came to be known, a marketing genius? Certainly the 1935–1939 Goodman band was a talented swing band, but other bands, such as Duke Ellington's or Benny Moden's, had been as gifted. The Goodman success story, and by extension the success of the entire swing movement, was largely one of timing. Much like a later king of popular music—Elvis Presley—Goodman's success was the result of being in the right place at the right time as much as it was the result of any new musical innovation or revolutionary performance technique. What his band played in 1935 had been played for some time and, perhaps, better.

Goodman enjoyed some advantages when he entered the Palomar Ballroom. He already had a record contract, first with Columbia and later with Victor. He was an excellent manager of talent, and there were few competitors—except for the Casa Loma Orchestra—in the swing marketplace in 1935. Goodman's biographer James Lincoln Collier also credits Helen Ward's presence as a salient feature of the band. The talented and attractive singer appealed to the major market of early swing high school and college-aged males. The female singer quickly became a staple ingredient for any band, and magazines such as *Downbeat* and *Metronome* featured them in cheesecake photos for the same reason. One also has to consider Goodman's timing, as his success came during a period of renewed optimism regarding the depression and America. One barometer of this change, according to *Metronome*, was "that skirts have been inching up from the ground to a spot approximating the knees." David Stowe's *Swing Changes* agrees, arguing that much of swing's appeal came from its upbeat tempo, which he links to general improvements in the economy and outlook due in large measure to FDR's New Deal agenda. Stowe emphasizes the importance of the development during this period of a musical elite, whose members ranged from college students at Ivy League schools to already established music critics and who used their positions to promote the new sounds and attach to swing the positivistic values connected with the New Deal.[7]

Another advantage Goodman held was his weekly "Let's Dance" radio broadcast. Although the show only ran until early May 1936, it was carried by fifty-three stations across the country and was featured during prime-time hours in the West. Many in the Palomar's audience had already heard of the band from the radio (although this does not explain why Goodman failed to draw crowds in Denver, Salt Lake City, or San Francisco). The sponsor of the program, the National Biscuit Company's Ritz Cracker, had paid for Goodman to secure new and hopefully popular arrangements, many of which came from Fletcher Henderson, who had used them with his own band. [8]

The "Let's Dance" program only lasted twenty-six weeks and did not make the Goodman band, but it did help them to develop an early following. The radio's potential to give mass exposure to relatively unknown singers, musicians, or bands, compared with pre-radio days when the audience was determined by the size in the hall that night, meant that two hours of radio time once a week reached millions of potential fans. Thus, the time provided by the band and money advanced by the sponsor paid off, as many young people, Collier points out, "saw Swing as *their* music, something that was anti-establishment." This corresponds to the trend during the first fifty years of the twentieth century, a trend that saw the rise and empowerment of a distinct social, cultural, and economic force called youth. The rise of the middle class and the systemization of industry and labor in the late nineteenth and early twentieth centuries helped to develop institutions of youth with their own culture, mores, and consumer goods. During the 1920s, many American young people saw themselves as the modern embodiment of the *now* and worked to transform their society to fit their needs. Different than the identity of their elders, this new youth identity carried over into the swing generation, as young people continued to support cultural institutions that fit their needs.[9]

During the 1930s, young people identified swing within the context of their generational identity. For example, when in early 1936 the editors of *Metronome* had difficulties defining swing, they were overwhelmed with letters from young fans upset at the magazine's lack of understanding. One fan wrote that he was confused by the article's reliance on traditional musical characteristics and offered up his own definition: "SWING IS THE SPONTANEOUS INDIVIDUAL INTERPRETATION OF MODERN DANCE MUSIC." This young man from Albany, Georgia, correctly placed swing within the context of his generation. By 1936, 65 percent of the nation's young people were more likely to be in high school near their peers than in the workplace around an older cohort, and thus they were more likely to see themselves as a separate social grouping. In the midst of the Great Depression, when nearly four million people between the ages of sixteen and twenty-four faced an uncertain future, many young people saw in swing the excitement and sense of immediacy that their lives demanded. The size and relative unity of the group—which made them an important subculture—made them attractive to advertisers and merchandisers, who targeted this group dubbed teenagers.[10]

The young people of the era defined the music in their terms. This did not mean trying to create a clear musicological definition, which was antithetical to their understanding of swing. They loved the music because it was *their* music, played for *their* enjoyment, and as one young woman who wrote to the *New York Times* in 1939 explained, "Swing is the tempo of our time." These young people knew little about its jazz legacy but enjoyed swing because it was fast paced, new, and one of the few things they could call their own. The writer of the "Name Bands" column for the *International Musician* wrote that swing music was "beyond his parents' wildest dreams" and that no previous generation had accepted the "hand-me-down" from its predecessor. "Swing stands for their GREAT DESIRE," he continued, and "expresses all things, releases energy, stirs emotion," but defies definition. [11]

This generational excitement resonated with the musicians, as the enthusiasm of the fans allowed them the freedom to create something new to satisfy the young people's demand. Audiences, Artie Shaw explained, demanded that bands play music for dancing in order to create a mood or "accompanying turmoil" that went with the music. Don Albert remembers that bands used their "killer dillers" to get the audience going, as the leader and musicians designed the song to "knock the audience out" and get them into the swing. Harry "Sweets" Edison concurs, saying that "the main objective of playing music back then was to make people happy."[12]

Others saw in the young people's passion for swing an opportunity to broaden their musical understanding and education. Floyd Hart, a high school music teacher in West Chester, Pennsylvania, convinced the local school board to offer a music appreciation course in modern dance music featuring swing. He decided that since his students "spen[t] so much time listening to it, [the teachers] might as well try to teach them what's good." This course introduced the students to the different elements that made up swing and showed them how to "correctly" analyze a song. Lilla Belle Pitts told other music teachers at the Music Educators National Conference to seize the opportunity and use swing to encourage students to play. She argued that "this [was] music made by the young for the young" and teachers had an obligation to try and accept it. Pitts labeled the music vital, energetic, and, like youth, immature. The music matched her students "inside and out." A student told her that he enjoyed the music because "we can go to town with a Swing band . . . symphony is for grownups." Pitts concluded by asking the educators to make an attempt to reach the students through their love for swing and to transform their appreciation for this music into other music.[13]

The editors of the *Etude*, the bastion of cultivated music educators, reluctantly endorsed a policy of using swing and popular music to reach potential students in 1942. When Dr. Thomas Tapper advised music teachers to use popular music in the classroom, he suggested they use the better songs, ones that were "clean" and "wholesome." His and the journal's advocacy did not mean that they accepted this music, but they saw it as a stepping-stone to better things. Giving proper instruction and using swing as a hook would help prove that "if you help children a little, the trivial will disappear from their interest." Further, if given the right conditions, there is "an inherent quality of fair if not good taste in most children who care enough about music to study it." Benny Goodman agreed and boasted a bit unrealistically that any child who learned how to play swing music would have little difficulty mastering classical music. The technical demands were the same, the King of Swing believed, and because of the popularity of swing with the adolescents, it could be used to introduce them to more complex musical training. In fact, by the late 1930s several swing arrangers and composers were applying classical techniques to their music charts. Record companies also saw a connection, as 70 percent of those who purchased swing records also bought classical music.[14]

Other adults hoped swing could be a positive force for the nation. J. F. Brown, professor of psychology at the University of Kansas, wrote, in his textbook *The Psychodynamics of Abnormal Behavior*, that because swing favored positive emotions like love and affection and rarely invoked violence, there was little to fear in the music. The *Musician*'s Alvin Levin saw the music as harmless and nothing more than the "emotional expression of those primal forces of human life that are intended to embody concepts of beauty."[15]

As the swing generation demanded more from the music, manufacturers of musical instruments and some musicians began marketing guidebooks for the budding player. Advertisements in magazines such as *Metronome*, *Downbeat*, *Swing-Out*, and a host of others featured items including Jimmy Dorsey's Saxophone Method, Bunny Berigan Modern Trumpet Studies, Bud Freeman Studies and Improvisation for Saxophone, and the Alvino Rey Modern Guitar Method to encourage the novice toward "The Right Road to Stardom!"[16]

There were many more people, especially those not of the swing generation, who were less excited by the young people's devotion to the music. Some agreed with *Vogue*'s Wilder Hobson, who identified the music as both the most recent phenom and one that "is not a precious form of art." Professor Harry D. Gideone, head of the Economics and Social Science Department, told the students at Barnard College in New York City that because of increased specialization and the consumer market, social values had eroded to the point where "someone will rise from commercialized entertainment or commercialized politics . . . to give us emotional outlets in mass demonstration and other ways." He pointed to the popularity of this new music as one such danger, saying, "Swing is musical Hitlerism." *Metronome* criticized a *New York Times* article, written by Gama Gilbert, that described the music as immoral. Gilbert associated the rise of "emotional unbalance, sexual excess, and even rape" with the popularity of swing and suggested that the use of marijuana was widespread among the musicians, who needed "artificial stimulus" in order to perform. *Metronome* attacked Gilbert for speaking to adults who know little about the music and for suggesting that if young people really wanted to swing, they had to "smoke marijuana."[17]

Ultimately, attacks of these types had little effect other than to crystallize the generational differences between the fans of the music and the adults who seemed shocked by it. One fan, in an attempt to help calm adult fears of swing, inadvertently helped to heighten them by suggesting that "swing [was] a new form of an eroticism as old as sex itself." Many adults were well aware of swing's erotic nature and saw it as part of the debasement of American society. Often using language similar to that used to criticize jazz during the 1920s, some feared that the primitivism of the music would lead to the general decline of American society. Those who feared the base nature of the music worried because they felt that neither the musician nor the listener understood the erotic road they were taking but were being led by the hypnotic and exciting sounds. Composer Virgil Thomson, for example, argued that underneath the "mannerism of style" that defined swing was a complex method and that most popular musicians were unaware of it or did not understand how it operated in their compositions. Consequently, he suggested that "swing music rarely has any literal swing in it. Certainly nothing like the Viennese waltz music has." He compared the "rhythmic measure-unit" beat of swing to the "music of the march, the dance, the religious or secular orgy." He described swing's effect on its audience: "Notice the high degree of intellectual and nervous excitement present in any swing-audience. The listeners do not close their eyes and sink into emotional or subjective states. They sit up straight, their eyes flash, they applaud the licks. They occasionally jerk on the absent down-beat, but on the whole they seem to be enjoying one of those states of nervous and muscular equilibrium that render impossible rapid intellection."[18]

The critical attacks leveled against swing were part of a larger debate dominating 1930s musical culture. With the rise and influence of the radio and popular music, many teachers, musicians, and leaders in the field were concerned that appreciation for cultivated music would erode. The popular sounds coming from the radio were musically simple and did not reflect the artistic standards set by those who controlled most of the musical associations, clubs, and orchestras. The debate over the relative musical merits of swing and its effects on children relate to this ongoing struggle within the musical ranks over the similarities and differences between cultivated and vernacular music. The same year that swing became popular the Works Progress Administration (WPA) created the Federal Music Project (FMP) to assist unemployed musicians. The director of the project, Dr. Nicolai Sokoloff, shaped the work-relief effort to the benefit of cultivated musicians over the popular because he found little value in popular music. Musicians who performed with the FMP orchestras, symphonies, and operas dominated the project payrolls, while the popular musician, unable to pass the rigorous, classical-based entrance examination, found little help from this agency. The American Federation of Musicians regularly challenged the direction of the project, but Sokoloff was like those teachers who saw little of value in swing, labeling anything popular as simple, common, and with little cultural value.[19]

To the swing generation, these critics missed the point. As Alvin Levin argued in *Musician* magazine in 1939, "as long as they remain music critics they will never understand the phenomenon of Swing music." Irving Kolodin, an early advocate of swing music, wrote in a 1939 *Parents* magazine article that the young people's love of the music was linked to the time-honored American ideal of individualism: "each listener enjoys the experience in his individual way, without concern for what the fellow in the next seat or across the aisle may be thinking." Kolodin scoffed at those who feared swing might lead to mind control or over eroticism, pointing out that the young people simply wanted to have a good time. What critics labeled as sexually immoral in the dances of the youth, Kolodin saw as "an uninhibited response to the impulse of the music, a participation in the performance . . . [and] what is more normal than a concerted response to music as rhythmic as swing?" He did suggest that the music lends itself to "exhibitionists" and "smart-alecks," but on the whole most of the young fans handled themselves with decorum and respect for others. He ended by quoting Benny Goodman: "They're only kids, and they want to blow off steam . . . and music like this gives them a chance to work it off in a healthful and perfectly natural way."[20]

To the generation that enjoyed the spirited sounds of swing, there was nothing to fear except those who attacked their music. During the 1930s, when unemployment and the problems of the economic crisis were daily issues, as were labor strife, a growing international conflict, and the specter of Soviet infiltration, many adults worried that the nation's youth might be taken in by a potentially detrimental music. The swing generation pointed out that *their* music just allowed them to have a little fun. What many adults feared was the difference in the music as compared to the sounds they grew up listening to; but, the swing generation reasoned, in many ways it was the same. They felt that swing, like the popular music crazes of the older generations, was a safe way for the nation's youth to celebrate its uniqueness and individualism and have a good time—nothing more, nothing less.[21]

Complicating the problem for the swing generation was the lack of a clear definition about what made something swing. Musicians, critics, and commentators were hard pressed to come up with a satisfactory definition, largely because of their need to justify swing as a musical and not a cultural phenomenon. The situation has not improved since 1935, as scholars, critics, and the musicians themselves still try to pin down a musical definition for swing. Some, like Gary Tomlinson, believe that to define swing one must first analyze the racial complexities within the definitional process of jazz. He argues that the creation of the "canon" regarding the characteristics of jazz oftentimes occurs without "serious regard for the contexts in which" the music was created or received. As a result, a "strategy for exclusion" has developed within jazz studies, establishing "walls" between what the critics believe to be true jazz and other forms of jazz-like music. Tomlinson details how four popular jazz curriculum texts perpetuate this tendency of exclusion by relying on many of the same jazz examples (taken from Martin Williams's *Smithsonian Collection of Classic Jazz*) and aurally categorizing the music in order to place the sound into a proper jazz framework. This process implies that the musical notes have meaning outside of the cultural processes in which they operate, and this "will always distance it from the complex and largely extramusical negotiations [which] . . . will always privilege European bourgeois myths of aesthetic transcendency, artistic purity untouched by function and context, and the elite status of artistic expression."[22]

To define swing, then and now, one must confront not only its musicological lineage, but also the social and cultural conditions of the people who created the sound, those who received or consumed it, and the market forces that promoted and profited from its popularity. This type of analysis is at the core of this study, but also makes the creation of a one line or paragraph definition of swing impossible. This was also the case during the peak of swing's popularity, allowing those who disliked the music to attack it as simply a fad to distract the nation's youth. Even the musicians were unable to agree on what was swing. Some saw it as musically similar to jazz, while others suggested swing had a more modern sound. Roy Eldridge said that as "the music advanced" so did the name. Zutty Singleton also saw swing as "just a modern term to denote jazz." But others, such as Jimmy Dorsey, saw swing within the generational framework, saying that "Jazz . . . means that old stuff," while swing was "modern" and organized.[23]

The most common means used during the swing era to define the music placed it into some historical musical context, which only reinforced its faddish interpretation. Replaying a now familiar story, many of those trying to define swing detailed how jazz began in New Orleans at the turn of the century and then moved up the Mississippi to Chicago where it became popular as jazz.[24] During the 1920s, jazz was introduced to a variety of new audiences and by the early 1930s it had emerged as a mature musical form. This new jazz featured "free, inspired improvisation," where the talents of individual performers were the "life-blood." This was the foundation of swing. Using this as background, critics such as Ethan A. Secor of the *Etude* were able to define swing as a "combination of melody and accompaniment" using staccato and syncopation to create the "swing tempo." The musicians had to play the song with "machine-like precision," he wrote, in order to convert "practically all passages of the eighth notes, or dotted eighths and sixteenths, into the generally accepted interpretation of the eighth note triplet with an eighth rest in the middle." After using more technical language to define swing, he added that the popular musician rarely knew "what he [was] doing."[25]

Many critics agreed with Secor's interpretation—namely, that the musicians themselves did not understand what it was they were playing, at least in musical terms. One's ability to swing, many felt, was not a learned skill, but one that came naturally. As James Poling reported in *Esquire* in 1936, "no musician, no matter how accomplished technically, can play hot unless it is in him, unless it is in his blood, his heart, his soul." According to another critic, even the audience had to "yield to [swing's] rather primitive moods and emotions." Sam Rowland went so far as to say that "unless you permit your emotions to run rampant and abandon your dignity" the ability to understand swing is impossible.[26]

Using Tomlinson's model, the context of these sophisticated definitions reveals an implied racism from many of the critics and within the larger societal framework. While able to acknowledge African American contributions to modern music, especially jazz and swing, most people were unwilling to allow these cultural creations the same level of sophistication reserved for European-based "serious" music and "real" composition. They saw in the simplicity of swing ties to African American primitivism, which while interesting was not considered art. American composer Elliott Carter, for example, scoffed at those who said that jazz and swing might represent the future of American music. He implied that one could take the music out of the jungle, but not the jungle out of the music. "Negroes," he wrote, "have always been a race of entertainers . . . [whose] tradition is outside that of serious music." Writing a review of the 1938 swing concert at Carnegie Hall, Carter suggested that the music was like a fish out of its water: "swing tends to lose its character and take on another." Carter was not alone in this assessment. The president of the Bach Society of New Jersey asked the Federal Communications Commission in 1938 to prohibit swing bands from playing European "classics," as the bands tended to destroy their beauty "by the savage slurring of the saxophones and the jungle discords of the clarinets." Joseph Rubba, in an attempt to describe were swing came from, wrote of "savages of South Sea Islands . . . the Dark Continent" and the streets of Harlem.[27]

Raymond Wheelock went even further, challenging the very nature of African American culture. He dismissed the "Afro-Negroid" explanation for jazz and argued that the American Negro had no African connection and had simply appropriated "European tonality, melodic sequence, and harmony." He saw the true source of jazz and swing in the "the world's most perfect specimens of mind and body," the Native Americans. African Americans only mimicked, as they had European tradition, the American Indian dance tradition to create jazz and swing. To his mind this theory saved swing, for now the music was connected to the great American folk music tradition, not a "cultural degeneration."[28]

Given this context, figure 1.1 helps to illustrate the cultural confusion held by many critics of swing music. Note the negative racial connotations of the figures in the panel labeled "When Jazz Was Jazz," when, as happy Sambos, they play a music they certainly did not understand, as evidenced by the red pepper being poured over the notes. Their appearance is suggestive of the minstrel darkie happily performing music for the entertainment of the white audience. In the next two panels these black jazz musicians go to Europe, where the music is exposed to more serious musical scrutiny and appropriated into sweet, orchestra jazz. In the last panel the transformation of the music has been completed. The "real" jazz played by those in panel one has now joined with the best elements of European harmonic discipline and reemerged as swing. The musicians are now white and, by association, safe. The African American inspired beat remains, but is tempered and civilized by European based musical sensibilities. The text of the article that appears with the illustrations reinforces this notion, suggesting that only

Fig. 1.1. Marvin W. Strate, "SWING—What Is It: The Jazz Prodigal's Return," *Musical America* 56 (May 25, 1936): 6–7. Drawings by George Hager.

when "men with a higher order of musicianship were attracted" to jazz did it begin to acquire widespread popularity. Before this, jazz had "crept out of New Orleans" and moved up to Chicago, where the musicians "simply played as they felt." This explanation had become so accepted into the mythology of jazz and swing that by the 1950s it became the basis for Hollywood scripts. As Krin Gabbard has shown, while "blacks play jazz more 'naturally,'" according to the film formula of the fifties, "it is the 'nature' of white musicians to surpass them" by transforming the music into a much more consumable product.[29]

There was a strong tendency therefore to view swing only as an interesting musical extension of jazz. This came as much from the cultivated music critics as it did from many of swing's earliest supporters. From the very beginning, critics such as Marshall Stearns, Milton Gabler, John Hammond, Ali Haggin, Otis Ferguson, George Simon, Barry Ulanov, Leonard Feather, and many more devoted themselves to the music. Some, including Hammond, were able to influence performers like Goodman, Basie, and Holiday, while others, including Gabler, Simon, and Ulanov, influenced consumers by writing reviews and selecting the best records. As longtime fans of jazz, these critics—and many more found in fanzines like *Metronome*, *Swing-Out*, *Downbeat*, or in popular news magazines like *Time* and *Newsweek*, or even in the *New Republic*, the *Nation*, and the *Daily Worker*—defined swing as an art form derived from jazz and were the first to help create what Tomlinson labels the exclusionary "canon."[30]

Eric Hobsbawn, writing under the pseudonym Francis Newton in the late 1950s, reveals other reasons for the canonization of jazz over swing music. Jazz, which he called a "folkmusic," was connected to the entirety of popular entertainment by its appeal to fantasy and protest. During the 1920s, jazz appealed to many because of its lack of convention, its implied protest and spontaneity. Much of what was jazz was popularized by either its incorporation into existing popular music or as a "separate art, appreciated by special groups of people." This stage of jazz began to lose its folk origins under the increased weight of urbanization (which changed the nature of the audience) and commercialization. However, the musicians retained their oppositional stance by their reliance on improvisation. All of this changed with the advent of swing in 1935, when, Hobsbawn argues, the "specialized jazz-lovers themselves became a commercial public" and this new creation adopted almost entirely the "instrumental techniques and arrangements" of earlier black jazz, especially that of Fletcher Henderson and Don Redman. Once swing became popular, the purveyors of commercial music "fell over themselves" to sell this popular jazz.[31]

Hobsbawn's argument that swing was simply created out of the more popular elements of the true art form jazz was not unique. Even before the editors of the *Musician* raised a similar point in 1939, many felt that the defining characteristic of swing was a good "press-agent." They questioned the originality of swing and pointed out that its popularity and lack of definition "may only go to prove that to change the label and get an original press-agent is the next best thing to creating an original product—or it may even be a better way." Some musicians also saw the difficulties between what they thought was jazz and swing. Mario Bauza, who played in Duke Ellington's band, called swing a "big promotion . . . a gimmick" to popularize Benny Goodman. Swing music, Bauza said, was "the same music we've been playing all along."[32]

Few, however, did as Tomlinson suggested and tried to locate the music within the cultural context which identified it, and more often than not presented the audience as passive consumers in the process. Thus they ignored the audience's ability to participate in the creation of the music and implied that the people were receptacles to whatever the culture industry offered them. To suggest that the music as notes was not part of a more complex cultural negotiation ignores both the market factors and the musicians.[33]

To define swing, therefore, is to confront an era, 1935 to 1947, and its social environment. The development of the music as a musical and generational moment has been forced to labor under its own mythology, from when it began to what defines it, and thus has blurred its social impact and cultural meaning. Whether Goodman is the King of Swing is less important than what factors allowed for the creation of this hierarchical lineage and what social meanings it may constitute. To separate the different bands who were all part of the swing revolution into good, better, and best musical categories defies their place within the consciousness of the people who both created and consumed the music. Jazz and swing were musically one in the same item, yet the generational factors that helped to create each of them made them very different and unique cultural products. Placing the music's creation within the context of its cultural creation leads to several avenues of exploration. What factors contributed to swing's popularity? What influence did the marketplace play in this process? What effect did class, race, gender, and ethnicity have in the creation and acceptance of the music? And finally, how did these factors, which operated outside the notes of the music, help us to better understand swing's place within the history of American society from 1935 to 1947? For the swing generation these factors certainly played a large role in their appropriation of swing as their music, as it became their generational symbol of unity and strength in an era where they faced the challenges of the marketplace, race, ethnicity, gender, and class. A new modern era was dawning, and these swing kids were going to be the ones defining the future. The cultural study of their generation will allow us to better understand the decisions that they made after 1945 and will better help us to understand our present historical situation.

Machine-Age Music

The Connection of Swing to Modernity

Understanding the generation that appropriated swing helps to broaden our view of the music outside of its jazz legacy. Perhaps swing's popularity and acceptance serve as an example of the appropriation of an avant-garde, or at least oppositional, culture by the dominant society. The whole story of the naming and defining of swing, according to Marshall Stearns, signifies the replacement of the negative, racial stereotype of jazz with the more acceptable moniker.[1] The last chapter focused on swing's generational qualities and the complexities of its defining characteristics in order to set in time and place the cultural product of swing. Part of establishing this time frame or consciousness is examining the language or ideology that the generation employed. What were their symbols? Ideals? Attitudes? And from where did they derive and become authentic?

To understand the voice of the era forces us to examine the modern means through which the music was created, disseminated, and accepted. Technological innovations such as the radio and phonograph, and new business practices that mirrored these modern means of production, not only helped to expand the potential audience and increase sales and profits, but changed the nature of the sound and legitimized modernity for the swing generation.

Roughly covering the period from about World War I until after World War II, the machine age in America symbolized the apotheosis of modernity. The modern mind-set held that through the unification of science and industry any problem could be solved using precision and logic. The machine and what it represented—efficiency, logic, and a better life for all— became not only an object, but a process and symbol for the modern age.[2] The production of time-saving consumer items like the vacuum cleaner, toaster, and electric iron sought to eliminate the drudgery of housework and free the individual to pursue other things. Perhaps the most significant of these new machines was the automobile, which, aside from its utility for the workingman, became a symbol of freedom and individuality.

It seemed as though man and machine working together could accomplish any goal. Representations of this unification were found in the geometric patterns of toasters and flatware, the machine purity captured by photographers, the functionalism of architects, the streamlined automobile and airplane designed to cheat nature of its drag, and the biomorphic image used for many of the consumer items, an image which reflected the joining of man and machine. People such as Frederick Taylor, Henry Ford, and Herbert Hoover personified the ideals of modernity, where the problems of men could be reduced with simple machine logic; and then, using the same engineering, men could design the cures.[3]

While any one definition of modernity is impossible, some clear patterns are apparent. Daniel Joseph Singal argues that modernity rose up in response to the fear of modernization, but its opponents also reveled in the machines' new capabilities. On one hand, they recognized that machines liberated humans from the drudgery of labor; but on the other hand, they feared that the rationalistic principles upon which the machine era operated could eliminate individuality. Stuart Chase, in his 1929 book, *Men and Machines*, wrote, "[T]he machine itself brings certain dangers and certain benefits." But to him and others of his time, the advantages outweighed the fears because man still controlled the machine.[4]

For many modernists the advantages of technology, especially in the arts, was difficult to ignore. George Gershwin wrote in 1930 that he did not fear the effect of technology in music, as "any instrument that tends to help [music] to be heard more frequently and by greater numbers is advantageous to the person who writes it." Man and technology could merge and create great art, for "mechanism and feeling will have to go hand in hand."[5] The Frankfurt School's Walter Benjamin's influential 1935 essay, "The Work of Art in the Age of Mechanical Reproduction," hailed the creation of standardized products as part of the liberation of the masses from the fetish nature of capital. He argued that art traditionally was based in ritual, but during the Renaissance it developed into the cult of beauty and thus became associated with money, power, and status. The multiple reproductions of a photo, film, or piece of music meant that the original lost its "aura" and each item was as authentic as all the rest. In the late nineteenth century, the United States developed a cultural hierarchy using the capitalist notion of accumulation as a guide. Those who owned, and therefore controlled, the great works of art became the guardians of culture and sought to sanctify what they considered "high" culture so as to better impose order over a society they feared was growing beyond their control. But, during the early twentieth century, largely as a result of capital, technology, and advertising, a more middlebrow, middle-class culture took shape. The sacrament of culture began to lose its allure with the increased reproductive abilities of film, literature, and even music, and so lessened the need for strict guardianship of the finer things in art. Benjamin was witness to these changes and argued that since the advent of the industrial revolution the ritual or cult value of art had been eroded by technology's ability to recreate or reproduce art, freeing art from "parasitical dependence on ritual." Benjamin wrote that "when the age of mechanical reproduction separated art from its basis in cult, the semblance of its autonomy disappeared forever."[6] The standardization and reproduction of goods, including art, allowed for them to become "a secular and real experience," shared equally by all who participated in their performance or exhibition; and thus they became more universal in their appeal. Much like the standardized soap, canned beans, or automobile, art could become an experience available to all society.[7]

The high point of modernity was the 1930s, when, as a result of the economic collapse, all aspects of American society had to be broken down to their simplest components and reassembled in a more efficient, productive, and streamlined manner. While this ideology was first applied to the political processes manifest in the New Deal, it soon spread to all aspects of American society. During this era the machine ideology of the earlier phase of modernity, which emphasized the factory efficiency of Ford and the systemization of technology required to transform the economy to consumer-directed industries, became part of the new order. No longer innovative, the *style* of modernity came into vogue during the 1930s through the repeated usage of modern images. This secured, according to Terry Smith's *Making the Modern,* "increasingly ordered patterns of reading from those consuming them, while at the same time modifying other modes . . . until a new regime of seeing became itself the norm." Modernity was made normal.[8] For swing this meant breaking down the complex improvisations that defined jazz into a more organized and formalized score where everyone knew their role and the performance could be repeated time and time again.

One of the key attributes regarding the acceptance of modernity involved planning and organization. America became the land of systems, where every industry, business, and task was divided into ordered patterns of understanding and then reassembled in an efficient and systematic manner. Order meant stability.[9] This systemization encompassed all aspects of American society, but central to the process was electricity. It energized America and transformed the manner in which systems were created and utilized. Electricity was the means by which the machine age reached the citizenry to better their lives. For example, in 1917 roughly a quarter of America's homes were electrified; by 1940 the number had risen to 40 percent. Many items used this electricity, including the refrigerator, which saw its sales increase by nearly seven million from 1924 to 1934. Radio also benefited from the electrification process. In five years, from 1920 to 1925, its audience grew from 1 station and a handful of listeners to 571 stations and 2.75 million listeners. These were not the only devices to benefit from electricity, as the modern home came to adopt the benefits of the energy by utilizing all sorts of "gizmos." By the late 1920s, electricity had become a basic household necessity. The power of electrification suggested economic progress and helped transform the nation.[10]

Those who became musicians during the swing era were part of this transformation. They, like the rest of society, saw the tremendous possibilities for the new technologies. Many musicians readily adopted technologies without fear of standardization. They saw in the new musical technologies an expansion of opportunity and better instrument control.[11] Their optimistic view was shared by many who saw in technology an improved way of being, making for easier work or home labors and, potentially, more money.

For musicians, the new technologies had to be utilized in order to stay competitive and display their willingness to adapt to the changing technological environment and the modern times. They, like the rest of America, *had* to become modern.[12]

One technology that had tremendous impact on musicians was the radio. For many Americans, including swing musicians, the radio was the means by which they were exposed to jazz in the 1920s and newer sounds in the 1930s. Maxine Sullivan recalled that in her youth in Homestead, Pennsylvania, she would lie awake at night listening to broadcasts from around the country. Tiny Grimes would sit up late with his "ears glued to the radio, listening to Duke Ellington, [and] Earl "Fatha" Hines," and this spurred him to try his luck in the music field: "I made up my mind I was going to be a musician." With no money for lessons, he used the radio to copy what he heard. Eskine Hawkins learned to play any song he heard on the radio without the benefit of any musical training.[13]

These recollections are not solitary occurrences. Many swing musicians learned the basics of their craft through technology. Jimmy Maxwell wanted to become a priest until he went to seminary high school and heard Duke Ellington and Louis Armstrong records. Hooked on the sound, he began to "ditch classes" to practice playing like them. "Sir" Charles Thompson recalled that while stationed at a Civilian Conservation Corps camp near Cape Girardeau, Missouri, he would drop nickels and dimes into the jukebox to hear popular swing songs of the mid-1930s. For Thompson, far away from the music hot spots like New York City or Chicago, the jukebox connected him to the newest and hottest sounds. "I learned this music that I was listening to . . ." he recalled, "and I began to create my own image of these creations." Taking what he heard through the jukebox, the radio, and the occasional live performance, Thompson created his own musical style; and while he did come from a musical family, it was the appropriation via technology that helped him develop his musical skills. Joe Williams used to stay up every night to hear Ethel Waters on the radio. When her songs appeared on the local jukebox, he played them "over and over again" to better grasp her phrasing and use of voice, all part of his training to become a singer. Most of the swing musicians would learn to play an instrument through their families or school, but recall that much of their professional

training came from copying sounds, riffs, and chords from the radio or phonograph.[14]

During the 1920s, when many swing-era musicians were cutting their
musical teeth, radio had come into its own, and music made up over 60
percent of all broadcast time. Network hookups began broadcasting live
music from coast to coast in 1925 with the development of the National
Broadcast Company, and in the next year with the Columbia Broadcast
Company. Musical performances once heard only by local audiences were
now broadcast nationwide via the network hookup, which by 1931 numbered seventy-nine for CBS and sixty-one each for NBC's two networks,
Blue and Red. NBC estimated that 41.4 million people regularly listened to
the radio, with over 80 percent of those tuning in at least once a day. Robert
and Helen Lynd's *Middletown in Transition* found that 46 percent of all the
city's homes had radio by 1930; this corresponds to Lizabeth Cohen's per-
centages of radio ownership in 1930 Chicago. By 1937, CBS reported that
more people owned radios (24.5 million) and were spending more time listening (five hours a day) than in any year previous. Their study also indicated that while the higher income families had more radios, the lower the
family income the more likely they would listen.[15]

Nearly at radio's birth, a debate began regarding whether cultivated or
vernacular music should be preferred in programming. Proponents of classical music argued that the utilitarian nature of radio lent itself for use in
promoting "good" music over the common sounds of popular music. These
classicists wanted the radio to become a "massive funnel into which centuries of music could be poured into the ear of the nation," according to Frank
Biocca. However, this cultivated vision did not match the desires of the
listening public, who sought out popular melodies and songs with lyrics.
Over four-fifths of those people in Middletown in 1935 favored popular
music over classical on their radios.[16]

Music was one of the most popular features of the 1930s radio programming, providing relatively inexpensive, easily timed, popular entertainment
to a growing consumer public. By 1942 over half of radio's programming
offerings were of the musical variety, with nine out of ten hours going to
popular sounds. Of the nearly ten thousand hours of musical broadcast over
station WEAF-WJZ in New York during 1942, only one thousand hours
were classical. Further, and perhaps this helps explain why popular music

received the nine to one ratio, "popular music evokes a large mail response from listeners but few letters are inspired by the classics."[17]

Radio music also conformed to what the underwriters of the medium—consumer-directed products—wanted for their shows: entertainment that was popular, relatively simple, and low cost. This formula worked with the development of a national programming schedule, as it increased the number of listeners and allowed the sponsors to better target their audience. During the 1930s advertising agencies worked with the performers to produce most network radio programs. They tried to create shows with built-in demographic targets, and with the aid of audience measurement techniques like the Cooperative Analysis of Broadcasting and the Hooperratings they were able to fine tune their programs to make them as successful, and therefore profitable, as possible. They saw in the radio a medium of sales—whether it be cigarettes or new a entertainment fad. Swing first reached its national audience through the "Let's Dance" program sponsored by the National Biscuit Company. The company was not interested in the musical form being presented, but in the potential listeners and their buying habits. If they enjoyed the show, they would be more likely to choose the item the show was introducing, the new Ritz Cracker. By the time swing entered the marketplace, the people trusted radio, and the medium had a tremendous homogenizing effect on American society. Regional and local barriers were lost to the networks as they "communicated the same stimuli throughout the nation." When the Federal Communications Commission surveyed the radio networks during the first week of March in 1938, they found that while one-half of all programming was music, nearly one-third was advertising. Radio significantly helped to promote swing by featuring many of the big bands and informing the record-buying public on exactly what songs were popular on shows like the Lucky Strike "Your Hit Parade" while selling cigarettes.[16]

When the Goodman band "made it" in 1935 and other bands sought to capitalize on the new sound, radio became the manner by which they got exposure. The purpose was to increase audience interest in a group or particular song so that live performances, the possibility of tours, and perhaps record sales would increase. Musician Charlie Barnet said, "You had to get on the air. . . . The live broadcasts were the things that brought people in." Bands and musicians would work for "unbelievably low money" in hotels and clubs that were wired for radio and then expect to make the money back by going out on the road to "capitalize on this exposure." According to historian James Kraft, these performances, called remotes, helped "to give rise to the swing era" by exposing large numbers of Americans to the sounds of the most popular bands. As the remotes became more popular, bands secured more gigs, or performances, in cities and towns where young people heard them over the radio and wanted to see them live.[19]

The musicians enjoyed these situations, both for commercial and personal reasons. Henry Gruen said the band valued these remotes because the "people would flock to see us because they heard us on radio." He, like many others, also felt a sense of pride when the radio announcer would introduce them and their solo during a particular song: "It helped you make a name for yourself." Since the swing bands made their money on the road, getting on the radio meant better and more gigs. Swing bands made only 16 percent of their income from the ballroom and other radio remotes while one-night stands accounted for over 29 percent of their revenue. This is not to suggest that musicians made no money on radio. Staff network musicians examined by a government study in October 1939 made an average of $125.90 a week, nearly double that of the others who helped make up the national staff. Yet this was not the norm, as independent stations paid only $78.37 a week. But for the swing bands, like Tommy Dorsey's band, which had a fifty-week contract with CBS, the pay was much less. But they saw their time on the radio as a means to promote live gigs. This made them valuable to the radio networks and stations, for they worked cheap and had little overhead. The bands were anxious to get on the radio to sell themselves, just as the advertisers were selling their products. Or, as Eddie Sauter put it, "[W]hat every band wanted was a cigarette commercial."[20]

The radio had other effects. Radio performance enforced a standardization of product and consumption. The musicians recognized that once they were associated with network broadcasting and the nationalization of advertising, their songs had to conform to the period of presentation, thereby limiting improvisation. The advent and utilization of swing made logical sense in this respect, as the detailed arrangements so fundamental for the definition of the music made it much easier to translate the music into seconds and minutes. Artie Shaw complained that the people who ran radio did so with a "stop watch" and were more interested in "selling soap than music." Because of this commercial aspect, the tone of the songs had to conform more closely to the advertising lead in. For example, if Ritz Cracker were sponsoring the show and the final song before the sponsor's break sounded sad or melancholy, the listener might not be as interested in the forthcoming sales pitch, and so the song had to be changed. Timing and emotion were everything; to run over, even by ten seconds, meant "infringing on another sponsor's territory." Eddie Sauter recalled that radio stations wanted songs under three minutes so as to not interfere "with commercials."[21]

There was a lot at stake in a band's radio performance, not only for the network and its sponsors, but also for the song-sheet publishers and, as the thirties continued, record companies. Columbia University's Office of Radio Research published a study in 1941 assessing the effect of modern technology on the music industry. Before radio, songs were plugged by vaudeville performers for two and or more years, which meant higher sales of sheet music (a hit sold more than 500,000) and fewer releases. As musical programming came to dominate radio, its interconnection with other industries also grew, meaning that more emphasis was put on trying to create hits. A newer song had about three to six weeks to become popular before it would no longer be promoted by the men whose job it was to get band leaders and singers to use the song. Even if a song became a hit, which because of the volume of new songs promoted now meant only 50,000 in sales of sheet music and 100,000 in records, its promotional life ran no more than a few months. The radio had changed how a song was sold, so that after it was introduced and played regularly, a business decision was then made to determine whether or not it was going to make it or not. If the audience did not respond, it would be replaced with another song facing the same risks. Performance became a stage in the advertising of the product—the song and by association the band or singer—in the hopes it would sell sheet music, records, band requests, and even advertising. Popular band leaders and singers would pick and choose those songs they wished to introduce and use, usually with an assurance that the publisher of the song would put out the necessary money to promote the song. A song without a multi-front promotion rarely sold. Within this new manner of production, even the songs themselves were produced by the publisher with the idea that volume and speed of production encouraged profit, and publishers created standards for the songs they would agree to promote. These "fixed canons of business" held that the melody should be no more than thirty-two bars; the line, easy to play and sing; and the lyrics, romantic or appealing as a story. Lazarsfeld concluded that songs were not left to the chances of the marketplace but were within the system of industrial production of consumer demand.[22]

The demands on the musicians increased as a result. They found themselves in competition not only with each other, in terms of being able to play their instrument, but with song publishers, radio sponsors, booking agencies, and consumers. Ultimately, it was those who could best conform to the demands of the modern system of production who were best able to reap the rewards offered by the increased exposure of national broadcasting and advertising. The swing musicians who succeeded in part did so by their ability to sell their wares to the widest variety of consumers: sponsors, advertisers, publishers, record executives, radio programmers, and the public.

Rivaling the importance of radio, the record industry began to exert more musical and commercial pressures upon swing musicians. Between 1929 and 1933 record sales fell by ninety million; but from 1932 to 1941 sales increased by 500 percent. The effect of the revived and modern record industry went beyond increased sales and company profits and was closely linked to the development of the entire cultural industry emerging during the 1930s and 1940s. People who bought the records of bands whose songs they heard over the radio played them on new models of record players, bought the sheet music, and, when the band came to town, bought tickets to the show. These interconnected industries encouraged a competitive consumer drive to stay musically connected, as an advertisement for Victor and Bluebird records suggested, "even though you're a thousand miles away from Broadway or Hollywood." In keeping with the advertised image of the American dream—that everyone had an equal opportunity to define themselves through consumption—the local "RCA Victor merchant always ha[d] the newest" song available for the consumer to "study . . . [or] play it again and again." Records, while not in and of themselves profitable to a band's musicians, kept the heat on the consumer to keep "in tune with the times," which translated, according to Trummy Young, into larger audiences for live shows, especially on college campuses. But in 1941 over 130 million records were sold, and many bands had created songs with the idea that they would become their signature pieces, almost like their brand name. A song became a band's killer-diller, or a guaranteed crowd pleaser, like Artie Shaw's "Begin the Beguine," or Tommy Dorsey's "Marie," or Cab Calloway's "Minnie the Moocher," to name a few. These songs set the band apart from its competitors and, with increased record sales, encouraged fan loyalty. The record allowed for the band's signature piece, like the Morton Salt girl or the Ford emblem, to become identifiable by the consumer as the real product.[23]

Records and phonographs had other effects. For the developing swing musicians in the 1920s and 1930s, the phonograph was, like the radio, a lodestone of new musical styles and ideas. Musicians from all over the country recounted the endless hours spent playing and replaying jazz or swing records in an attempt to recreate what they heard. This also became part of many swing musicians' training. The famous Austin High gang—Frankie Teschemacher, Bud Freeman, Jimmy and Dick McPartland, and Jim Lannigan—all of whom later played in numerous swing bands, were initially exposed to jazz through records at a local youth hangout. They purchased jazz records and would try to learn the songs by playing portions of a song, stopping it, and then continuing through the next bar. The same held true for Art Hodes and Wingy Manone, who were introduced to African American jazz via the constant replaying of records: "[W]hoever gets up first puts the 78 on the turntable and winds it up." These musicians and many like them would listen, try to repeat what they heard, and then, if possible, go see the person live to get the full effect.[24] To a young Woody Herman, the recorded sounds of Duke Ellington and the Washingtonians proved "very exciting and very different from anything else [he] had heard or felt." While growing up in a Polish-German family in Milwaukee, he listened and learned not only from Ellington's records but from a wide variety and "got to hear people like Benny Goodman for the first time."[25] Some record companies, understanding that many of those who purchased records were musicians or students trying to develop their craft, recorded accompaniments for practice. Acompo Records promised "An Entire Orchestra at Your Command" for just $1.50.[26]

These records exposed the many styles and variations of jazz to people whom probably would not have heard them in an earlier time. Russell Procope, growing up in New York City, listened to records as a youth in order to "pick up on what was happening." He would buy any jazz records he could and from these learn his technique. Albert "Budd" Johnson said he and his mates would try to copy what they heard on records by slowing the phonograph down. This way they "would copy anybody's solo that was good . . . this was really a school." He learned the solos of Coleman Hawkins, Fletcher Henderson, and Louis Armstrong and replayed them until they were committed to memory. Buddy Tate followed the same regiment. He and his friends would each buy a different record and then slow its tempo down to where they could follow it. "I could learn the solos from the record," he said, "because I could play it so slow and you had to learn it." Eddie Barefield took the money his mother gave him for formal lessons and went to the movies instead. Later, when he went home, he listened to records and copied what he heard. He assured his mother that these songs were part of his paid-for lesson.[27]

Records played a crucial role in the formation of the swing sound from the beginning, when young people first heard and learned how to play jazz. When they became the musical leaders, they advised their fans to follow as they had—by record. Gene Krupa urged young drummers to practice using records as it allowed for the player to get the "feel" of playing live.[28]

But there was a vast difference between the records of Goodman, Miller, and Basie and the jazz greats in the 1920s. Those swing musicians who sampled jazz sounds in the 1920s did so from imperfect recordings. Those musicians who recorded in the 1920s and early 1930s recall how the primitive studio conditions changed their live sound in order to be captured on record. Particularly in the 1920s, when most recording equipment could not tolerate loud sounds and was limited as to the number of tones the equipment could pick up at once, sessions were done live with the full band competing to be captured on the disc. Bill Crow relates in *Jazz Anecdotes* that when American jazz bands first started playing in Europe, they encountered musicians playing jazz copied from the flawed recordings, full with "hollow" horns and woodblocks.[29]

Electrical improvements by the 1930s allowed for a more complimentary sound, yet the production of accurate recordings was still in the future. Eddie Sauter recalled that recording conditions in Chicago in 1937 at the Padded Cell studio included thick padding covering the walls to absorb any reverberations. These sound deadeners, to Sauter, "took up all the tempo of the instruments." The recorded material was unable to capture the energy of the live performance, which he felt cheated the fans: "people think that's the way they played; it isn't so, it was a recording technique."[30]

The timing of songs was, like with radio, affected by the record industry. In order for a song to be commercial, it had to follow certain guidelines. When jazz first became popular, it relied on its live sound, where songs could be improvised and there were few time constraints. However, when jazz and, later, swing became viable record business commodities, certain constraints were necessary from the commercial and technological standpoint. The rules for the system of production were quite new to the musician, who had up to this point been largely spared the decline of power that came with the increased industrialization of America. But with the introduction of sound recordings, both for movies and for home consumption, significant changes in the production and control of their goods began to affect their craft. Some would profit and prosper, while many others would not. Those who prospered recognized and were able to work within the confines and limitations created by the new system. The key to recording work was efficiency, speed of turnover, and adaptability. In order to produce the items necessary for consumption and maintain low prices, demands outside the creation of music began to affect the craft.[31]

In the first place, going into the recording studio required capital investment. This meant that the person or company paying for the recording wanted something marketable, popular, or designed to fit a target audience. The musician or band found that the hotter, or more improvisational, a song, the harder it was to record because of shifts in timing, missed cues, and fluctuating volume. When asked to repeat the song because of a technical problem, for example, many found it difficult to recreate the same hot number. Musician George Lewis believed that the more times a band was forced to retake a song the more it deviated from its original intention and emotion. He attributed the changes to the introduction into the recording process of "the man"—the engineer. While this specialist may know music, Lewis argued, his constant need to adjust the levels and sounds and the constant demand to start and stop made it difficult for the musicians to maintain focus, and thus they "sort of los[t] it." The further from the first live take, the less original the song.[32]

The capital required to record and the influence of the engineer led to standardization in the studio in order to maximize time and money. The longer a band spent in the studio, the more expensive the cost and the more difficult to recoup the initial investment. In order to maintain costs, the songs came under increased technical and commercial scrutiny. With the increased popularity of the jukebox and its nearly 350,000 machines—which consumed at least one-half of all records produced in 1941—in soda shops, restaurants, and bars, bands were "encouraged" to keep their presentations under three minutes. While the jukebox operators could not force such an activity, it was common knowledge that songs that went beyond the formula had a difficult time getting onto playlists or jukeboxes. Jack Kapp, who had made Decca the second largest producer of records by 1939, tailored the label's business to the jukebox. This practice also lowered Decca's production costs and created a positive relationship with his primary customers, the jukebox owners. As the technology required to produce records became more complex, more nonmusical experts entered the system. Engineers now exerted increased influence, as it was their job to use the recording technology in the most efficient and profitable manner in order to create a consumable item as defined by the producer. By the height of the swing era, musical production relied as much on the producers, engineers, jukebox operators, radio stations, and record executives as it did on the performers. One could be part of a great band, but without the support and investment of these others, the sound would not come across.[33]

With so many interests to serve, many times the producer or the engineer clashed with the intent or creativity of the musicians. Charlie Barnet's producer burst into the studio and demanded to know why his band was playing "all this doodley doop," which happened to be a Benny Carter arrangement. The producer scolded them for wasting time and money and said their job was simply to record the melody as written. Bob Crosby and his band found many ways to get around their producer. Once, when the producer refused to let the band record a swing version of "Maryland, My Maryland," Crosby simply renamed their arrangement "March of the Bobcats." Since the producer was not a musician, he couldn't tell it was the same song, and it went on to become one of the bands biggest hits.[34]

Once recorded, pressed, and released, the record faced other pressures that altered its authenticity. How and where the record would be marketed determined success or failure. Given that few records were played over the air during the 1930s, to sell records required extensive promotion from those people whose job it was to make sure retailers were giving prime space for their products and working up promotions to sell the song. The jukebox, for example, held between twelve and twenty-four selections and was subject to quick turnover. Jukeboxes allowed the stocker to determine which record was getting played the most and which was not being played. Forty percent of all records made in 1936 went right to the jukeboxes; this rose to 60 percent by 1939. Those songs that did not get played were quickly removed and returned to the record company. The producers of these machines—120,000 jukeboxes were produced in 1935 by six companies—had tremendous power in the production of the music, as record companies sought to satisfy their demands. Tommy Dorsey knew that for his records to become popular they had to be on as many jukeboxes as possible so that when the young people went "out for lunch or recess and they pack[ed] into these soda parlors feeding nickels into" the machine, his band's selection would be preferred over others.[35]

The success of swing, so tied to the modernization of recorded popular music, helped lead to a homogenization within the music itself. While contemporary jazz critics like Gunther Schuller detail the many different types of swing-jazz, to the musicians themselves, technology had made any regional style a mute point. Anyone from anywhere could play any style. The Kansas City style was not limited to musicians growing up in the region, but included the entire country through road shows, radio, and records. Theoretically then, a musician growing up in Kansas City had as much of a chance of playing the Chicago style as kids growing up in Chicago.

The loss of regionalism in jazz is tied to the influence of technology on the musicians, both in terms of popularity and standardization, and stands at the center of swing era and its interconnection to modernism. Miles Orvell, in his study of American culture from 1880 to 1940, argues that during the first third of the twentieth century, those who considered themselves modern attempted to move "beyond mere imitation" that came with the systemization of industrialism—"the manufacture of illusions"—and sought to create "works that were themselves the real things." Machine technology had made such rapid advances that by the early 1900s the marketplace was dominated by industrially created consumer items that had once been hand-crafted. While the introduction of the machine allowed for lower prices and an expansion of sales, the authenticity of the object came into question.

Orvell challenges Benjamin's mid-1930s analysis of art in the mechanical era, arguing that reproduction was an attempt by the artist to utilize the machine in order to produce an authentic piece of art that could be mass produced and therefore exposed to a greater majority, but remain authentic.[36]

The musicians discussed earlier who used the phonograph or radio to learn styles fit nicely into Orvell's analysis. Eddie Barefield scoffed at the tendency by some to divide jazz into styles: "That's one of the . . . biggest fallacies that I ever heard in my life. When it comes down to jazz, this thing was universal. All I can say is jazz evolved as it went . . . [s]o when Benny Goodman came in and they called it swing, but he only was swinging the things that Fletcher Henderson was swinging in the twenties."[37]

The need for the musicians and the generation of the thirties to call their music swing can be seen as their need for authenticity—to make this new incarnation of a traditional sound a "real thing." Musicians and budding musicians borrowed from one another through electronic media because they could, because it made them better players, and because it helped to create the modernist authenticity that made something swing. Each artist heard in the other's samples what they themselves hoped to create in order to carve a specific sound for themselves. And, while swing demanded precision, arrangements, and the unity of a large ensemble, it also featured that special moment when the soloist was presented to the audience or listener. This provided the freedom to be authentic while recognizing the confines of their creation. A symbiosis took effect, as swing musicians were able to accept the limitations placed upon them by the machine while at the same time utilizing the machine to create something new.

Technology and modernism thus changed the fabric of the artist and the audience. Within the swing band, individual improvisation was standardized into the text of the arrangement. When Benny Goodman was asked what he wanted out of his swing band, he said he needed a combination of a good rhythm section, an arrangement, and the opportunity for musicians to solo—much like factory organization where the individual contributes to the making of a product. The worker does what he or she does best, and this individual contribution aids in the creation of the total object, whether music or an automobile. Earlier forms of jazz depended on the individual interpretation of the music, but swing needed the members to work together to produce the music. And while no one would argue with Bud Freeman's assertion that "the big bands needed individualists," their necessity was more linked to a star's cult of celebrity and marketability than to the desire to cater to the needs of independent soloists.[38]

Swing was the music of the machine age, or at least the music of modernism. What helped to make swing was not as much the individual artist's interpretation or production, as the sound of swing had been played well before 1935, but the social construct of the band, the audience, and American culture. A young, predominantly white and working-class audience saw in Goodman and those who followed him what they wanted in their music. Producers, desirous of a consumable product, catered to what the people sought out in their music: social acceptability, fun, and participation. Jazz has been called the folk music of the modern age since the 1920s for its frenzied pace and reckless abandon. Yet swing, if any music, deserves this title as it incorporated nearly all aspects of modernism into its culture and allowed the audience more participation through identification than did jazz. Gene Fernett, in his fan's description of the great black dance bands, links the music to the Empire State Building, Packard automobiles, Joe Louis, and a host of other *big* things of the era. "It was the bigness," he wrote, "that we admired."[39] And while composers of formal music called themselves modern, they failed to capture the richness of the machine age, the energy, indeed, the bigness. But swing, as Horace Kallen wrote in 1942, "cuts itself loose from every rule and canon that tradition has brought down or craftsmanship confirmed."[40] It became *the* modern sound for a modern generation.

Technology had changed the nature of swing music. The modernist paradox of swing was that as it became more popular, the medium of its dissemination required regimentation (on radio) or captured the sound forever, unchanged (on records). Moreover, since many of the musicians learned how to play jazz or swing from records, they were inspired less from the improvisational nature of the music and were drawn more to the formula performance exposed to them through the radio or phonograph. This empowered the audiences, as swing's reliance on technology allowed the listener to have more power over the performance. If the trumpet player was not popular with the audience, perhaps for reasons other than musical ability, his solo could be cut and replaced by a lesser, but more popular, musician. There were stars of swing but, unlike those in earlier jazz, some of these might not be great musicians but rather great *performers*, such as Cab Calloway, catering to the desires of their audience. As George Lipsitz has argued with reference to the theater of the late nineteenth century, as culture came to be less based in ritual—something Benjamin saw as liberation—"commercial culture sought credibility with its audiences by promising at least the illusion of connection with the past."[41] The audience wanted a shared cultural experience, one that they could claim as their own. Swing became this shared modernist musical culture.

Swing musicians understood the dangers of this modernist interconnection of technology, capital, and their craft. Musician Jimmy Maxwell recognized that while electrification and technology enabled him and other musicians to enjoy a career in music, he "didn't like" the amplified instruments. "They sound fake to me," he said. Maxwell and others feared that the technology would forever alter the sound and that bit by bit the music would lose its soul: "[T]he greatest music in the world is the voice . . . and the heartbeat . . . and everything is an imitation of the voice and the heartbeat. And as long as you're blowing your breath into the instrument or you're plucking on the string of an instrument, you could control the feeling of it. You know, you could put the expression [into the music]".[42] The technology displaced the individual in the musical process. Teddy Wilson agreed, worrying that the increased use of the machine might replace "the live person." He linked the development of electricity to this dilemma, saying its ability to create more efficient instruments "should not be allowed to take over the expression of the human soul." And, while he made these comments much later than the 1940s and perhaps in relation to the increased proliferation of technology into American life in the sixties and seventies, he was present in the 1920s through the 1940s as these modernist issues were introduced, discussed, and eventually accommodated.[43]

What both the modernists and their critics ignored concerning technology was the influence of capital in the control process. Some feared that the standardization of products, hailed by many as liberating, would in fact destroy creativity. Given the influence of marketing and advertising during the Great Depression era, and the close interconnection of swing, the radio, and the phonograph, the manipulation of the marketplace needs to be analyzed with more scrutiny than has traditionally been given. Goodman understood the nonmusical factors in his band's popularity and knew that while he and the band had no "special ambition" except to "play music" their newfound popularity changed the context of performance: "[S]omething happens when you find out what you're doing is no longer music— that it's become entertainment. . . . Your whole attitude changes."[44] Responsibility came with the acceptance. People wanted to hear the songs Goodman was known for in the style they had heard either in previous live performances, over the radio, or at home on their phonograph. This created a whole new set of difficulties for the musicians and their audience, for within the context of the period it was impossible to separate the music from the consumable product. Nor could the artist escape this process.

Swinging the Marketplace

Advertising and Selling Swing

At the heart of the swing generation was its proximity to the consumer marketplace. That Goodman did not invent something new in swing and that his enthronement as the King of Swing was more a result of promotion than invention raise questions about the role of capital in the emergence of swing. Mario Bauza, of Duke Ellington's band, believed Goodman's success was based on "a gimmick. Swing, they called it swing. So they started commercializing the word swing. Swing, swing, they made a King of Swing, they made a picture, and then they have all these bobbysox dancing in the aisle. Everything—everybody can know, so the thing was well planned."[1] In Bauza's mind there was something else behind Goodman's success that had little to do with the music but concerned the marketplace. In attempting to understand swing, it is necessary to explore the role of commerce within the specialized musical marketplace of the depression era, especially with regards to the ideals of modernity and the emerging cultural industries.

Connecting swing to its generational qualities and the ideals of modernity helps to define it as a cultural force, but it also demands an examination of the growth and development of popular music as an industry. Taken in this context, swing can be viewed as one of many "brand names" used to market a seemingly new product. During the 1930s, industrial and product designers utilized modernist images to change the forms of objects without modifying their functions. Oftentimes this meant simply repackaging a good under a new ideology which made it appear as new, improved, or modern. As an early advertisement makes clear (see fig. 3.1), with the radio microphone in the background and the text extolling the virtues of Tommy Dorsey's trombone made with "new ideas," the connection between the ideals of modernity (with its generational appeal) and the new music swing (with its generational appeal) is made plain. Little had actually changed in the construction of the instrument, but what made it modern was who and what it was attached to—swing musicians and swing.[2]

To view swing as a brand name for a highly marketable product means placing it within the business culture of the era. During the 1930s, when one would assume that businesses and industries, as well as consumers, would be pulling back on their desire to consume, there is compelling evidence to the contrary. Because the economic factors of traditional capitalism had failed, capital changed its focus from increasing production (to lower cost and increase sales) and toward the encouragement of consumption. This meant redefining the people's needs to accommodate consumer items that had earlier not been necessary. This new way of being encouraged Americans to consume as part of their patriotic duty. As Charles McGovern has argued, advertising played a key role in suggesting that "being a good American meant being a good consumer."[3] A 1935 Works Progress Administration survey, which sought to determine a living wage for American relief workers, helps to explain this transition. The WPA researchers suggested that within the modest income paid to the worker for necessities, additional monies for tobacco and other leisure-directed activities, like a trip to the movies, be included. People's needs had changed to include more luxuries, as Robert S. Lynd had pointed out in his 1933 study for Hoover's Committee for Research on Social Trends. He argued that by the end of the 1920s America's families came to see work as "buying a living" and that businesses changed their strategies to meet this new ideology by focusing less on the creation of goods and more on distribution, hoping to get people to consume even if they had little excess income or direct need for the product. This change helped lead to an increased proliferation of brand names, the multiplicity of

Fig. 3.1. *Metronome* 52 (June 1936): 10

product lines, and the institutionalization of entertainment in the form of radio, movies, and sports. Within these, the consumers played an ever-increasing role in the determination of the economy, as they were no longer free to choose but *had* to choose.[4]

In order to assist this shift in consumptive consciousness, the marketing and advertising industries had to create new means of production. Mass marketing played a major role in the shift from customers to consumers. In the modern system, products were produced in mass amounts, utilizing machine technology, and required mass consumption to maximize profit. In order to ensure predictability and control over consumption, brand-name identification became important. Demand was less free and tended to be directed by the manufacturer utilizing modern business practices such as market research, label and art design, psychological studies of consumptive behavior, and advertising. The process of selling became, like so many other aspects of the emerging modern America, directed by experts utilizing scientific methodology to best meet their needs. One of the key ingredients for this process involved creating customer loyalty through brand-name association. In order to break the consumer's reliance on the local store-owner's bulk supply of goods and encourage the purchase of packaged goods, producers used the introduction of brand names, advertising (which stressed the qualities of the goods), shelf placement, and coupons to increase consumer interest. The brand became the means by which the customer could expect the standardized product associated with the purchase, as well as a guarantee of its quality. Ivory soap maintained the same quality in every package, and the consumer knew that in choosing this brand, satisfaction was guaranteed.[5]

Swing conforms to this brand-name packaging ideal. Since the name itself had little meaning, those who followed Goodman's success used swing as a brand name. As its popularity grew, the music industry sought to stabilize the consumer's buying habits by standardizing the new musical style. The success of the standardization of the product—swing—thus made it easier for consumers to make its brand-name association.[6]

Central to brand-name identification was the creation of consumer loyalty. During the early twentieth century, as industrial capitalism gave way to consumer capitalism, advertising and its creators began to exert more influence in the marketplace. The invisible hand dismissed in industrial capitalism was replaced by the visible hand in consumer capitalism. Advertising became more important for the creation of new markets rather than for simply fulfilling market demand. Roland Marchand, in his examination of the rise of the advertising industry, labeled the persons responsible for the ads "apostles of modernity," whose job it was to introduce, advise, and sell new products without raising class antagonisms. The advertising images they utilized sought to reinforce and intensify existing patterns and conceptions, and by their acceptance they communicated broader social values. The ads sold the American dream and informed the consumer how to fit in and what products were best, and they encouraged the consumer to fear social alienation. The message inherent in the pitch held that the blame for the lack of success, whether financial or personal, lay within the individual and not the larger society. Ads promoted products which guaranteed satisfaction, albeit for a price, to aid in the individual's quest for self-esteem. The American dream was advertised, bought, and sold to the individual, who was free to choose whether or not to consume. However, the risk of alienation by not consuming in part guaranteed consumption. As advertisers began to see themselves within the context of the managerial revolution—to control and direct the economy—their concern shifted from selling or persuading and more to informing the consumer. As Advertising Agency president H. A Batten said in 1941, "advertising is a specialized technique for mass communication." But since so few ad persons were from the ranks of those consuming, they chose to focus not on the product but on the consumer. To inform thus became to sell.[7] When placed in this context, Bauza's statement of who created, advertised, and marketed swing for the generation of the 1930s meant that not participating in swing and, for example, preferring one's parents' music meant possible social alienation.

The influence of the advertisers was not restricted to the promotion of the music, but included the many music students and budding musicians around the country. Radio promoted swing as a brand name for record sales and live gigs, but print ads were more directed at those persons interested in becoming musicians. The government estimated in 1929 that there were over seventeen thousand music stores in the United States, with chain stores controlling only 4 percent of the sales.[8] But what this data did not reflect was the prevalence of brand-name items within the stores, namely the instruments by Martin, Buescher, Selmer, and a host of others. C. G. Conn, a leading musical instrument company, recognized in the late 1920s that in order to survive it was necessary to create new markets. Conn founded a band director's school of music in Chicago in 1928 to encourage school programs in music and sent salesmen to towns across the country to create excitement about musical education. The result was all-time high sales of Conn instruments. But the depression flattened sales and eliminated many school music programs. Young people still wanted to play, so the new markets Conn and other manufacturers sought were out there, but they had to figure out how best to capture them.[9]

Since the makers of instruments knew that budding musicians were out there, they sought to market their wares in magazines that catered to them, sometimes called fanzines or pulps. This was not a tactic reserved for the musical instrument companies, as many industries turned to more specialized mass circulation magazines to advertise their wares. *Sports Illustrated, Bride's Magazine, Mademoiselle, Glamour, Baby Talk, Esquire, Women's Day, Popular Photography, Family Circle,* and many more begun to cater to a distinct reader to better target advertising. Within the entertainment industry, Hollywood spurred the creation of such magazines as *Modern Screen, Movies, Romantic Movie Stories,* and *Movie Mirror,* while radio's audience read *Radio Guide* or *Radio Mirror.* These titles were part of the pulp magazine explosion of the 1930s, where the total number of magazines declined, yet readership increased. For the pulps, which tended to cater to more distinct and popular audiences, circulation grew from eight million in 1929 to over fourteen million ten years later.[10]

Swing had its special interest magazines as well, and they became the medium through which the swing generation stayed informed about the personalities, performances, and new products. *Downbeat* was one of the first to cater to jazz and then swing audiences in 1934. It featured plentiful photographs, especially of the female singers, and regular reader contests for the best musicians, singers, or bands. In 1935 *Metronome,* which was founded in 1887, changed its direction to follow the swing crowd. More sophisticated in its analysis and covering other musical issues, *Metronome* had fewer photos and catered to the serious swing fan. There were other fanzines, but *Downbeat* and *Metronome* were seen by both musicians and the music industry as the most important. As such, these received the bulk of advertising for musical products, musical instruments, and accessories. Robert Draper's analysis of the rise and importance of *Rolling Stone* to rock and roll places the magazine's success within the context of record companies' willingness to utilize the periodical for the introduction and promotion of records. The same holds true for swing's fanzines, but as record sales were still in their infancy and radio was the primary means to introduce and increase sales, the swing fanzine's advertising space was filled with musical products ranging from instruments to how-to-play booklets, sheet music, instrument accessories, and new technology. The bulk of the ads were directed at those who hoped to be a part of the swing movement.[11]

Advertisements in these swing magazines conform to the patterns described by Marchand, Strasser, Ewen, Lears, and others. They utilized the traditional advertising practice of encouraging brand loyalty by outlining the excellence of one product over another, the profitability of a specific brand, and the new technology associated with purchasing a particular brand. As with any other product, there were many competitors in the field and the potential consumer needed to be informed as to why they should choose this particular instrument. In an industry like musical instruments, the competition was for a relatively small and stable marketplace and the desire to control consumption was high. Thus, the companies tended to rely on similar formulas to inform their audience as to the choice of products.[12]

One way that the companies and advertisers worked to assist in the consumer decision was to utilize "endorsements." Featuring stars like Benny Goodman or Tommy Dorsey, they informed the potential consumer of the benefits associated with their chosen product. A 1937 advertisement for Selmer instruments featured a quarter-page photo of Goodman under the banner "Swingmaster" and suggested that "Benny play[ed] Selmer exclusively" as did twelve others in his band. Selmer used Goodman frequently in their ads, informing the reader that in order to get that "brilliant tone" they needed to get the endorsed brand. Many of the ads offered a coupon for a free booklet on swing music redeemable at the nearest dealer. Selmer included a "free trial offer" and a teasing prophecy: "current material shortages indicate the desirability of equipping yourself now." For Conn Instruments (see fig. 3.2), since Goodman himself did not use their product, the ads suggested that his success was aided by the "finest instrumental equipment" used by many in his band.

While the market for youngsters and musicians to buy traditional instruments such as brass and woodwinds was strong, newer markets created by swing included the clarinet, trombone, and drums and offered manufacturers the opportunity to build lifetime brand loyalty. The ads for these instruments conformed to the "real Life" technique utilized to present an "un-

Fig. 3.2. *Metronome* 53 (April 1937): 8

problematic window of reality." The ads featured the performers as they were, using plain speech to describe what they liked in the product. Simple in form, these types of ads held the widest appeal and were used by most musical manufacturers. Slingerland was endorsed by "the world's two greatest drummers—Gene Krupa and Davey Tough," while Gretsh-Gladstone utilized the lesser known but musically talented Chick Webb to endorse its product. This ad is also striking as it reflects the increased use of black musicians for product endorsement in the pages of *Metronome*. By 1940 the pages of both magazines were filled with endorsements from many musicians for a wide array of products. As figure 3.3 shows, the endorsements themselves became part of the swing movement, as picture trading cards of the musicians were available from the manufacturer.[13]

Once America entered World War II in 1941, instrument manufacturers used patriotism to encourage brand loyalty. Conn changed its slogan from "band" instruments to "war" instruments and described how the company had turned over its facilities to create war materials. Conn was doing its

Fig. 3.3. *Metronome* 56 (March 1940): 20

part, the ad implied, so the consumers should do theirs. The E. K. Blessing ad is a good example of how the war was used to increase brand loyalty. While detailing the toll of war, the ad hints that the end is near and soon the boys will be back and ready to play Blessing trumpets.[14] These are two of the hundreds of ads that appeared during wartime. Each extolled the virtue of each company's patriotism and conformed to the sacrifice, duty, and hope formula for most ads during the period.

But in the era preceding the war, when the reality of the depression was a powerful motivator, instrument manufacturers' ads detailed the potential profit from using their product. The depression forced changes among the ad agencies, as companies demanded results. In response, the agencies began to use alienation and fear as motivators for consumption. Using "thick black type [and] scare headlines" the ad industry attempted to prove their worth to the companies by encouraging consumption using the most basic and carnivalesque techniques.[15] For example, when Selmer featured their spokesperson Goodman in a 1938 ad for their clarinet mouthpiece, the copy stated that "80% of the highest-paid sax and clarinet players" used their product. Selmer had made the same claim a year earlier, but had added the comment, "You'll earn more with a Selmer." Not to be outdone, competitor Buescher ran ads proclaiming, "Yes! Buescher Players are Definitely in the Money" because their instruments were more versatile and "designed for today's music." Another instrument company, Bundy (fig. 3.4), was more to the point. Featuring a well-dressed man exiting a band bus, the copy begins with "Tom's in big-time today" because when he first began to play he choose Bundy." Now, the copy drips, he "makes $15,000 a year." With the music store lit up behind the man's left shoulder, the ad makes clear the connection—good equipment bought at authorized dealers leads to economic success. In a clear example of the use of desire for capital rewards and envy as a means to sell a product, figure 3.5 makes plain that the instrument is the player. Another ad simply announced, "Micro Products Pay Big Dividends."[16]

One manner used to stimulate consumer interest created the fear of falling behind or not preparing for the future. Sometimes ads used cartoons to convey this idea. Developed as a result of the crash, these lowbrow tactics initially promoted soaps and cereals. But as they proved successful, the cartoon ad expanded to help sell higher priced items like musical instruments.

Fig. 3.4. *Downbeat* 8 (February 1941): 4

The comic approach favored "testimonials [and] the promise of self-transformation." Martin band instruments used this formula continuously with their "Joe Doaks" campaign (fig. 3.6). He was the type who knew everything and refused to be taken in by an advertiser's claim for new or improved. But

Fig. 3.5. *Metronome* 56 (May 1940): 3

ultimately, his lack of vision prevented his success and he soon fell behind others. Other ads followed this simple formula. Roth instruments told the story of Johnny McGee and his switch from the cumbersome drum to the easy to handle and carry cornet. Using cartoon figures, the ad visualized the

He's the kind who thinks that all makes of band instruments are about the same . . . that he can play just as well on one as another . . . and that there really hasn't been enough change or improvement in instruments to bother about since he bought his last horn a few years ago anyhow . . . and so on. Oh yeah-h-h? We all know him. He's a great fellow, a good musician, and an asset to any band. But—boy oh boy, what an eye-opener he'll get when he tries one of the new Martins . . . a sure cure for the fellow inclined to be skeptical, who thinks all this talk about new and highly perfected models is a lot of ballyhoo.

No matter what you play—saxophone or brass—you must know how Martin has stepped out far in advance of the field, building instruments definitely superior in construction and performance to anything ever produced before. All you have to do is try one. The instrument itself will convince you of Martin leadership. No matter what you play, how well you play or where you play, you'll find a Martin gives you that extra perfection and recognition every conscientious musician strives to attain.

Put "trying a Martin" on your "must" list today. Convenient purchase plan makes it easy for you to enjoy the prestige and many benefits of owning and playing one of these fine instruments. Keep in step with progress!

MARTIN

BAND INSTRUMENT CO.

DEPARTMENT 903   ELKHART, INDIANA

Fig. 3.6. *Metronome* 53 (September 1937): inside of back cover

difficulty of lugging drums around and how after he traded them in for the cornet he "went places." Selmer confided that "winners know what makes the difference between ordinary and extraordinary playing." It's not luck or image, but the brand of instrument. Vandoren's use of the cartoon features the testimony of Eugene Vandoren, "a world famous woodwind authority," and the transformation of Freddie the saxophone player from hack to star. Meanwhile, their competitor Buescher introduced its new "True Tone 400" in the early 1940s by announcing that it had been in development for eight years and that "16 major improvements" had been made as a result. Even the president of the company gave his endorsement, calling the 400 "Our Greatest" accomplishment. The new 400 was advertised as the instrument of the future. [17]

Of course, World War II interrupted the future hailed by these visionary ads, but this did not discourage them from continuing to stimulate consumer interest. While Conn and several others used their patriotism to remind readers of their loyalty, others began to ask if the reader was ready for the postwar. In a 1944 ad, King imagined the approaching victory parades and the "prospect of home and fireside, the pursuit of normal pleasures, the promise of ecstatic reunion" and wondered if the reader was ready: "Look to music to play an important part in American life after the war." Martin began much earlier, in 1943, to promote its "$25 After-the-War Purchase Bond" to servicemen everywhere. If someone played a Martin, all they had to do was write to the company, tell them a little about themselves (to be used in future advertising), give them the serial number of their current instrument, and a twenty-five dollar redeemable bond would be sent to their home for use after the war. Martin wanted to make sure that every man was ready for what Robbins Music Corporation prophesied—the "post-war MUSIC BOOM." Buescher also hoped for a prosperous postwar period; its machines were "ready to turn from war work to the world's best band instruments almost overnight." For those working in the defense industries and finding consumable goods scarce, the instrument ads suggested that with peace right around the corner, new and improved musical instruments were in the making. But planning was essential to this, as figure 3.7 suggests. Other Martin ads asserted that their instruments would "herald the new era of Peace." Armstrong Flutes assured its consumers in 1945 that as "The Big Day Draws Closer," Armstrong Flutes would be ready and willing to return to prewar consumer production.[18]

An interesting technique utilized by those advertising musical instruments was to visually link the products to modernity. While the majority of the ads featured in the magazines followed the more traditional models outlined

HIS
POST WAR PLANNING
IS BUILT AROUND
MARTINS

Occasionally, between strikes at the Jap, there's a chance to dream. A few minutes to find a spot of shade and make plans.

The other day we received a letter, written during one of those breathing spells, by a member of an AAF Band on a far Pacific island. He'd been a school band director before the war.

And after it's over?—well, his post war plan is a music store! He wants to sell Martins. He's writing us now about a dealer franchise. *The part of his letter we quote at the right will tell you why.*

It wouldn't mean so much, perhaps, if his were the only letter like this. But, actually we get many from men serving in all war theaters. They're all impressed with the high quality of Martin band

> May 22, 1945
> Somewhere in the Marianas
>
> The Martin Band Instrument Company,
> Gentlemen:
> In the Army I have learned that the best men have a high regard for Martin Band Instruments and those that play them consider them tops. Knowing the men as I do, I respect their opinions and, like them, believe the Martin horns have a big future . . .
>
> Sincerely,
> *(name on request)*

instruments—and especially the way Martins stand up under the rigors of war service.

Yes, Martin horns have a big future—and there's a big future for the players, as well as the dealers, who tie up with Martin.

THE *MARTIN* BAND INSTRUMENT COMPANY
ELKHART, INDIANA

Fig. 3.7. *Metronome* 61 (August 1945): 2

above, there appeared a large number which utilized the streamlined, rounded-edged, futuristic visions of modernity. The Excelsior Accordion hailed itself as "Modern as Tomorrow" (fig. 3.8) and promised improved tone and sound. Note the clean lines, which suggest the increased capabilities, and the

Fig. 3.8. *Downbeat* 3 (July 1936): 9

rounded edges that catch the eye. As an ad it was designed to conjure up associations of modernity with the train, plane, and automobile.[19]

There are several ways to analyze these visual artifacts. Jackson Lears outlines how in the mid-1920s ad designers began utilizing modernistic images as "a bag of tricks the artist could use to set an ordinary product apart." The design of the ad placed the product within the larger context of design aesthetics, hoping to detail the "glamour" of the object without having to change its design. The items advertised, regardless of their function, "carried a double aura of cosmopolitan culture and avant-garde style' " writes Lears. Further, he argues that the "appropriation of modernist forms" announced the union of business/industry with the artistic aesthetic and linked the functionality of the commodity to its artistic, advertised design. Miles Orvell points out that during the 1930s, manufacturers redesigned and repackaged goods to reflect a more modern look, either to remain competitive with others making the same product or to expand their product line into previously under-tapped markets. This process was most obviously implemented in the automobile industry, where the utilitarianism of Ford's modern assembly line was transformed by the new model design ideology of General Motors' Alfred P. Sloan. Henry "Buck" Weaver, of General Motors' Customer Research Division, provided compelling evidence, during the early part of the 1930s, that younger consumers favored the more modern and streamlined designs in the items they purchased. "Almost without exception," he concluded, "[Young people] favor . . . the more radical designs." Not much had to change with the product except the exterior or the packaging, and an advertising campaign designed to display the "modern" changes.[20]

Musical instrument manufacturers were part of this same process. In 1930, Conn responded to the decline in instrument sales by reinventing its saxophone. They did away with the older floral design engraving and replaced it with the slogan "the modern style for the modern player." There were no technological changes in the instrument, only cosmetic ones designed to make it look redesigned, new, and modern. Other instrument manufacturers followed suit. In 1935 King proclaimed the new Zephyr saxophone; but, aside from a few cosmetic changes, it was the same as an earlier marketed Voll-True II model. But the advertisement for the new King said the Zephyr was "Lighter, Faster . . . Better." In 1939 King introduced another new Zephyr, only this one had more elaborate engraving, but it still promised better tone, faster playing, and perfect balance.[21]

Advertisements in *Metronome* and *Downbeat* reflect this modernist production technique. All of the musical instrument companies utilized not only the word, but also the idea of modernity throughout much of their ads in the late 1930s and the 1940s. Many of these ads tried to soothe the consumer's fear of change. In order to convince them that the "new and improved" version was indeed better, the consumer had to be sold modernity in order to take the risk of purchasing. Just taking a picture of the new item and saying how much better it was did not convey the generational angle so essential to stimulating the youth marketplace. To place the new item in context with the times, as figures 3.9 and 3.10 display, meant visualizing the past as less than modern. In the first ad, Uncle Harry is seen as a visionary as he moves from the horse and buggy to the more modern automobile. It meant a change in lifestyle, a readjustment, but in the end everyone who

Fig. 3.9. *Metronome* 60 (June 1944): 26

It was the McCoy in 1911

But it won't do to-day.
A *Rudy Mück* horn is built
to take you places, with up-
to-the-minute performance.
Ask your dealer for a convincing trial

TRUMPET $187.⁰⁰
CORNET $187.⁰⁰
CASE $20.⁰⁰

J.R.Mück &Sons Inc.
125 East 126ᵗʰ St.   New York City

Fig. 3.10. *Metronome* 53 (July 1937): inside of back cover

saw the ad as it appeared in 1944 recognized the advantages of the auto over
the horse. J. R. Miick and Sons trumpet company presented the same type
of image in 1937. This time the car is old-fashioned and simply could not
hold up to the standards of today. Martin's "Reed-ripper Zeke" (fig. 3.11) is

"TWENTY-THREE *Skidoo!*"

No new horn fer me!"

SAYS *Reed-ripper Zeke*

Zeke denies that his old gillope saxophone retards his prog- ress and adds—*"My Uncle Goober played 'er fer ten years and then gave 'er to me. Say, she's a dandy. You orter hear me slap tongue on 'er. Some jazz, kiddo. And when I play my laffin' break with the flutter tongue on the end, the folks sure do swing their pardners."* All this is very well but, un- fortunately for Zeke, his future looks none too bright. He can't see very far in the first place and apparently he's well satisfied to keep the hay in his ears, play Uncle Goober's Sax and stay right where he is. Most of us aren't built that way. We know that band instrument construction has greatly im- proved and that instruments considered tops a few years ago are way behind the times now. Competition these days is plenty stiff and to reach the top and stay there we can't be like Zeke! We must keep in step with progress, and combine our own artistic ability with the finest instrument obtainable, a *MARTIN.* Arrange to try one today sure. Compare it with your old horn. Liberal trade-in allowance, easy purchase plan.

MARTIN
BAND INSTRUMENT CO.
DEPARTMENT 1103   ELKHART, INDIANA

Fig. 3.11. *Metronome* 53 (November 1937): 5

a fine sax player, but "his future looks none too bright" because he refuses to buy a new instrument. Back in the 1920s when his uncle blew the horn, it sounded great, but others know "that band instrument construction has greatly improved and that instruments considered tops a few years ago *are way behind the times now.*" The choice is the consumer's, but Martin reminds the reader that "competition these days is plenty stiff" and the musician must use whatever modern means necessary to stay one step ahead of the others.[22]

Other ads placed their product within the pantheon of progress; an idea intrinsically bound to modernity. Here the images deviated little from standard copy, usually displaying a photo of the instrument, written copy distancing it from its competitors, and an invitation to visit the local retailer. What differentiates these from the more standard ad was their validation of modernity. Terry Smith reminds us that by the mid-thirties modernity was legitimized throughout business and industry as a representation of progress. Much of this legitimization involved a compromise of the aesthetic to the mass market, which meant that by the end of the thirties the terms *modern* or *progress*, and the visual imagery associated with them, were normalized and accepted as part of the American social fabric. They were no longer terms or ideas to fear, but signposts to follow. Musical instrument companies participated in this practice by heralding their products' new designs or new features, while changing little. Buescher (fig. 3.12) called the consumer's attention to the "New Models on the Horizon" in 1939. In actuality, little had changed in the trumpets; but, when placed within the design of the ad, where they appear to float on their own, they appear new and modern. In 1944, Buescher announced that it had created the "Sax of the Future" because it had to delay its new series 400 saxophone—heralded as their "greatest achievement"—in 1941 and 1942 to turn production over to making bombers. But now that the war was ending, Buescher reminded readers that it had invented the most modern sax well before its competitors. The same held true for the reed crisis. Musician Edmund Hall recalls that during the war he was forced to try plastic reeds because French ones were in short supply and domestic reeds weren't very good. While he eventually returned to French reeds after the war, during the shortage he found the plastic reeds inexpensive, reliable, and flexible. This was exactly the type of response that the plastic reed manufacturers hoped musicians would have, so many followed Maccaferri's lead by repeating the name of the product—"Futurity"— and describing how its patented improvements created the "perfect reed." To give the product more authenticity, a patent number was included with the company seal. This product had a proud past and a scientific future.

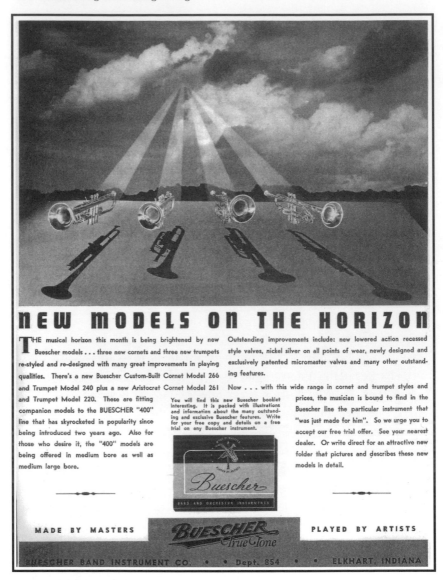

Fig. 3.12. *Downbeat* 6 (August 1939): 15

Cane reed manufacturers soon found themselves having to employ similar tactics, making sure the reader knew that while they were made from cane and not science, the Symmetricut reeds provided "soft, sweet, solid . . . unlimited response!" It was the process that made the Symmetricut, much like the plastic reed, work so well: "It's the exclusive Ciccone cutting and shaping process that makes the most of this superlative cane, and produces reeds that are uniformly perfect."[23]

Others used modern artistic imagery to promote their goods. Advertisers and industrial designers had already begun to utilize rounded corners and additional layering effects to connote a sense of the modern. This process, which Smith labels "modernism through stylization," demanded little change of function from the product but made it appear more streamlined. This modernity of design allowed for advertisers to promote their customers' products by associating them with modern symbols and imagery. Buescher displayed its trombone with its foreground full of the symbols of modernity: big car and well-dressed, wealthy, and successful people (fig. 3.13). King's new 1941 saxophone was linked in name and image to the streamlined, speedy, and modern "Zephyr" train (fig. 3.14). The product had not been changed because of cost and artistic limitations, so the ads simply appropriated symbols of modernity and used them to market the item as new.[24]

Other advertisers choose to link their products more closely with the image of the machine itself. Tonalin proclaimed its reeds to be the superior product based upon their utilization of modern techniques. "Science Triumphs," the ad begins, and the Tonalin Enduro was "revolutionizing the entire reed industry." Apparently Symmetrical reeds were also on the reed cutting-edge, as figure 3.15 attests. The juxtaposition of the factory vise holding onto the reed has a modern look of clean lines, angled positions, and a similarity to modern art. This type of stylization, called Moderne or the International Style of modernism, held high the ideals of "honesty to the materials and simplicity of form." The image should represent the "principle of functional expressiveness" The tactic visualizes all the aspects of modernist art—clean lines, machine precision, simple beauty underlying a complex and efficient machine, and a gentle nonthreatening image—to suggest that the product is more than just an instrument, it is *the* connection to the modern.[25]

The machine itself could be absent, for it was more important to suggest the natural and simple beauty of the product by its association to the principles of modernity. Figure 3.16, for example, emphasized the round, polished finish of the Micro oil products, showing their efficient design and using simplicity of presentation. The ad suggested the past, in the script lettering

Buescher Trombone Model 445   Background Photo Courtesy Cadillac.

THE BUESCHER "400" GIVES YOU A NEW

Perfection in Brass!

*Y*OU will agree . . . the new Buescher "400" Trombone is absolutely the world's finest example of the horn maker's art. Try it. Listen to the beautiful full tone. Important in accounting for this tonal quality is the famous Acousta Bell . . . a bell that is tempered for tone by expert workmen and according to a secret process developed by Buescher research engineers.

The new "400" Trombone is designed for high register clarity. In the high register you'll discover a tone that broadens without going into brilliance—a quality every top-flight professional needs.

A newly designed slide with a much longer bearing surface eliminates chance of binding in sixth and seventh positions. Made of a special nickel silver alloy which gives a smooth, glass like surface and resists corrosion.

Send Postal for FREE NEW BOOK
Here is a fact-giving booklet that every musician should have. Shows by detailed pictures and descriptions just why Buescher instruments blow easier and play better. You'll like the straight-from-the-shoulder presentation. Send for your free copy. A penny postal card will do the trick. Mention instrument in which you're interested.

To achieve a new high in ease of blowing the slides are carefully fit to .002 to .004 of an inch tighter than ordinary slides. Then each sli is automatically worked into its receiver with a special Buesch machine and finally by hand. Special lubrica and the finest abrasive known to mankind are us to assure a smooth, swift, closely fitted, air-tight sli

To assure many years of service, nickel silver used on all points where there is apt to be we These are but a few of the many important reas why the new Buescher "400" Trombone is a r help in improving musicianship. To really app ciate the fine perfection of the new Buescher "4 Trombone you must see it and play it. Our F Trial Plan makes this possible. See your lo Buescher dealer. Or write direct to the Factory complete details.

Fig. 3.13. *Downbeat* 6 (September 1939): 33

"tru-art," while making sure the consumer recognized Micro oil products as "modern oil" with "no waste." An ad for the Olds and Sons "featherweight" trombone, the advertisers juxtaposed the clean lines and stylistic, streamlined image of a bird with the trombone. This "lightest-fastest trombone

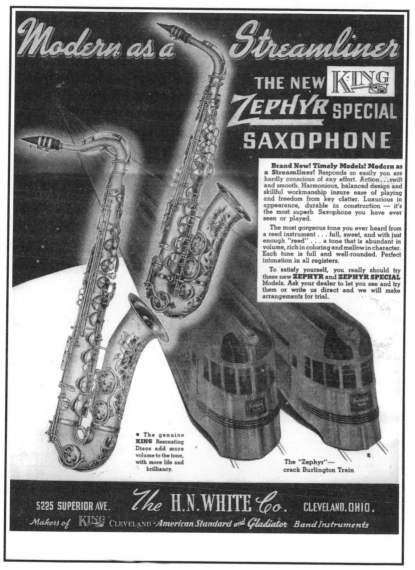

Fig. 3.14. *Downbeat* 8 (June 1941): 7

ever made" appears to operate, like the efficient bird, with little effort, although the machine technology that produced this ease is in plain view. A similar technique is used for figure 3.17, where a close up of a Buescher trumpet is used to detail the simple, functional beauty of its new 400 series.

Fig. 3.15. *Metronome* 62 (July 1946): 2

Not to be outdone, competitor Selmer featured just its pads as part of the "Overture—to a new Musical Era" (fig. 3.18). The use of the product as an artistic modern image is used in figure 3.19 for the Penzel-Mueller Company. The rounded opening of the clarinet suggests the symmetry and naturalness of its design, while the straight lines open the image up for an interesting geometric, modern angle. The instrument as an artistic object reveals its functional simplicity, its beauty, and its connection to the modern. For the Conn ad (fig. 3.20), the modernist imagery is even more striking. The instruments appear as though they are being shot at the viewer. One cannot help but notice the compliment of round and straight, angle and curve, simplicity and complexity, all in one photograph. All of this suggested the

Fig. 3.16. *Metronome* 51 (October 1935): 60

visual imagery necessary to carry the product into the future by connecting it to the industrial and artistic designs of the modernist present.

Nothing changed in the Conn instruments, but the association of them to modernism, an association which by the 1930s and early 1940s had become increasingly normal, encouraged an association with technological innovation. And, since these advertisements appeared in the fanzines of swing, itself a modern creation of sound, sight, and technology, the ads projected the image that swing was natural, liberating, and entirely modern. One of the best ads to project this appeared in early 1946 for the venerable Buescher 400 series. Since Buescher could no longer suggest its technology was "new," as it had in 1941 and 1942, the advertisers attempted to connect

Fig. 3.17. *Metronome* 61 (December 1945): 3

the instruments with other machines of the future. "For an age of better things" (fig. 3.21) suggested the postwar optimism but went further to project a modernist future full of streamlined and functionally designed machines, with their trumpet as the embodiment of this expected heightened modernity.[26]

Fig. 3.18. *Downbeat* 8(February 1941): 5

These ads not only helped to identify swing with modernity, but also aided in the mainstream appropriation of the generational music. The existence of these ads in *Metronome*, *Downbeat*, and a host of other magazines represents the validation of the music. The instrument manufacturers had traditionally spent most of their ad dollars in journals for band directors,

Fig. 3.19. *Metronome* 61 (January 1945): 3

music educators, or school bandleaders. With swing, the promotion of the individual desire to play an instrument existed outside the traditional means of expert control. These ads rarely suggested that lessons might be necessary to play like Benny Goodman or Chick Webb but implied that by purchasing

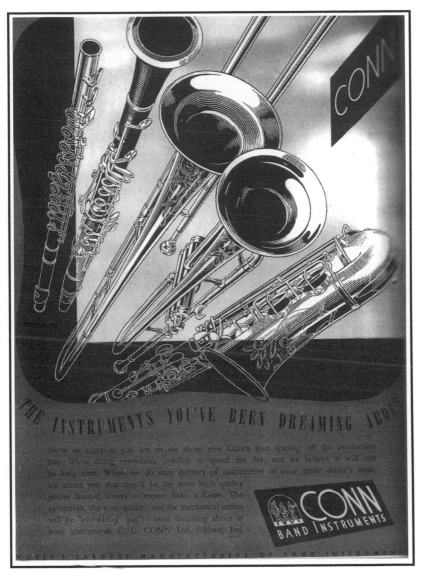

Fig. 3.20. *Metronome* 61 (October 1945): 2

the item the consumer would be connected to the swing movement. The brand, style, and look of the instrument were as important as the ability to play. The product consumed suggested to others a certain ability, status, and modern connection. To play the older instruments meant the player was

Fig. 3.21. *Metronome* 62 (March 1946): 7

behind the times. The new and improved models suggested their players were modern, hip, and successful.

Don Albert recalls that Conn supplied him and others with free instruments in exchange for these types of endorsements. This, of course, translated into increased sales. *Metronome* reported in 1937 that sales of instruments had increased 25 percent in 1936, and sales were up 102 percent since 1932, largely as a result of swing. Sales in 1937 grew by nearly 75 percent from sales in 1935, grossing over $34 million. Company sales records from Conn are limited or nonexistent, but by looking at the serial numbers of its reed instruments from the years 1935 through 1948 and comparing them to the serial numbers of the instruments sold between 1916 and 1930, the role swing played in the rebound in sales is evident.[27]

The influence of the marketplace, or Bauza's "they," was not restricted to advertisers. Another important component to the success of swing as a generational movement was its important connection to the growth of the culture industry, particularly Hollywood. During the depression era, movie attendance grew by over seventeen million, as the studios produced more films than ever before. With technological improvements like sound and, later, color, some films became events unto themselves—openings—and Hollywood stars became influential and important celebrities. Most of the offerings were of the B-grade, whether they were in the Western, gangster, comedy, or monster genre, and were produced in formulaic fashion. Several scholars have emphasized the growing reliance of the industry on appealing to working-class consumers, as the number of theaters in these neighborhoods tended to be higher than in wealthier areas.[28]

While the movies had utilized jazz, the film industry's acceptance of swing represents the interconnection of the three primary entertainment media of its time: radio, records, and film. The role of radio in the promotion of swing was significant for the stimulation of record sales and concert appearances (as well as selling other nonmusical consumer products), but film provided a visual aesthetic that spoke directly to the youth, an emerging market many industries were trying to capture. *Metronome* recognized this growing connection between film and swing in a 1937 editorial which outlined the economic value of having a swing band open up for a movie. The film tended to draw larger crowds, made more money for the theater, and gave the band wider exposure. The Paramount theater in 1936 used swing bands as draws for its films and the results were significant: $8,500 gross for the movie without the Casa Loma band versus $55,000 profit when the band opened for a movie. With these numbers in mind more and more theaters hired popular bands to serve as openers for new films with the resulting increase in profits. In some cases the bands were seen as carrying weak or poor films.[29]

But the movies also robbed many musicians of work. Once again the modernist dilemma regarding technology, which sought to enrich the musicians and also made them unnecessary, was at the center of the crisis. Previous to the introduction of sound to films, musicians found ample employment performing in theaters. The American Federation of Musicians estimated that about twenty-four thousand musicians worked in this vein.

But as the technology improved these musicians were replaced by canned or mechanical music. By the end of the 1930s the popular musician faced a real quandary—movies about and featuring swing exposed the music to more people and thus expanded the potential for performances and profits; yet the films themselves represented a means of replacement for live music. It was a problem that they would never quite solve.[30]

Hollywood sought an easier method for increasing the draw of movies without having the theaters pay for the live entertainment, namely, bringing the music and musicians into the films. From 1936 through 1949 Hollywood released over fifty films that used swing in their titles, including *Swing It* (1936), *Swing Hotel* (1939), and the ever-popular *Synco-smooch Swing* (1945). Countless numbers of other films used jazz or swing music and musicians as part of their presentation. Krin Gabbard's recent examination of the film industry's treatment of jazz and swing offers an interesting look at their role and meaning within the context of American society. In the introduction he outlines the story of Kay Kyser, one of the biggest draws of his day and someone who starred and featured in swing music in seven films, more than any other band or leader. Yet, as Gabbard points out, because the canon does not recognize Kyser's form of jazz as among the best, he is rarely mentioned in jazz and/or swing histories. But Kyser, who was among the leaders in record sales and audience polls regularly, said his band "could swing just as hard as the orchestras of Glenn Miller and the Dorseys." In terms of his influence on the popularity of the music, Gabbard argues, "Kyser cleaned up swing music and made it acceptable to a large, Middle American, white audience" via film.[31]

Within the movies swing was promoted on a variety of levels, yet one of the strongest involved dance. The essence of swing was its youthful dance energy, and Hollywood sought to introduce new dance styles. These dance fads helped perpetuate swing as a generational musical form and gave identity to its participants—the audience. Dancing helped define their role in the creation of the music, for while the musicians and bands created the music without direct input from the audience, the audience's desire to dance encouraged the arrangers, leaders, and musicians to create music and songs that they hoped their fans would make popular through their participation.

One example of this tendency was the emergence and popularity of the Lindy Hop. The dance originated in the late twenties in Harlem and was named for Charles Lindbergh, but the swing generation called it the jitter-bug or swing dancing. Hollywood sought to use the energy of the dance to excite its youthful audiences, encouraging more young people to attend the films where the dance was presented. One of the first problems with its presentation was the highly individualistic and improvisational nature of the Lindy. To present it on the screen meant certain standardized versions had to be created and performed to meets the studio's needs. The Lindy Hop was simplified and made to exhibit youthful exuberance and good clean fun. To do this, a Lindy Hop dance troupe from New York City called "Whitey's Lindy Hopppers" was brought to Hollywood in 1937 to work in films such as *A Day at the Races* (1937), *Hellzapoppin* (1941), and a score of others. By 1943 the dance had become popular enough across the country to warrant a *Life* magazine cover, inclusion in dance class curricula, and increased appearances in films.[32]

That swing became a staple in the film industry is no surprise, for it was tied to the emerging modern entertainment industry. Whether it was music, radio, magazines, or film, this modern consumer industry had developed an interconnected system of checks. These gatekeepers helped determine what would be sold to the consumer. Those involved in the preselection process—producers, engineers, rackers and jobbers, jukebox owners, distribution companies, record reviewers, fanzines, film corporations, and many more—helped to shape the consumption of the swing product. This fit with the argument of Theodor Adorno, Max Horkheimer, and others of the Frankfurt School: culture had lost its autonomy and had been absorbed into the base of the capitalist system. "All culture," Andreas Huyssien writes concerning the Frankfurt School's interpretation, "is standardized, organized and administered for the sole purpose of serving as an instrument of social control." Since culture is caught in the capitalist cycle of production for profit, creation is sold to the profit motive.[33] To Adorno and Horkheimer, the cultural industry's connection to consumerism was "part of the broader oppressive 'totality' of capitalism."[34]

The flaw in this argument regarding swing concerns both the availability of products and the role of the people themselves. Geoffrey Nowell-Smith argues that the difficulty of applying the cultural industry thesis to film is that talent, which cannot "be produced to order," determines the product. There are many examples of films that fail, regardless of their promotion, stars, or even positive critical review. The story formula, whether Western or contemporary, rarely satisfied the consumer for long periods. The same was true for popular music and swing. There were countless numbers of bands that played the territories, the small dance clubs, and the remote towns in America. Only a handful ever became nationally recognized. The same held for the musicians. For every Bunny Berigan there were perhaps hundreds of wanna-bes who never got beyond their local communities or played as sidemen in regional bands. Even if records were not as important as they are for today's music industry, the competition for a place in the jukeboxes was intense, and for every hit there were hundreds of misses. To further complicate the Frankfurt School's view of cultural manipulation, Michael Denning's recent book, *The Cultural Front*, argues that members of the working class came to dominate the cultural industries in the latter part of the 1930s and 1940s, and cultural formation was altered to accept these newer versions and visions of the American experience.[35]

Instead, the rise of the swing generation suggests more the legitimization of an avant-garde idea than a creation by a monolithic cultural industry. During the 1920s jazz had been popular and profitable, yet as an attitude or way of being it still remained part of the underground. As the music evolved and came to be regarded as swing, it was initially seen as oppositional. The music industry had much more vested interest in the continued promotion of Tin Pan Alley tunes than in promoting a new identity with overt racial connotations. Under the scrutiny of Adorno and Horkheimer, this music had little chance of success, coming as it did from groups outside the traditional cultural industry. Yet swing music became the generational music of the 1930s and 1940s, not through manipulation, but through the ability of the dominant culture to absorb oppositional ideas and legitimize them. This concept, sometimes labeled cultural hegemony, recognizes that the cultural industry is unable to completely manipulate everything that is produced. Instead, it minimizes the risk of failure by making legitimate the public's particular cultural taste. If that taste is critical of the existing social order, by its acceptance as popular it is validated by the dominant and loses much of its oppositional force, while still retaining its countercultural value. This Gramscian conception of hegemony, according to Walter L. Adamson, "is not a static concept but a process of continuous creation which, given its massive scale, is bound to be uneven in the degree of legitimacy it commands and to leave some room for antagonistic cultural expression to develop."[36]

Jazz, as swing, was oppositional because initially the established gatekeepers did not accept it. When it achieved popularity with the nation's youth as a safe way to "blow off steam," it was legitimized, and this allowed for its dissemination as a consumable article produced and marketed to the young consumer. These young people wanted to fit in with the acceptable youth culture promoted to them through magazines, radio, and film and appropriated the consciousness of swing.[37] Teddy Wilson, part of Goodman's band, saw it in a more monolithic manner: "[T]here's no telling what will open up, and the only thing is when the businessmen take hold of it, it will be the same old thing again. They will control the public taste, the exposure to what is available, and they will control the production of it and the publicizing of it and the marketing of it."[38] But he was speaking as someone who had witnessed the buying and selling of swing several years before. He failed to take into account the generational influence and energy that was as much a part of the business as anything else. Swing was a consumable product, but the generational attitude—the swing way of being—that went along with the music was not for sale. The easiest way to view this consciousness is to read what they wrote about their music. A 1939 *Musician* article captured their consciousness when it suggested that those who criticize the music "will never understand the [swing] phenomenon" because it creates a "circle of men and women . . . [as] it becomes a people's music."[39]

By 1939 swing had helped to revive the music industry (live bookings, employment, and records), provided inexpensive entertainment for radio, played a role in the movies of the era, and was part of the economic transformation from customer to consumer. Swing's role in this was not a calculated business decision, but one of accommodation to the fluctuations in the marketplace whereby the consumers, or people, played a significant role. Swing did this by utilizing the most recent technology without sacrificing the ideal of individuality. This modern connection appealed to the young people in America, and they adopted swing as their modern music. There were other factors at stake within this scenario, namely, the interaction of class, ethnicity, race, and gender, an interaction that also made swing the modern music of America.

The American Swing Dream

The Role and Influence of Class in Swing

The generation that made swing the popular music of its time was the product not only of unique musical and modern circumstances, but also of the changing nature of America's social construction—the American dream. Many of those who came of age during the swing era witnessed in their childhood and early occupational years, 1900–1930, the very changes affecting the definition of American society. These swing kids witnessed their parents' labor or began participating in the economy themselves and, as a result, developed certain ideologies, regarding class and work, which grew out of their working-class backgrounds. Given the necessity of collective behavior and cooperation during the dual crises of the Great Depression and World War II, the swing musicians' ability to join with others outside their normal circle of acquaintances to create a cultural product exemplified this changing social consciousness. America as a whole was undergoing profound shifts in its understanding of class, and this was a key ingredient in the development and acceptance of swing music.

Admittedly, the question of class and American society during this time period is a difficult one. More often than not, class becomes part of an analysis of consciousness based on the ability of the workers to collectivize along lines more closely defined by the European experience. And, given the totality of the cold war experience and the extent to which class as a political ideology became taboo, it is not surprising that the American conception of class has taken a backseat to the more obvious European model. But what these types of analyses ignore are the unique characteristics of the American experience and modernity, especially in regards to the heterogeneous nature of America's workers, language, customs, and the all too pervasive influence of abundance.

Scholars have begun to redefine the working-class experience in the first third of this century, placing it, as Lawrence Glickman argues, within the context of "the American Standard of Living." His analysis of the development of working-class identity from 1880 to 1925 argues that the transition from wage labor as wage slavery to one pegged against the ability of the worker to consume and participate in the economy changed how labor was viewed within the American political economy. Workers' representatives now clamored for a wage that would enable them to more fully participate in the economy and give them a standard of living that allowed for goods other than needs. As a result, "these workers emphasized the centrality of material well-being to class consciousness" and "placed themselves at the center of any consideration of the nation's political economy." The same held true for the influx into the system of immigrants and African Americans, who helped remake the concept of working class in their acceptance and rejection of these ideals.[1]

Class identity defines the working experience during the early third of the twentieth century. Lizabeth Cohen's work on the formation of class identities in Chicago details the manner in which workers adapted to the economic changes from the 1920s to the 1930s and how these adjustments transformed America's political and cultural landscape. By attempting to reconstruct their daily life, Cohen views the working people of Chicago as multifaceted and powerful in their ability to mold mass culture into products and identities that did not alienate them from their parent's ethnic, racial, and/or class experiences. While changes did occur, the consumptive pattern of Chicago's working class during the interwar years reveals their increased participation in the consumer marketplace in a manner such that they "did not deny their existing class and ethnic identities nor find themselves unconsciously incorporated into middle-class society." It was during the hard times of the 1930s that workers began to frequent chain stores, signaling, some have maintained, their acceptance of middle-class ideals. But, Cohen argues, while they may have increased their consumer behavior along more "mass" lines, they retained their oppositional status by increasing their participation in organizations such as the Congress of Industrial Organizations (CIO). While the consumer habits of the working class increased along standardized lines—chain stores, network radio, Hollywood, magazines— they also allowed for the creation of a much more "homogeneous working- class culture [that was] distinguishable" from the middle-class one.[2]

During the 1930s a distinguishable working-class culture emerged. Largely under the auspices of the Popular Front, but generally outside of its organizational tendencies, the children of the first generation of ethnic or regional migrants to the nation's urban areas took up positions of relative power in the emerging cultural industries. These sons and daughters of the working class, encouraged to finish high school by new state-mandated laws, found themselves within the mass entertainment industries as workers producing goods to be consumed by other workers. While not involved in the production of heavy machinery or automobiles, they were nonetheless workers in their identity and belief structure. There are a variety of examples to support this idea: the success of the CIO; the abundance of populist movies like *The Grapes of Wrath* or *Citizen Kane*; literature by Ralph Ellison and John Dos Passos; the Ghetto Pastoral; or even the labor agitation of Disney's cartoonists. What all of these suggest is an allegiance to the working-class ideals of social democracy, collective behavior, and anti-fascism. These new mental laborers produced goods for the new workers empowered by the ideals of the CIO, workers who saw themselves in the cultural formations. The 1930s and early 1940s produced working-class images and ideals and left a lasting legacy on American culture.[3]

By the 1930s American class-consciousness was clearly different from the European model. American workers sought to participate in the growing consumer-based economy, and their labor unions' ability to legitimize this desire by arguing for better hours and wages meant increased participation within the organized national political parties. While they may not have viewed themselves as working class in the same manner as their European cohorts, their lived experiences defined their class, and while consumer and voting patterns help to measure their influence, they do not tell the whole story. In a 1941 *Fortune* poll, nearly 80 percent of the respondents identified themselves as middle class. But the magazine provided only three choices—upper, middle, and lower. When Richard Centers redid the study in 1949 and added another class, working class, the results found middle class dropping to 43 percent while 51 percent identified themselves as working class.[4]

What this suggests is that during the era of the Great Depression and World War II, the ideals of working class and the American dream were challenged and redefined. The issues and ideology of the working class became part of the American dialogue. The workers, whether they be New Deal Democrats, members of a labor union, or moviegoers, were not simply blind consumers of the middle-brow way of life, but they helped to create their own avenues of production, influencing and creating markets targeted at their desires and lifestyles. This was especially true during the depression, as the hard times defined their class identity in opposition to the creators of the collapse. Combined with the proliferation of mass consumer and cultural products, their ideals became more homogenous and held political and economic power. Their expectations rose in conjunction with their increased social and political voice.[5]

Taken this way, class was central to the experiences of a majority of people in the United States. And, if taken out of the context of organizational strategies in opposition to capitalism (the traditional measure of class consciousness) and placed within the context of the American situation, class becomes more of a signifier between the people's differences based upon their wealth, education, or occupation. Although this seems to put more emphasis on status, given the American situation and the close connection between consumption and class, there is, as Richard Polenberg points out, a "reasonable congruence between the two."[6]

Contemporary sociological studies from Middletown to Yankee City came to the same conclusion: "class membership determined virtually every aspect of an individual's life." Where one went to school, the subjects studied, opportunities in the workplace, spouses, clubs, magazines, activities, and other variables were subject to the confines of one's class. Movement outside one's class, while not impossible, was infrequent because most individuals were in constant fear of unemployment and increased job alienation. Of 122 working-class wives interviewed for *Middletown*, 83 said they or their husbands "never [knew] from day to day whether [their husbands'] job [would] be there." The only hope seemed to be promotion, but this, too, proved elusive. Out of the 4,240 persons employed during the first six months of 1923, only ten openings for foreman existed, a 1 in 424 chance. But the company felt that only 531 men were qualified for the promotion. Most workers knew they had little chance of job improvement. One wife lamented that her husband had been doing "the same thing over and over for fifteen years, hoping he'd get ahead, and he's never had a chance; so I don't suppose he ever will." This tendency was mirrored in other industrial cities, where the number of skilled positions rarely matched the increased number of qualified workers. The workers saw the futility of their work and became more disillusioned about their futures. As one wife related, "He'll never get a better job." They also recognized their obsolescence to the machine, telling the Lynds that "the work of a modern day machine-tender leaves nothing tangible at the end of the day's work to which he can point with pride and say, 'I did that.' " Work, for Middletown's laboring class, was necessary for survival, but held little attraction.[7]

The structure of life was influenced by the wages paid to the worker. While wages increased during the first thirty years of the century, they were well below the middle-class wage-earning culture. For the common road laborer, that meant a change from 20 cents an hour in 1914 to 36 cents an hour in 1931, while manufacturing wages went from 25 cents per hour to 46 cents. For workers in heavy industrial production, wages rose less than 1 percent or dropped significantly when combined with the standard of living, periodic layoffs, and the lack of growth in the period right before the 1920s. Throughout this period more than 42 percent of all American families made less than $1,500 a year, which barely covered the basic necessities of home, automobile, and food. The annual wages for workers in most occupations rarely went beyond that $1,500 mark, with most matching the annual pay of the non-union manufacturing class in its 1928 high of $1,325 per year. During the depression these numbers went down; by 1939 the average factory worker made $1,250 for the year, while only 4.2 percent earned $2,500. In that year, over 58 percent of those men employed in the private sector earned less than $1,000, and 78 percent of the women earned even less.[8]

When the Lynds returned to Middletown in 1936 they found little had changed. Occupation still determined nearly all aspects of life, and with the decrease in opportunities caused by the economic collapse, those persons labeled workers found their vision of the future clouded. The number of males in the workplace exceeded the number of positions available, and although there seemed to be a renewed optimism among the workers after 1935 (several plants reopened and new ones began), the chances for advancement among the working class remained slim. The Lynds' feared that the old American adage of starting from the ground up was evaporating, and, if the trend continued, workers would be within the "permanent boundaries of nineteen-dollar suits, $2.50 shoes, and a secondhand 'Chevie.'" This situation was not lost on those who labored for the cities' companies, as more workers began to place less emphasis on the skill differences between their jobs. They saw their situation simply as work: "You have a job—if you're lucky—and you work." Since getting ahead was unlikely, the pursuit of leisure activities occupied more of their time and energy and became a means to associate with their peers.[9]

The consciousness of the working class had direct influence on swing both as music and as a culture, for it was within this context that most swing musicians and their fans grew up. Those who became swing musicians were like the majority of Americans who were born between 1904 and 1919 in America, representing the largest working-class generation in American history. They witnessed how hard their parents worked for so little and saw how much respect they deserved for what they did. Many times, when the swing musicians recalled their parents' occupations, they did so with a level of respect that reveals their class-consciousness, so akin to the ideology of the 1930s. Gil Evans, for example, remembered traveling through Idaho and Montana mining camps with his cook mother and miner stepfather. The work was unstable and he had to get up at 3 A.M. every morning to help fix breakfast. Gene Ramey knew his father as a teamster, but admitted that most of the work he was able to secure around Austin, Texas, in the late 1910s was that of farmhand.[10]

When one examines the lived experiences of those who became swing musicians, most of whom were born into the above cohort, a clear connection is made to class. I created a statistical database of 278 musicians from a variety of swing-era bands—Benny Goodman's, Count Basie's, Duke Ellington's, Bob Crosby's, Artie Shaw's, the Dorseys', Cab Calloway's, and even Guy Lombardo's band—and tabulated their life stories to categorize their parents' occupations and the musicians' level of schooling, musical training, race/ethnicity, where they were born/raised, and what instrument they played. The information was derived from a variety of sources, including collections of firsthand accounts, such as those found in the many Stanley Dance books, credible autobiographies and biographies, the many published oral histories, and those yet unpublished ones housed at the jazz oral history collections at Rutgers and Tulane Universities.[11]

Examining the results of this basic survey, I detailed the role class played in the lives of the swing musicians. In 233 cases, where the occupation of a parent during a swing musician's childhood could be determined, over 51 percent remembered their parents as laboring among the working class, with another 10 percent recalling they came from the lowest rung on the occupational ladder (see tables 4.1 and 4.2). When one adds the white-collar workers and clergy, who were socially distinct but not economically ahead of the unskilled laborers, the percentage of swing musicians who came from this segment of the population goes to nearly 80 percent. Using this data, one

Class	Number Of Musicians	% Of Musicians
Data missing	45	16.2
Poor/transient	28	10.0
Working class	144	51.8
White collar	50	18.0
Professional	11	4.0

Table 4.1. Swing Musicians by Class

	Poor/Transient (%)	Working Class (%)	White Collar (%)	Professional (%)
African American	13.6	61.4	23.6	1.4
Southern or Eastern European Immigrant	7.3	67.3	14.5	10.9

Note: Of the 278 musicians examined, those who mentioned minority ethnic backgrounds were broken down into two sections: Southern or Eastern European immigrants (out of a possible 231 cases, 55, or 23.8%, were included) and African Americans (out of 232 cases, 129, or 55.6%, were included).

Table 4.2. African American and Southern or Eastern European Immigrant Swing Musicians by Class

can argue that the majority of swing musicians came from working-class or lower backgrounds. This ideology helped shape their conceptions of self, work, and money.

Many of those who made swing were informed by their class backgrounds, which became part of their own adult identity. It would be difficult for them to forget the experiences of their childhood. They witnessed firsthand their parents', or their own, struggles to find and keep work. Count Basie, who grew up in the resort town of Red Bank, New Jersey, during the 1910s and early 1920s, watched as his father's job as coachman for a local judge became obsolete with the rise of the automobile. Denied his primary source of income, the elder Basie became a caretaker for wealthy people's homes during the off-season and prepared the homes for their summer arrival. Count Basie's mother supplemented the family's income by taking in laundry. When Basie described the situation, he did so with pride, as his parents' hard work and dedication allowed them to own their home and provide a stable environment for their children. Jay McShann remembered the hard work of his father, as a driver of a delivery truck for a Muskogee, Oklahoma, furniture and carpeting store, and the countless times he had to go out of town for extended periods. Jess Stacy's father worked on the railroad in Missouri, and Jess was born during a train layover. His early years were spent near the abandoned boxcar that served as the family home. By the time Jess had reached his teens, his father's eyesight had failed and the railroad let him go. The family survived on the income of Jess's seamstress mother and his job as a messenger for Western Union. Benny Goodman remembered how his father brought in less than twenty dollars a week for the family of twelve as a factory tailor. This forced the family to move frequently, from one low-rent flat to another. He recalled there were times when "there wasn't anything to eat" but spoke with pride of his father's work ethic.[12]

These types of experiences are hard for children to forget, and Goodman admitted never losing that feeling of seeing his father unable to put food on the table. Given this environment, Goodman's father was dedicated to making sure his children would not follow in his footsteps and did everything in his power to getting them out of the cycle of poverty in which he was locked. For Billie Holiday's teenage parents, their youth and lack of money complicated the task of raising their newborn. But Holiday recalled with pride the fact that her mother would "scrub floors" and help others having babies "so she could pay her way." In fact, once her daughter was born, the mother had to continue to work at the hospital to finish paying off the bill. According to Holiday, by the time she and her mother went home, she was able to "sit up in the carriage."[13]

Another indicator of class membership was that many swing musicians grew up on the move, following their parents in search of steady work. Of the 278 musicians in the survey, just over 50 percent were born in the North (East Coast, Midwest, and Mideast) while the number increases slightly, to 54 percent, for those who were raised in this region. But, when broken down by class, the percentage of working-class and poor musicians is higher in the North (see table 4.3).

This increase reflects internal migrations from the South, primarily among the working class and poor; but what these numbers do not reveal is the tendency among working-class families, such as Goodman's, to constantly move within the same region or city. For example, Benny Carter's father's frequent job changes—from low-paying janitor to night watchman and postal clerk—allowed the family to stay in the San Juan Hill area of

	North (%)	South (%)	West (%)
Born there			
Poor/working class	77.70	72.15	70.96
Middle class	18.75	27.85	22.58
Professional	3.55	0.00	6.46
Raised there			
Poor/working class	85.00	66.10	52.17
Middle class	11.60	32.30	39.23
Professional	3.40	1.60	8.60

Note: North includes Maine, Connecticut, New Hampshire, Rhode Island, New Jersey, Vermont, New York, Pennsylvania, Massachusetts, Michigan, Ohio, Indiana, Illinois, Wisconsin, Missouri, Nebraska, Kansas, Iowa, Minnesota, and North and South Dakota; South includes Delaware, West Virginia, Virginia, Kentucky, Tennessee, North and South Carolina, Maryland, Georgia, Alabama, Mississippi, Florida, Arkansas, and Louisiana; West includes Texas, Oklahoma, New Mexico, Arizona, Montana, Wyoming, Colorado, Utah, Idaho, Washington, Oregon, California, and Nevada.

Table 4.3. Where Swing Musicians Were Born versus Where They Were Raised

New York City, but they were constantly on the move. Elmer Miller traveled with his family throughout the Midwest in search of steady work. He was frustrated in his attempts as a carpenter, a railroad foreman, and even a homesteader. When Glenn Miller was five, his family lived in a sod hut in Tryon, Nebraska, outside of North Platte. They stayed there for five years and eventually moved to Grant City, Missouri. While picking beets, Miller decided on a career in music, spending his lunch hour and all his free time playing an old trumpet. "It got to where Pop and I," his mother later recalled, "used to wonder if he'd ever amount to anything." The family then moved in 1918 to Ft. Morgan, Colorado, where Miller attended high school and graduated in 1921. These years were also spent working in a beet sugar factory and playing end on the school football team. But by graduation Miller was off in search of his musical career. Stan Kenton's father wandered with his family throughout the Midwest and Far West in search of work. During this quest the elder Kenton sold tombstones, worked as a mechanic, roofer, and carpenter, attempted to own a garage, grocery store, car dealership, and butcher shop—all resulting in failure. Finally the family settled in the Los Angeles area where the elder Kenton found steady work. The father wanted to make sure his son would not follow in his footsteps and frowned on his musical skills, wishing that Stan, as his sister remembers, would "be a postman," where he felt he would have steady employment and a retirement fund.[14]

The elder Kenton's concern that his son not follow in his footsteps was a real concern among the laboring classes, for, as the Lynds' point out, many wanted more for their children. The confusion came from how to go about attaining something better. Most working-class children would "stumble on" or "fall into" the particular jobs that became literally their life's work. Or, more likely, as Judith Smith's examination of Italian and Jewish immigrants and their children during the 1920s and 1930s reveals, they followed in their parents' laboring footsteps. Smith's study of Providence, Rhode Island, workers reveals that in 1935 "27 percent of employed Italian sons and daughters" and "14 percent of Jewish sons and daughters worked at the same occupation as their fathers." This proved a real concern for future swing musicians as well. Vic Dickenson tried to learn his father's bricklaying business when he was sixteen or seventeen, but the experience of carrying a seventy pound "hod full of mortar" up a ladder, which gave way and caused him to injure his back, soured him on that career choice.[15]

Sometimes these class connections had advantages. Sam Wooding's father was a butler in Philadelphia, but young Sam refused to follow in his father's footsteps and ran off to Atlantic City to be a musician. Finding little success, he got a job as a waiter in a hotel. "I used to go up and help my father," he said, "so I knew something about waiting, anyway." His father's training proved beneficial, for he was able to not only make some money, but sneak food out to musician pals in a leather pocket on the inside of his coat. For Doc Cheatham, following in his father's medical doctor footsteps proved too difficult, and by his teens he was actively pursuing music as a career. By 1921 he was traveling with bands, landing in Chicago in 1923 broke and without hope. After working a variety of menial jobs for three years, he finally landed a full-time music gig.[16]

While fearful that their children might follow their career paths, para-doxically, the precarious nature of employment encouraged parents to ad-vise their children to follow in their paths. Hilton "Nappy" Lamare, who played banjo and guitar for Bob Crosby's band, hoped to follow in his father's and grandfather's footsteps by becoming a printer. While he had no aversion to the craft, he found music more interesting. Willie "the Lion" Smith's mother asked her husband to add him on as his helper on weekends at the local pork slaughterhouse, both to make sure her husband did not drink his checks away and to provide job training for her son. Smith worked halving pigs at a rate of four hundred a night. Cozy Cole was sent to New York City after his high school graduation in the hope that he would follow in his uncle's barber profession. He worked awhile, then quit to work as a shipping clerk. He left this job as well, for all he wanted to do was "play drums."[17]

Sometimes following in the parental footsteps meant working in the en-tertainment industry. Harry James was born and quickly went to work for the Mighty Haag Circus, where his mother performed as a trapeze artist and his father led the band. At an early age James began working as part of a contortionist's act. His father promoted him by age seven to the band, where he pounded the bass drum. At ten he became a full-fledged member of the band as a trumpet player and later replaced his father as the soloist. Buddy Rich was raised in vaudeville, and by the time he was ten years old he was already a seasoned performer. But for Drew Page, coming from a working-class family in Ada, Oklahoma, playing music was seen as an escape from the reality of working in his hometown. He answered an ad in *Billboard* magazine for oil-field workers who could also play musical instruments and was sent to Salt Creek, Wyoming, where he dug ditches and worked as a cook. He never got the chance to play his clarinet.[18]

Working-class women faced more obstacles in going beyond the generational occupational pattern. Although employment opportunities for women improved after the First World War, the effect was limited. And, for working-class women, a job meant they now had two jobs, raising the family and supplementing the household income. When the Lynds revisited Muncie, Indiana, in the mid-1930s, they found that women were being crowded out of several professional fields—dentist, designers, and engineers—and were being driven out in their traditional field of teaching. However, their numbers were growing in the domestic and personal service jobs. The depression hit women especially hard. By 1931 there were over 2 million women out of work. Until the 1935 creation of the Works Progress Administration (WPA), they could expect little help from the government. Most Americans felt that working women should give up their jobs to men and spend more time in the home. But under FDR and with the assistance of Harry Hopkins, Ellen Woodward, and the president's wife, Eleanor, women's employment issues took on an increasingly significant role by 1935. The WPA created a specific division for their employment, called the Women's Division, whose job it was to target unemployed women for WPA jobs. By 1936, 459,938 women were on the WPA rolls, with one-third of them employed in the professional sector. While the great majority of women assisted by the WPA were employed in projects involving traditional women's work—as food canners, librarians, seamstresses, and educators—many others found opportunities in theater, music, and writing through the Federal Art Project, which included nearly 41 percent women. One of these professional projects, the Federal Music Project, gave some American women composers and musicians their first opportunity to hear their compositions and play alongside male musicians. The era was a mixed bag for women, for it both reinforced traditional roles for women and liberated them through agencies such as the WPA and Social Security (headed by Frances Perkins) and through the First Lady's social agenda.[19]

For most women, especially those from the working class, the changes during the 1930s were barely noticeable. Many were locked into a social vision as wives, mothers, and little else. Swing vocalist Viola Jefferson remembered her mother's struggle in a coal-mining family outside of Carbondale, Illinois. Witnessing the day-to-day events of her mother's life "turned [her] against the idea of being a mother or a housewife." When she was sent to Chicago to live with her sister at age fourteen, she quickly married a "city slicker." And, even though she had already made a name for herself as a singer, "being the original country girl and coal-miner's daughter," she agreed to abandon her singing career to take care of her husband. This lost its allure quickly, and less than a year later she began singing under her maiden name. Her husband objected and gave her an ultimatum, him or singing. They divorced and she sang. The great Billie Holiday was torn between which parent to follow: her mother as a domestic or her father as a musician. When her mother sent for her to come to New York City and got her a job working as a domestic, Holiday hated the job. She described her boss as a "big, fat and lazy" woman who yelled at her all the time. "I didn't want to be her maid, or anybody's," she recalled. "I figured there had to be something better than this." After losing that job, her mother took her to Harlem to board with a woman who turned out to be a madam. Within weeks the young girl became a "twenty-dollar call girl." Even after the madam took her cut, Holiday made more money in a day than she could make all month as a maid. But when she refused to service a black man connected with those "running" Harlem, she was arrested and eventually sent to prison on Welfare Island. When she got out, she went back into the trade, but sent all her profits to her mother. When her pimp discovered this, he beat her and threw her out. She ended up at a poker and gambling house out on Long Island where she waited tables, cleaned, and occasionally sang at the local Elks Club.[20]

Many of those who became swing musicians found, like most members of the working class, that they had to work throughout much of their childhood. The income generated by the children of the working class was often seen as a necessary supplement to the family's income. This was certainly the case with future swing musicians. By age nine, for example, Clark Terry earned his own room and board by charging pennies to haul away people's ashes. As the seventh child in a family of ten, he lived with his oldest sister and her husband and had to earn his keep. As a twelve-year-old, Quentin Hall's job was to light and clean seventy-five gas lamps in his hometown of Springfield, Illinois. His paycheck went directly to his mother. "Sir" Charles Thompson shined shoes, washed cars, operated elevators, caddied golfers and was a bellhop during his youth. He also served with FDR's Civilian Conservation Corps. Willie Smith remembers that during his childhood in Charleston, South Carolina, he woke up every day at 4 a.m. to deliver papers on two routes; later he got a better job working with his father hammering down boards. Andy Kirk's first job was working on a sugar beet farm outside Denver when he was fourteen. He worked from sunup to sundown hoeing the beet fields for $1.50 a day. When he returned to Denver to begin his sophomore year, he continued to work; before school he cleaned the lobby at the St. James Hotel, and after school he worked as a porter and delivery boy for Regal Shoes. Benny Carter was hired as a replacement worker in a railroad camp in Youngstown, Ohio. A recruiter came to his New York City neighborhood searching for young men wanting work at $1.00 a day, and since that was well above the prevailing wage, Carter and others readily joined. However, the recruiter failed to mention that they were to be used as strikebreakers and Carter returned home as soon as he could.[21]

Having to work while still young instilled in some the desire to escape the world in which they and their parents were trapped. In the late twenties and early thirties, some people took to the rails to find work or in search of adventure. Following the example of tens of thousands of other Americans desperate for work, several future swing musicians hopped freight trains in search of employment. Buck Clayton tried it as both a means of escape from Parsons, Kansas, and way to find better opportunities. He and a friend ran away from home in 1929 and made their way to Los Angeles. Both were seventeen and found their job options limited to menial jobs. After several months, Clayton returned home by bus and took a job in the local rock quarry. Jay McShann and a friend jumped a train heading east from Oklahoma in the mid-1930s to find work. They were only sixteen and found few opportunities in Knoxville, Tennessee, so they tried to ride the rails back. In the middle of the Blue Ridge Mountains, the railroad detective kicked them off the train. They waited for another train that took them to Nashville and from there jumped a train back to Oklahoma.[22]

But the most interesting story comes from John Simmons. In 1935, when he was about seventeen, Simmons took to the rails to find work. Eighteen miles outside Amarillo, Texas, he and his traveling friend were kicked off a train heading west. The rail dicks (detectives) threw several other "hoboes" off as well, and the group began to walk back to the town. While they were walking, a dust storm hit and the twenty or so men "joined hands and started to walk," fearing that standing still might mean they would be covered with sand. They wandered without direction and finally saw a farmhouse; but when they got to the house, they were turned away. Finally, they decided to stand pat and wait for the storm to subside. Afterward, they hitched a ride on a truck back to Amarillo to catch a ride on a train back to California. Around Indio, California, they were told by a friendly rail dick not to get off there, for the sheriff would arrest them, but to jump off when the train passed through Lincoln Park. Simmons remembered jumping off and "running and the only thing that stopped" him was a billboard for the "El Ray Roofing Company."[23]

Some children of the working class turned to crime as a viable career option. In the famous Yankee City study done by Lloyd Warner, his analysis of crime and class reported that of those arrested, over 89 percent came from the lower classes. Of these, over 60 percent came from ethnic minority rather than native backgrounds and were "the most liable to arrest." Many swing musicians as youngsters flirted with extralegal activities and saw them as a dangerous, yet real alternative. Artie Shaw believed that he could have become a criminal as easily as a musician, while Benny Goodman believed that given the "neighborhood where [he] lived, if it hadn't been for the clarinet [he] might just as easily have been a gangster." Art Hodes described the area of West Chicago where he grew up as a place where "hoodlums grew like vegetables in a garden." Since many of the future swing musicians grew up in neighborhoods similar to Hodes's, some joined gangs as a form of neighborhood unity and protection. Willie "the Lion" Smith joined a gang made up of black students from the reformatory and elementary school he attended. They fought Italian and Irish gangs for territory, most times with parental approval.[24]

Athletics was also viewed an as viable and quick means of escape. The development and popularity of professional sports opened up many opportunities for working-class youths, and the message was not lost on many of those who became swing musicians. Duke Ellington, who came from a middle-class African American family, thought his future lay in baseball, football, and track because "athletics were what the real he-man were identified with, and so they were naturally the most important to [him]." Others, perhaps with fewer options than Ellington, saw sports as their meal ticket. Sy Oliver, later a talented trumpet player, boxed professionally in Cincinnati, mainly fighting old-timers in preliminary bouts. Eddie Barefield was trained by his father to be a fighter and while in elementary school fought older boys for pennies in a hat. As an amateur in Des Moines he fought 120 fights. He tentatively moved into music on the advice of a friend, but with mixed results. Taking up the piano, Barefield quit after a year because, he said, "the fellows thought [my teacher] was a sissy and they began calling me one, too. I didn't want to be a sissy, so I went back to boxing." Budd Johnson, while not a boxer, had similar peer troubles. When he took up the piano, his friends told him that all piano players were gay, so he quit in order to avoid guilt by association.[25]

Within this world, school was just not practical for many swing children. Barney Bigard was twelve years old when he went to work for fifty cents a week in his uncle's cigar factory as a tobacco sifter. He was promoted to roller, which paid a rate of eight dollars per one thousand cigars, and worked there until he was seventeen. He only quit to pursue music and because he "got tired of making cigars." Hoagy Carmicheal, raised in a middle-class home, found high school a waste of his time and quit to work on a cement mixer and then in a slaughterhouse. He did these jobs without joy: "I sweated and I worked and I was cheerless." For young Cab Calloway, school was where he went between jobs. He would wake in the morning and ride the street cars peddling the Baltimore *Sun* until ten in the morning, then go to school—"when [he] felt like it"—and leave around noontime to get the afternoon *Sun* and the *Star* to hawk. After this, he would ride the streetcars to the Pimlico racetrack to sell racing forms and watch the races. Around 6:30, he would shine shoes at Pimlico until eight or nine and then go home. He did this from the time he was eleven until he was fifteen. He said "to hell with school" because he wanted to earn some money and school got in the way. While his mother wanted him to get an education, he wanted to make "that money." He was sent to reform school at age fifteen and began considering music as a career.[26]

School even prevented some from developing their musical, and profitable, careers. Eddie Miller was already established as a fine clarinetist and alto saxophonist in the New Orleans area by the age of fifteen. He traveled throughout the South with several bands and, by the time he was seventeen, was married and a father. Jimmy Rushing had to walk through the red-light district of Oklahoma City on his way to school, and the sight of pretty girls and the sounds of music were too much of a temptation. One day he knocked on the door of one of these brothels and asked if he could come in and play the piano. But his father did not like the thought of his son skipping school to play music in a bordello and ordered him to never play the piano again. Two weeks later Rushing left home to become a musician. Garvin Bushell, who was shuttled between his parents and grandparents, finally found himself working in a tobacco factory by the age of fifteen. Upon hearing this, his grandparents sent him to Wilberforce University's high school division, but Bushell left the school to work in Dayton to save for a new clarinet. When his father heard that he had left school again and taken up music, he went to Ohio and brought his son back to New York to finish school. But Bushell refused. He worked at a variety of jobs until he finally got into the Harlem musicians' network. By the time Stuff Smith was fifteen, he had quit school to go out on the road with the Aunt Jemima Revue band, and by eighteen he was fronting Alphonso Trent's band in Dallas. Jack Teagarden set out on his own as a professional musician at the age of fifteen, after his father died and the family moved to Oklahoma City. The King of Swing learned at an early age the value of a well-paying career by witnessing the long hours and short pay his father received. His father also did not want his children to get stuck in the poverty of day labor and encouraged them to work to get ahead by taking the boys to the local synagogue and later Hull House for musical training. In 1923, Benny Goodman was working regularly as a musician around Chicago; this forced the thirteen-year-old to miss school. After the death of his father, he quit in order to play music full-time, making eighty to one hundred dollars a week. Arthur Rollini decided to leave school in his final semester due to his father's death. While he had hoped to finish and then go to Columbia, his father's long illness meant his mother went without a "breadwinner for the past three years," so Rollini quit school and took a job as a musician for a band going to England. He sent three-fifths of his salary home to his mother.[27]

That school held little appeal, or that education was not seen as the avenue of success, is nothing new in the study of American society. And during the Great Depression, while school enrollment went up and students remained in school for a longer time, upon graduation many found themselves with few job opportunities. The resulting trend for those under age twenty-four and without work meant that "they were too old for school and too young for jobs," according to the Lynds in *Middletown in Transition*. Johnny Board, who played clarinet and saxophone, remembered graduating from high school in 1936 with no job and few chances to get one. He finally found a job delivering goods for a local Walgreens on a per delivery basis.[28]

Many swing musicians grew up in situations where the internalization of class failure was present, and upon their maturity they sought something better than what they had witnessed. Drew Page, a journeyman trombone player, remembers his father walking six miles to get to work at five in the morning and returning home at seven at night, six days a week, for twelve dollars. Page's house had no electricity or hot water; and, when the pipes froze, he and his brothers would "crawl under [the house] and thaw the ice out . . . with newspaper torches." Dizzy Gillespie felt guilty because his mother had to work so hard to make ends meet. The family of four had to live on the $1.50 a week she made washing clothes for a white family. Gillespie tried to find work, even as a young child, but found few opportunities. "I tried everything I knew to help Mama. The trouble was I just didn't know very much." Vic Dickenson was born outside Dayton, Ohio, where his father supported the family as a corn farmer. During his childhood in the early 1920s, the Ku Klux Klan held rallies and burned crosses in the woods near the family home. Three of his siblings died in childhood, while he suffered from pleurisy and was forced to miss much of his early schooling. By mid-decade, his father quit the farm to become a day-labor plasterer. Andy Kirk went to work because he felt he had to help his aunt who had taken him in when his mother died and his father abandoned him. Sammy Price's father abandoned the family with nothing, forcing the young man to wonder "what [his] mother would do without the support of [his] father." His response was to get a job shining shoes. He was only ten years old.[29]

For someone like Stan Kenton, whose family moved around a lot, or Dizzy Gillespie, whose father died when he was a boy, the experiences of youth convinced them that the working life offered little stability. In fact, instability characterized many of the swing musicians' childhoods. Charlie

Parker's father left home early in his childhood, and his mother, who had previously worked long and hard as a cleaning woman to support her son and her heavy-drinking husband, now had to work harder. She moved the family into a cheaper apartment and took a second job as a cleaning woman at the Western Union office. Pee Wee Erwin was initially raised by his grandparents as his mom worked long hours and his dad had left home to work in Philadelphia. When his father returned from World War I, he moved them throughout the Nebraska-Kansas area in search of permanent employment. Finally, in 1924, the Erwins settled in Horton, Kansas, where the father landed a job of managing a local music store. When Carol Chilton was two weeks old in 1907, her mother and grandmother took her to adoption court, where a probation officer, Lucille Chilton, took the baby home. Although never legally adopted, she was raised in a middle-class environment and had parents who loved and cared for her. But Chilton was never able to escape the feeling of abandonment.[30]

In a few cases both parents died leaving their children without any means of support. Dicky Wells's parents died within a year of each other, leaving the boy virtually on his own. Other youngsters, for example, Sandy Williams and Cat Anderson, were sent to orphanages. Williams's parents died in the 1918 flu epidemic and the couple's eleven children were sent to orphanages throughout the Washington, D.C., area. Williams went with his brothers to the Delaware Vocational School, where he stayed for two years. He left the school and went back to Washington, D.C., where he went to school during the day and worked in the mornings and evenings. But he soon gave up school entirely, as his work in a theater pit band by the age of seventeen earned him thirty dollars a week. Cat Anderson's parents died when he was four, and he and his younger brother were sent to an orphanage in Charleston, South Carolina. Like Williams, Anderson recalled the days in the orphanage battling to protect his brother, which was how he got the nickname "Cat." The school, like many others, had a children's band which traveled throughout the South on fund-raising tours. By the time he was a teenager Anderson was already a seasoned touring musician.[31]

These stories and many more like them were not unique to the swing musician's childhood. Most working-class children experienced similar situations. Some experienced worse. What these stories underscore are the realities of their working-class upbringing, the instability that permeated their

youth, and their desire to escape this way of being. For many swing musicians the decision to become a musician was driven less by their need to be
accepted into society and more by an understanding that playing music was
the best way to put money on the table. When Jack Teagarden's father's
died and the family was forced to move around the Nebraska-Oklahoma
area in search of steady work, he felt it was his responsibility to support his
widowed mother and his four siblings. He struck out on his own at the age
of fifteen.[32] Few stories are as sad as the day Lee Collins's mother died:

The last I remember about my mother was on the day that she died. She drank some
milk that was left out on the back porch. I'll never forget how soon after that she
started to groan and ran to me, pulling at me to go get my father. Then she lay down
on the bed with my brother Teddy in her arms . . . I ran all the way to where he was
working. I told him to hurry home, something was wrong with mama that she was
crying and could not get up. So my father ran back to the house, with me trotting
along behind him as fast as the legs of a six-year old could go. But mother was
already dead when we got there. My littler brother was trying to nurse from her; that
was a sight that will never leave my mind as long as I live.

His father, a cornet player, was left to raise four boys, all under six years of
age. His mother had asked his father to promise to never let the boys play
music, believing it evil. Once she died, however, his father taught all the
boys to play; two later became professional musicians. When he proved unable to raise the boys, they were split up amongst relatives in the New Orleans area. Those who raised Collins were not very concerned about his
welfare, and he soon found himself in the company of local roughs, gam-
blers, and musicians. Fats Waller did not lose any parents, but did lose six
out of eleven siblings. The surviving children were watched over by the now
overprotective, grieving mother. She allowed her children little freedom and
was "determined that her five surviving children would grow up to adult-
hood." But she developed diabetes and the youngsters were forced to take
on greater responsibilities, including working. This led young Fats to the
Harlem nightlife and a career in music.[33]

For many swing musicians, growing up meant finding some way to make
money. Because of their class and, perhaps, lack of formal education, traditional occupational options were limited. These factors led many young people to jazz and swing, which, according to critic Martin Williams, are "the

music of a people who have been told by their circumstances that they are unworthy." In this music they found a home. Those who were talented enough could make decent money doing something they enjoyed. The musical safety valve appealed to many, and some began realizing their dream earlier than others, sometimes causing friction at home. Elmer Snowden was earning more per day than his father made per week by the time he was nine years old. This weakened his father's traditional role and made him feel inadequate. When Snowden returned from a day of playing, his father smashed the guitar in frustration. A family fight ensued and the mother sided with the young wage-earner. She bought her child a new instrument because his wages enabled the family to live better than they could on the wages of her husband. With the new guitar, the young Snowden got a better job as a theater musician, earning ten dollars a week. With his role superseded, his father quit his job and allowed his not-yet-teenage son to earn the money for the family. Others wanted to play music but were too poor to purchase instruments, so they made their own. Clark Terry recalled, "My brother . . . devised a drum out of a worn-out ice pan . . . (which) atop a tall, upside-down bushel basket made an excellent snare drum. Old chair rungs were great substitutes for drumsticks. To get a tuba sound, we took a big, round tin beer mug, wrapped a vacuum hose around it, blew through it, and got fantastic bass noise. I made a trumpet by coiling an old hose and putting a kerosene funnel on one end . . . and a pipe on the other end for a mouthpiece."[34]

Playing music became a means to make a good and, in most cases, respectable living. In Chicago during the 1920s, musicians held high status in the black community, and for Eddie "Lockjaw" Davis this was enough of a reason to want to become a musician: "I wanted the instrument for what it represented."[35] Many times musicians could earn more money by their teen years than their parents, and since they had witnessed their parents laboring at jobs they disliked, music as an economic factor was superceded by its ability to allow them to escape the drudgery of their parents' labors. As a child Artie Shaw was a talented musician, but when he asked for a saxophone in high school, his father protested, believing music was a waste of time better spent earning money. He eventually agreed to let Shaw buy the instrument if the boy agreed to work off the money as an errand boy. Shaw worked hard and soon earned the forty dollars necessary to pay off the debt.

He then quit the job because he knew that "this saxophone was [his] car-fare." The next year he won five dollars at a local amateur show. When he told his father, and subsequently played some numbers for him and his bud-dies, the elder Arshawsky looked at his son and laughed. They called him "American gonniff," which Shaw translated to mean "if people are stupid enough to pay good money to listen to crazy noises," so be it. Eddie Miller, who played clarinet for Bob Crosby, grew up with a father who enjoyed music but did not think it a good career choice. He thought "they were all bums" and encouraged the young boy to focus on his studies. But by fifteen Miller was on the road. Art Hodes's father demanded that the boy either go to work or school, that he could no longer spend his time in local burlesque houses or theaters playing music. Hodes tried a number of jobs but found all of them too difficult for too little money. He returned to school, where he began picking up gigs to play for the students. Eventually, he was asked to play piano for a band at thirty-five dollars a week. The most he had ever made as a worker previous to this was seventeen dollars a week, and he "never liked any of" the jobs. He was making twice the money doing some-thing he truly enjoyed. "Most people have to work," he said, "I *play* for a living."[36]

The status associated with being a musician was not lost to those future swing musicians growing up in search of career options. Watching their parents work for little money and experiencing firsthand the internalization of class frustration encouraged their search for a career where a "person [could] do something he enjoys . . . and get *paid* for it," according to Jimmy McPartland. He came from a home broken by divorce and alcoholism and witnessed firsthand the devastation of his working family's struggles. Stan Kenton watched his father's dreams of self-reliance and success shatter, forc-ing him to take a job that was steady but dull in Los Angeles. The elder Kenton did not want his son to end up like him, but all Stan could "dream about [was] the possibility of maybe making a little money at playing the piano." While still in high school he began "hustling around" to get gigs, and after his graduation he took a six-week job with a band in San Diego, a job that set him on the path as a musician. Duke Ellington choose music over a scholarship to the Pratt Institute in Brooklyn because he was making so much money "playing piano, and by booking bands for dances." Going to college seemed a waste of time and money.[37]

These types of stories are replayed time and time again in the reflections of many of those who became swing musicians. All follow a similar formula: sometime during their youth they recognized that playing music not only was something that brought intrinsic joy, but could bring money, popularity, and even social acceptance. Andy Kirk, who worked hard after his mother's death and quit school in his sophomore year to earn money, somehow knew that music was his means of escape from the difficulties of working so hard for so little. While still in his teens and living on his own, he bought a saxophone, practiced at night as best he could, and eventually landed a gig. He was soon playing throughout the Denver area and even landed a permanent spot with George Morrison's band at one of the best hotels in the city.[38]

For many of these young people, witnessing the struggles of their parents and, in many cases, themselves led them to reevaluate the parameters of the American dream. The term itself was coined in the 1930s, signifying the change that the country was undergoing at the time in terms of economic direction. The dream held that through hard work and dedication one could achieve (consume) whatever one desired. In a way, the creation and acceptance of the American dream discouraged militant class consciousness as it promised a society where every person's chances of success were equal and the fruits of one's labor were spread evenly. The barometer of success was the accumulation of consumer goods that differentiated the classes—Chevrolets versus Cadillacs. Interestingly, in the midst of the greatest economic crisis the country had seen, the focus was on not scarcity, but abundance. In the earlier chapter, I argued that the images of modernism were used to sell swing musical products and that the language of the ads encouraged consumption in the midst of crisis. This tendency was not reserved for the musical instrument industry alone, for the 1930s was an era punctuated with new things to consume.[39]

But the American dream also reflects the imaginary quality of the distribution of goods and wealth in America, especially during the thirties and forties. Many within the working class recognized the illusion of this promise and began to work toward equalizing the social and economic situation. Those involved in labor saw in their daily choices the dilemma of their situation: to seek advancement meant working with the bosses which meant turning their backs on their communities, families, and friends. They recognized that the problems of their day were laid at the foundations of capitalism, but the call for socialism did not resonate within them. They, like most other Americans, continued to believe, at least in theory, that while the American dream may be an illusion, with their activism in the CIO and other industrial unions and the growing coalition within the Democratic party of FDR, perhaps a more balanced and fair society would develop. They began to place more agency on the role of the government and their union to affect their lives in a positive way, but they continued to believe that the ownership of private property, even by their bosses, was a privilege that made America unique.[40]

Socially, America underwent fundamental redefinition in the same era that it was defined by the dream of capitalism. Workers tended to believe they deserved the fruits of labor, yet found a society unwilling to provide the necessary job options to meet the demands. They wanted to consume the items being sold to them through the media, yet their ability to participate was blocked by the limited job opportunities and the desire not to lose the connection to their usable past. In *The Hidden Injuries of Class*, Richard Sennett and Jonathan Cobb argue that the working class understood that wealth and goods were not distributed fairly but felt personally responsible for not being able to live up to the American dream. This internalization muted the ability of the workers to work toward changes in the system and confirmed in them the continued desire to make it in America.[41]

But it was not an all or nothing situation. The working class during the depression era mediated between their own perceived sense of failure and their desire to work through organizational structures such as the CIO and the Democratic party to bring a greater sense of parity and fairness to the American landscape. The 1930s thus changed the nature of the negotiations between the owners and operators, as the culture and society of the era took on a more equalitarian patina and the producers of culture began to "sell" this vision as well.

Within this, swing and the depression era are inseparable. The crisis itself helped create a rediscovery of America, a rediscovery that involved all aspects of society. Roosevelt utilized this mind-set among the people to further his New Deal program, itself an appeal to the CIO mindedness of the era. In his Fireside Chats and in the programs he chose to support, the president suggested that a new America could be seen on the horizon, one that promised a fair share for all the people. This indeed was a "new deal," and he asked that Americans reevaluate their past in order to understand their future. Cultural and political intellectuals, such as Alfred Kazin, Marc Blitzstein, Clifford Odets, John Dos Passos, Aaron Copland, Richard Wright, Carey McWilliams, Orson Welles, and a host of others, joined worker-artists, such as Woody Guthrie, Roy Acuff, Patsy Montana, Benny Goodman, Duke Ellington, Billie Holiday, Josh White, Aunt Molly Jackson, and others, in proclaiming that the new era was underway. This ideal was prevalent throughout much of the vernacular and cultivated culture of the time—from Hollywood to Main Street. Disney, Superman, Batman, Monopoly, Henry Fonda, Jimmy Stewart, Bette Davis, Rita Hayworth, John Ford, John Wayne, *Anthony Adverse*, Roy Rogers, and so many more spoke to ordinary Americans in terms they could and did understand—they *were* America. Scholars including Warren Susman and Charles Alexander have likened this movement toward Americanism as part of a dual movement: on one hand, the people sought out national symbols of unity; and, on the other hand, they developed a sense of patriotism in a era of intense national loyalty. In order to survive, common symbols and myths needed to be created and validated in order to justify the continuation of the American experiment. The 1930s also saw the rise of a hyper-nationalism, best exemplified in the rise of fascism in Europe, in Stalinism in the Soviet Union, and within the United States among demagogues like Father Coughlin, Huey Long, and others.[42]

The desire to unify within these struggles is key to understanding how the workers came to not only be a part of the CIO and the Democratic party, but become the guideposts for American culture. The rise of these distinctly American manifestations—whether they be New Deal programs like the Federal Music Project, the Civilian Conservation Corps, or the National Youth Administration; Hollywood films like *Mr. Smith Goes to Washington*, *Gone with the Wind*, or *The Petrified Forest*; or swing and hillbilly music—can be traced to the early part of the twentieth century and must be seen as a continuation of the trends begun in the era before World War I. The activities of the Americanism programs begun in the 1910s, combined with the capitalistic welfare promises of the 1920s, informed and empowered ethnic, gender, and racial identities that reached their maturity during the age of Roosevelt. No longer outsiders or alien to the ways of American life, these Americans, who were working class in their consciousness, sought to and did make the country over in their own image. This did not usher in the age of socialism, as some radicals hoped, but incorporated the ideals of the working-class experience into the belief structure of the dominant society. The 1930s thus legitimized the worker experience and made it part of the American experience.[43]

Swing music played a central role in this transformation. It was the music of the working class during the 1930s, which helps to explain its popularity and appeal. The musicians, like their audiences, were well aware of the precarious nature of their labor, and so viewed their fans and their career choice with respect and dignity. Their childhood experiences taught them not to take for granted the benefits of their skills, and they also knew that they did not want to follow in the hard, laboring footsteps of their parents or siblings. When the crash brought more unemployment to the country, including themselves, these musicians realized they had to mold their music as best they could to the mood and tastes of their audience. Artistry was one thing, rent was another, and the swing musicians understood the clear line that separated these two realities. Those who came of age during this depression era accepted that they had choices but also knew that they were limited in the number of possible options, especially if they came from the laboring classes. Popular musicians, like those who played swing, made an exciting and decent living in an era of economic uncertainty. They also worked at jobs they felt were better than those of their parents, jobs which they associated with an increase in social status. They recognized that theirs was the music of the people, for they had come from the people and felt a unique bond with their fans, audiences, and other musicians.

This image of class manifested itself in a unique form of labor solidarity during the era. James Kraft's study of the musicians' response to the changes in musical production and their attempts to find power in the American Federation of Musicians (AFM) details stories of failed expectations, frustrated bands, lack of economic rewards, and the encroachment of technological obsolescence. To resist these changes and empower themselves, the "musicians had forged a labor ideology" which did not reject capitalism or the rewards of the system but sought to protect their craft. Under the AFM's leadership in 1937, musicians won a contract, with radio affiliates and record companies, that protected jobs, raised wages, and increased worker solidarity. From 1936 to 1941 AFM membership increased from 105,000 to 135,000, and the union, under the strong leadership of James Petrillo, believed it was forging a future for its membership. Time would tell.[44]

But these class understandings were not without contradictions. Some found that working in a swing band was physically and emotionally difficult, while others were aware that the money they were promised rarely materialized or was less than they had expected. When trombonist Lawrence Brown was lured into joining Duke Ellington's band in the mid-1930s, he did so on the promise of seventy dollars a week. But he soon discovered that that wage was only guaranteed on working weeks and that all other expenses came out of his own pocket. Later, in 1939, he got a raise to one hundred dollars a week.[45] There were other less tangible contradictions. The basic structure of capitalism and modernity, for example, meant that most of the performers were torn between the idea of worker solidarity and profit and also torn between the use the machine to expand the music's popularity and the displacement of workers that would come as a result of this technology. They worked with a union that promoted better wages and job protection but was still racially segregated and paid persons of color lower wages. The contradictions of their class tie into the convulsions that make the 1930s and 1940s interesting and challenging and underscore the difficulties of modernity. Musicians, like other workers during the era, found themselves caught in the changes that affected the entirety of labor. Changes in capitalism meant that the art of the music was replaced by the work of production that led to the desire for goods in the marketplace. The musicians' role had to decrease in order to maximize profit, and the swing musicians found themselves caught in the middle. They were joined together by their class experiences that focused on work but were also driven apart by the individual competitiveness of capitalism.

Swing is the story of the people's music during an era that seemed to promote the ideals of the masses over the desires of capital. Yet as the depression waned and the situation abroad grew more serious, the consciousness of the people began to shift as well; they defined themselves more in relation to the freedoms associated with their consumption and less in relation to the unification of their experiences. The survival of swing as the music of its generation would depend on its ability to adapt to the changing consciousness of the people and, more significantly, on the changing definition of who exactly constituted "the people" and what their roles were to be in the rapidly modernizing world.

The Swing Stew

Ethnicity, Race, and Gender within Swing

The swing generation was made up of a variety of types of people. Artie Shaw, for example, was born on the Lower East Side of New York City and spent his formative years among "kids with long, foreign-sounding names . . . Romanoff, Liebowitz, Carranello, Esposito, Schechter, Wiecznowski, Anzelowitz, Fiorito, O'Clanahan, Borazybski." Maxine Sullivan recalled that while growing up in the steel town of Homestead, Pennsylvania, she lived next door to and sometimes with Polish, Hungarian, and Italian workers. "There might have been segregation between the so-called affluent and so-called poor," she pointed out, but not "among the poor class of people . . . [who] were workers." Trummy Young spent his early youth in the Yamacraw section of Savannah, Georgia, next door to Italians, Indians, blacks, and Chinese. They all "went to the same schools" and played with one another. He remembers one time "blacking up" an Italian friend in order to get him into the black theater to see a Tom Mix movie: "[W]e loved cowboys, you know."[1]

These stories of ethnic, racial, and gendered situations point to the complex arrangement that was part of the swing generation and its music. Those three brief stories are representative of the diversity within the swing bands and, by extension, American society. Yet how could different ethnic, racial. and gendered groups overcome generational tensions to join together into a unified swing band? This chapter will seek to explore how these groups came together, how this process solidified swing as the music of its generation.

That different groups of people, identified by where they came from in Europe, Asia, Africa, or Latin America, have their own cultural traits, celebrations, languages, and identities is not the point behind trying to determine ethnicity. That part of the definition is clear. What remains unclear is how these groups, which by their categorical nature (i.e., Italian, Chinese, etc.) encouraged homogenized definitions, overcame their heterogeneous backgrounds to coexist in the new world. Those who migrated to the United States from 1880 to 1920 came from diverse national cultures that, though the immigration statistics might reveal their common national identification, were often separated by local or regional differences; thus some immigrants perhaps had animosity toward each other. Their identities were also constantly undergoing change both in response to the American situation and by choice. As the last chapter makes plain, class became one means by which these different groups created new definitions and navigated ties that in the Old World would have been impossible. Swing is representative of this same phenomenon.[2]

Between 1880 and 1920, over twenty-three million people immigrated to the United States. Of these, the largest percentage came from central, eastern, and southern Europe; a large percentage also came from Russia (17.4 percent), Italy (19.4 percent), and Austria-Hungary (18.2 percent). The largest northwestern European migrant group came from the United Kingdom (5.8 percent). These national identifications point to the diversity of those coming to the United States and also detail the wide range of ethnicities within each of the national identities. Most of these migrants shared language, religion, and folkways, but differed in how they viewed each other within the regional context of their European experience. They were not homogenous. Once in the United States, most settled in the Northeast, but a significant number migrated to interior states such as Ohio and Illinois. Few migrated to the South. They tended to concentrate in the cities, where demand for labor was highest. In Cleveland, Ohio, the population was two-thirds ethnic; in New York City, three-fourths; in Newark, New Jersey, three-fifths, Other cities, such as Chicago, Toledo, Detroit, Pittsburgh, and

Boston, also had large immigrant populations. By 1940 almost one out of every four Americans was a first- or second-generation immigrant.[3]

Given the number, diversity, and urban tendencies of immigrants, it is no wonder ethnicity-immigration scholars have struggled to define the process by which these groups became part of the American experience. The first explanation came from studies done in the 1910s by University of Chicago sociologists led by Robert Park. They devised a three-stage "race relations cycle," labeling it the "Melting Pot" theory. During these stages—contact, accommodation, and assimilation—the minority ethnic and racial groups accepted the basic societal mores and norms of the dominant culture. No two groups or individuals assimilated at a set pace, yet Park's study observed that all groups adopted—at least superficially—the traits of the dominant culture. This Americanization "melted" down the ethnic and racial cultures in the big pot called America. Henry Ford attempted this very recipe in the late 1910s at his factories. At large festivals Ford employees would sing their native songs while dressed in their native costumes. At a certain point, they would exit the stage and shortly thereafter reenter dressed as Americans (gray jumpsuit overalls) singing American songs in English. Ford's Personnel Department, or Sociological Division, went so far as to investigate the home lives of its immigrant workers to ensure assimilation. As the Ford situation attests, there was a fine line between Park's idea that the immigrants slowly melded their consciousness with the ideal of America and the reality that they were coerced by economics.[4]

At the heart of this debate is whether the scholar views the immigrants as coming to America seeking freedom and liberty or as alienated and desperate people fleeing repression and thus willing to shed their previous way of being. Oscar Handlin's *The Uprooted* suggested that while the immigrants adopted certain American traits, they remained somewhat alienated to America because of their ethnicity. In more recent years, scholars advocating ethnic pluralism have refuted the idea of the melting pot, arguing that ethnic and racial groups were/are not melted down. Immigrants, in fact, sampled the ideas and attitudes of the dominant culture to better retain their ethnicity. For the pluralist, the argument is less about melting down and more about what cultural and social ethnic identities remain.[5]

Others argue that while the immigrants may have thought their migration permanent, nearly a third from 1821 to 1924 actually repatriated. For many immigrants, America did not represent their dream but was a place to go to for a short time to earn some money and then return home. This alters the conception of the immigrant from a poor and helpless transplant to an active agent attempting to negotiate the complex world of capitalism. Many of the immigrants were males in search of work, men who dreamed of returning to their native land but were sucked into the American capitalist system. Now part of America, they attempted to retain their ethnic identity while adopting the American capitalist ethos. Lawrence Fuchs and Werner Sollors have pointed out that the immigrants were not so powerless in this process but chose to adopt American civic culture while retaining many of their ethnic cultures. This allowed for the creation of a more modern conception of immigration and assimilation, one which empowered the migrants by suggesting that they mediated between the somewhat alien world of America and their native identities. There is a need to place the immigrant within the individualized context of the experience, where constant renegotiation of the meaning and depth of ethnicity takes place. Thus the migrant experience becomes not a melting pot, or even a salad, but tiles of different colors all combined to make one mosaic.[6]

Another migrant to the nation's cities came from the American South and, while fitting into the mosaic ideal, faced racist pressures that European immigrants and their children could escape. In the aftermath of the Civil War, and the subsequent failure of Reconstruction to deal with the issue of free labor, the South in the late nineteenth century resembled a fiefdom where blacks toiled as sharecroppers or tenant farmers with few opportunities. By the end of the century, 90 percent of the nation's blacks lived in this region of the country, with 80 percent of these living in rural areas. The new century offered new opportunities and new ideologies; however, the specter of racism did not vanish. Between 1900 and 1930 nearly 1.5 million southern blacks moved to the North and West, mostly to urban areas like New York, Chicago, Cleveland, Detroit, and Pittsburgh. By 1930, New York City, Philadelphia, and Chicago had black populations over 200,000. This migration to urban areas was not restricted to northern cities, as southern blacks migrated to Atlanta, Memphis, Houston, or Birmingham in large numbers as well. The peak of this movement, called the Great Migration, took place in the period between 1920 and 1930, when nearly 749,000 southern blacks moved north.[7]

There were many reasons for this exodus. The decline of the plantation economy brought on by the advent of machine technology and the plague of the boll weevil forced rural blacks off the land they had worked for generations and into the urban areas in search of jobs. There were other southern pushes as well, including inadequate educational facilities and fear. As Booker T. Washington said at the turn of the century, whenever a lynching occurred, "a score of colored people [left] . . . for the city." This reality did not end in the 1920s or 1930s. Charles Thompson recalls growing up in Ohio and playing with children in his neighborhood regardless of color. But when his family moved to Columbia, Missouri, in his senior year of high school, the racial differences became problematic. He began to see signs for toilets and water fountains marked white or black only. When he heard about a lynching of a black man thirty miles outside of town, he realized he had "to be a man in order to protect [him]self" and "desperately tried to find some way to get out of that town, to go where [he] thought things were better." Aside from the real fear that Thompson describes, the labor demand stimulated first by World War I and then by the immigration restrictions imposed by Congress in the early 1920s added up to a 63 percent increase in black migrants to the North between 1920 and 1930. These migrants were not powerless in this movement but migrated to the North and West in search of better opportunities for themselves and their families.[8]

What they found in these urban areas varied in much the same way it had for the European immigrants, but their experiences were exacerbated by racial tensions oftentimes caused by class competition. Joe William Trotter provides an overview of the different interpretations of this migration. The first, called the race-relation model, was begun in the 1930s and emphasized community studies and general social and economic explanations for the movement within the context of ongoing race relations. The sixties and seventies were dominated by the ghetto model, which built upon the race relations argument and sought to detail what had happened in these urban areas in regards to housing, educational, and social segregation. The proletarian approach, developed in the late seventies and eighties, placed the migration into the larger historical perspective of the development of the industrial working class and the problems it faced. And, like the immigrant experience, the analyses tend to fall into two generalizations: (1) the migration was a bad experience resulting in poverty and the destruction of family life patterns; and (2) the migrants retained much of their cultural values and sampled the new urban society.[9]

These new migrants faced the difficulty of securing housing and employment in a society driven by prejudice and racism. They were segregated into specific areas of the city not always by choice, as was the case with some of their working-class European cohorts, but by coercion. The same held true for employment, as blacks found it difficult to secure stable and well-paying jobs. Despite these and other problems, the migrants were able to build their communities into thriving and exciting communities and in some places, such as Harlem or Chicago's Black Belt, were able to make them into entertainment centers for the city. Russell Procope remembers the transformation of Harlem in the 1910s—the excitement of going to bed at night and in the quiet hearing the "piano players, all up and down the street." When Garvin Bushell's father brought him to Harlem in 1919, he immediately recognized he was in the mecca for musical and social creativity. After trying a number of low-wage clerk jobs, he and some others organized a five-piece band and began securing gigs. His experience was not all that uncommon, as John Chilton's *Who's Who of Jazz* details. Chilton examined the lives of 427 black southerners who played jazz and were born before 1915: 63 percent migrated to the North after 1917, while only 6 percent moved North before 1916, and another 17 percent migrated after 1931. This exodus helped to define and create the jazz of the 1920s and 1930s by instilling a sense of community among the migrants and exposing them to a variety of urban entertainment opportunities. But for all of the excitement of the new northern urban vistas, these communities and their residents also suffered from overcrowding, poverty, and limited job opportunities.[10]

When W. Lloyd Warner in his *Yankee City* series analyzed the composition of typical American cities in the 1930s and early 1940s, he sought to discover who made America's cities and industries operate and at what economic level they lived. Warner and his team of researchers found that the lower middle and upper lower classes comprised some 60.72 percent of the population. If one adds the lower class percentage of 25.22, nearly 86 percent of the people in a typical American city toiled below middle class.[11]

And who were these people? The ethnic composition of the classes in Yankee City showed that in the upper lower and lower lower occupations, ethnic minorities dominate by over 70 percent. Poor native whites predominated the lower middle class, Irish and Jews tended to dominate the upper lower, and Italians, Russians, and Poles tended toward the lower lower class. Blacks also tended to occupy the lower lower classes, finding most of their employment in the manual labor field. The statistics compiled and introduced in the last chapter show that among swing musicians the vast majority tended to come from these same economic classes. As for upward mobility, Warner admitted that "few persons not of English origin have made their way into" the upper classes.[12]

Most contemporary and scholarly observations point out that during this time period ethnic and racial groups tended to aggregate in the lower working classes. And, as similar studies have shown, class plays a very large role in the attainment of education, occupation, and even church membership. Recently, a number of studies have examined how these groups, unified by class yet divided by race and ethnicity, came to coexist and by the 1930s cooperate with one another in labor, politics, and cultural activities while still harboring ideologies that encouraged separation, racism, and sexism.[13]

Among the best studies is Lizabeth Cohen's *Making a New Deal*. She outlines how these groups interacted in Chicago in the years previous to the Great Depression and what changes came about as a result. She details how, although these groups of people worked and lived near one another, they worked to retain their autonomy. For example, over 65 percent of those employed in the blast furnaces and rolling mills in 1920 were of foreign or mixed parentage, while over 20 percent were black. In the slaughterhouses and packinghouses the story was the same, ethnics made up nearly 70 percent of the workforce, while blacks made up another 23 percent. Black and ethnic women also worked in these types of industries. In those same slaughterhouses and packinghouses, of the 2,696 women employees in 1920, over 77 percent were ethnics and just over 18 percent were blacks. After work, these folks shared neighborhoods, for where one worked usually indicated where one lived. Yet rarely did the groups live side by side. Many immigrants chose to live close to their work and among those who shared their culture and lifestyle. But for others, this was less a choice and more a result of economic necessity, fear, and social pressure. For black migrants this was especially true, as the creation of their neighborhoods came through coercion rather than choice, even though blacks retained much of their southern ideologies and ways of being in the new urban areas and often chose to live and socialize with other southern blacks. Between 1910 and 1930, Chicago's Black Belt became home to two-thirds of the black population; this, in many cases, was not close to where they worked. Thus, while occupation and class pointed out the similarities among the laboring classes, in the era after Word War I, Cohen writes, "[r]ace, ethnicity, job and neighborhood served as boundaries, not bridges, among industrial workers in Chicago."[14]

In the era before the crash, those new to the urban American experience sought to preserve their native ways of being. Outside of the workplace, few immigrants ventured beyond their enclave and had little contact with those not of their group. They had their own newspapers, restaurants, grocery stores, pharmacies, and churches. The emerging record industry operated within this context, catering to immigrant and racial music tastes by releasing specific recordings to target populations. But as the twenties progressed, the ethnic businesses saw more of their customers choosing outside competitors. Cohen uses the arrival of grocery store and department store chains as an example of how the ethnic stores either merged with their competitors or went out of business. This occurred in black neighborhoods as well. The marketing of national brands through radio and newspapers coincided with these chain expansions and challenged the hegemony of the racial and ethnic enclaves. Whether it was through Campbell's Soup or a White Castle burger, these neighborhoods were becoming Americanized.[15]

This economic and modernist conversion process did not take place without protest, but many of the immigrant children found the American items too appealing to ignore. While their parents encouraged or forced them to speak their native tongue at home, for example, more ethnic children were making the connection between being able to speak good English, and thus hide their ethnic identity, and attaining work or social acceptance. Many in their community were afraid that their children might change their first and last names to more American sounding ones and in other ways attempt to hide their ethnicity and become American. Some believed that the popularity of musical and visual cultures was to blame for these changes. They feared the effect that the radio, phonograph, and movies were having on their children, perhaps encouraging them to forget the ways of the past and their people. The immigrants' children were less afraid of other groups, including blacks, and found themselves entering into situations that would encourage mixing. This was not reserved for the ethnic enclaves, but was part of the general decline and falling away of Victorian racial and social ideals during the 1920s.[16]

Many of these children began to search for ways out of their particular enclave, and popular culture provided one such means. This was not a new phenomenon, for outsiders had often used culture as a means by which to gain both acceptance and profit from the dominant society. Early twentieth-century America proved no different, as a variety of entertainment options were opened or made open to the ethnic immigrant. The rise and popularity of ragtime and the career of Scott Joplin are sometimes overshadowed by their institutionalization by Tin Pan Alley and its songwriters, who tended to be Jewish. Over 75 percent of the lyricists and 50 percent of the composers of Tin Pan Alley's songs appear to have been Jewish during the 1920s and 1930s. Among the top five in the business, Cole Porter was the only non-Jew and accredited his success to his ability to write in a Jewish way. The same was true of the motion picture industry, and other ethnics were involved in baseball, vaudeville, and boxing. Regardless of the popular medium, ethnics played a primary role in its popularity and profit. For many migrants, popular culture became the means to get out of the drudgery of daily labor and, perhaps, into mainstream society. Some have suggested that the migrants' marginality aided in their ability to create popular amusements, as they felt less bound by the limitations imposed by the established society. As the culture industry grew and the migrants became more accustomed to the American way of being, the ethnic barriers separating performers and audiences also declined. This is not to suggest that they merged into one culture, but that a sampling of attitudes, ideologies, and cultures began to take place.[17]

It was during the 1930s that the mature version of this process became apparent. But it was earlier, during the migrants' childhoods, that the process began. The same holds true for the swing musicians. When one examines the stories of swing musicians and their cultural interactions during their childhoods, one begins to view the process by which they would be able to come together and create swing as adults. This process did not happen overnight or at the same pace throughout the country or music industry, but slowly and then in bursts until, finally, some musical integration had taken place.

Benny Goodman's use of black musicians serves as an excellent case in point. While there had been racial mixing among jazz performers in the 1920s, these had largely been jam or impromptu sessions. In the early 1930s John Hammond was responsible for bringing together white and black musicians in the recording studio, among them Benny Goodman. This experience, as well as Hammond's encouragement that Goodman's band use Fletcher Henderson's arrangements in 1935, led to Goodman's hiring of pianist Teddy Wilson in 1936. Originally part of an intermission trio at the Congress Hotel in Chicago, Wilson shared the "public spotlight" with drummer Gene Krupa and Goodman. Wilson soon became a regular member of the band. Hammond's role cannot be overstated in this integration, for while Goodman's booking agency, MCA, was telling him that adding black players would ruin his young and promising career, Hammond assured him that it would pay off. Hammond was right. Later Goodman added vibraharpist Lionel Hampton and guitarist Charlie Christian. There was some resistance to these black players, primarily from promoters and some audience members. The producer of the Camel Caravan radio show urged Goodman to drop the black players because of several letters of protest, but the band remained mixed. Jimmy Maxwell, who played with Goodman during this time, recalls that the race mixing meant the band lost most of its bookings in the South, which cut band income. Once, when a hotel manager refused to let the black members of the band pass through the lobby to get to the ballroom, Goodman told him to "screw" himself and threatened to leave. A solution was worked out.[18]

But what Maxwell remembers most is that Goodman and the other band members "stuck up for them." While they were still featured as part of an intermission sextet, the symbolic nature of the act made it pathbreaking. Hampton recalled that when he first started playing with Goodman in the Madhattan Room of the Hotel Pennsylvania in 1937, it was the first time blacks and whites played together in any cultural medium, from baseball to movies. He also believed that this integration "started a lot of things happening." By the end of the thirties Goodman integrated his big band with pianist Henderson, Christian, and later trumpeter Cootie Williams, drummer Sid Catlett, and bass player John Simmons. Goodman's band, with black musicians included, toured the country with some difficulties. One such problem occurred in Dallas, Texas, during the centennial celebration in 1937. Several local police objected to the openness of several white fans' adulation of Hampton and Wilson. When one white, a professor from the University of Texas, invited them to sit and drink some champagne, the situation became troublesome. With tempers flaring, only the intervention of a police official and jazz fan stopped further problems. The next day the police chief apologized to Wilson and Hampton. Goodman believed that "for a lot of people that came to hear us, the quartet was a special kick—and when we played, nobody cared much what colors or races were represented just as long as we played good music. That's the way it should be."[19]

This does not suggest that either the audience or the musicians were unaware of the differences. For many swing musicians it was precisely the fact that they were different that made them unified. They were able to "appreciate each other by how" they sounded, "not by [their] ethnicity," recalls bassist Milt Hinton. Since Goodman was the "King," his acceptance of blacks into his band was akin to U.S. Steel accepting the United Steel Workers; or General Motors, the United Auto Workers. Other bandleaders saw their chance to integrate their bands. Artie Shaw wanted Billie Holiday, and when the singer left the Basie band in 1937, she joined up with Shaw. In order to make her feel welcome and to offset any problems, she became the roommate of Cliff Leeman's wife, singer Nita Bradley. When they traveled in the South, she rode with several of her band mates; and when restaurants along the way would not let her eat in the dining room, "[they] all sat in the kitchen with her." Later Shaw added Roy Eldridge and Lips Page. Soon most of the top white bands, including Charlie Barnet's, Gene Krupa's, and Jimmy Dorsey's, had one or several black players. Audiences reacted, according to Wilson, with "tremendous" interest and general acceptance. Hampton recalls how "white people would . . . stand around the bandstand" without prejudice, supporting the band.[20]

These types of stories tend to overstate the alienation and difficulties that many young people from ethnic minority backgrounds faced. For most, the lack of acceptance based on race or ethnicity led to shame or embarrassment. Artie Shaw recounts how being born on the lower East Side of New York City into a Russian-Jewish dressmaking family made him feel out of place when his parents decided to move to New Haven, Connecticut. As an eight-year-old boy, Shaw discovered that being Jewish meant being different; and when his classmates first heard his name called out, they "laughed." This led Shaw to feel ashamed of his ethnicity and work to try and gain acceptance into the Anglo American society, even though he knew doing so would cause him to lose some of what made him what he was.[21]

The ability of ethnic groups to become accepted into the dominant culture was a bit more complicated. The era that bred the swing musicians and their generation was not one that encouraged assimilation or integration. In fact, for blacks and other ethnics, American society was neither open nor assimilationist. Blacks faced the constant threat of lynching and operated in a culture that did not believe African Americans could ever be equal. The rise of the new Ku Klux Klan in 1915 and a host of "scientific" justifications for racism—best exemplified by Madison Grant's 1916 *The Passing of a Great Race*—enabled racism to achieve a level of respectability it had not enjoyed since before the Civil War. By 1923, the KKK could claim some three to six million members dedicated not only to anti-black ideals, but to anti-Semitic and anti-Catholic ideals as well. Jimmy Maxwell grew up in Tracy, California, in a town dominated by white migrants from the lower south. His family, being Catholic, became targets of Klan activity along with the Mexican and Japanese farmers. When his father found out that his supervisor on the railroad was a Klansman and reported him, the Klan responded by burning a cross in the front yard and threatening the family. These types of incidents were not uncommon, as many intellectuals, such as Theodore Stoddard, Charles W. Gould, and Clinton Stoddard Burr, fueled the fears of their white middle-class readers by suggesting that the mixture of races and ethnicities in America was sapping the strength from the country. Much akin to Josiah Strong's earlier *Our Country* (1886), these authors feared for America's future because of what they viewed as declining intelligence as a result of mongrelization. The fear of immigrants overrunning the country, argued earlier by the likes of Frederick Jackson Turner, Jack London, E. A. Ross, John R. Commons, and many others, received a new voice in the 1920s, culminating in the Immigration Act of 1921 and its conservative revision in 1924. President Coolidge, upon signing the bill, commented, "America must be kept American."[22]

The fear of blacks and other ethnics—who were primarily Catholic eastern or southern Europeans or Russian-Polish Jews—which manifested itself in books, clubs, and organizations during the period of the swing generation's youth, had distinct social and cultural effects. While Park and his Melting Pot sociologists were popularizing their theories of assimilation, blacks and other ethnics continued to be alienated from the dominate culture. Two stories illuminate the fear and polarization that held sway during this time. Both stories involve young black men riding the rails in the early 1930s in search of employment, and both involve the accidental realization that they were in the South. Future swing musician John Simmons was heading west when he and a friend had to catch a different train in Dalhart, Texas. They were trying for a passenger train, as it would go faster and directly to Los Angeles. When they tried to board one of the freight cars, the rail dick saw them and shined his flashlight on them, scaring them away. When he saw their "complexion," he gave chase and soon several others joined. Simmons and his pal alluded the posse by hiding in the cattle pen under the cows amidst the manure. After several hours of waiting, several Mexicans helped them to get a train out of Texas. Buck Clayton tells a similar, if not more frightening, story. Catching a train in Denver, he and a friend thought they were going to Los Angeles; when it came to a stop, they discovered they were in Texas. They hid near the rails, waiting for a train heading west. Suddenly they saw two cops cars approaching, and before they could do or say anything, they were put into the car and driven back to town. The police accused them of raping a white woman and brought them to the rail station, where about seven men formed a circle around them and ordered them to dance. Afraid of what might happen if they didn't, they complied. After several hours of this and attempts to get them to confess, the police ordered them to begin walking towards the outskirts of town while some white residents followed in the cars. Clayton and his friend were convinced they were to be lynched. After they were marched well outside of town, the mob returned to the town. Clayton figured that the white residents were hoping they would try to run, so they could shoot them as escaping criminals. "We didn't run," he said, and after several hours of waiting, they caught a train headed back to Denver.[23]

These types of stories were not reserved for the South. *Middletown* outlines the popularity of the KKK in that typical American city, where the fear of the "Catholic situation," as well as the anti-Semitism and racism typical of the Klan, received support from good, upstanding Christian white citizens. When W. Lloyd Warner analyzed assimilation in his *Yankee City* series, he discovered that the further a racial group moved away from the light Caucasoid, English-speaking, Protestant type, the longer it took for assimilation. For example, among light-skinned non-English-speaking Catholics (French, Germans, and Belgians), assimilation, ethnic association, and subordination were moderate. But as the types became darker—southern European, Near Eastern, Slavic, Latin American, Asian, and black—ethnic ties grew stronger, assimilation slowed, and subordination increased. Warner's study detailed a typical city where blacks and other ethnic groups were not melting in and had developed an ethnoracial caste system.[24]

It seems clear that when an ethnic group faced limited economic mobility, they tended to adopt the mannerisms of the dominant culture. Acceptance of the new culture, or the denial of past culture, improves an individual's chances of gaining a better life. When poverty is associated with stigma and prejudice, the tendency to lose the ethnic attachment is made stronger, as individuals are willing to sacrifice their ethnic identity for economic security.[25]

This economic accommodation resonated within the swing generation. Black musicians and arrangers accepted the less than equal status, compared to their white counterparts, because that role held more promise and security than many other nonmusical positions in their community. White performers, such as Shaw, Goodman, and Krupa, would de-emphasize their ethnicity and try to appear "American." Benny Goodman's marriage into the Hammond family was important for just this reason—acceptance and assimilation. Goodman's acceptance into and by the blue bloods of Westchester County, New York, became so complete that he soon began to talk like his new family. Shaw describes in his autobiography how, when he decided to be a musician, he also figured he would have to change his name. While he told himself it was because it was too long, or difficult to pronounce, he really knew that he was "ashamed of being a Jew," and by changing it to Shaw, he could hide his ethnicity.[26]

But why would Goodman want to deny his ethnicity? Or what made Arthur Arshawsky change his name to Artie Shaw? Was it simply the desire to succeed? Or were there other motivations? Certainly the idea of success played an important role in their decisions. Among many ethnic groups, the alienation of being different could be breached by success. If one was a great boxer like Joe Louis, a gifted baseball player like Joe DiMaggio, or a talented musician like Duke Ellington or Benny Goodman, the ethnic barriers, while not totally removed, would certainly lower. Goodman believed that all that counted was whether or not someone was a good musician, and during the performance no prejudice existed, yet he himself denied his own ethnicity to become part of the accepted majority. For many, the social and personal marginality experienced as a member of an ethnic minority group encouraged activity in the creative arts, which, since the arts relied on audience approval, meant increased social insecurity. This duality—creative release leading to increased alienation—came less from feeling inferior and more from a need to fit into the dominant society.[27]

For many swing musicians, being an outsider allowed them to channel their energies into creative endeavors. Dizzy Gillespie hated the racial caste system in South Carolina during his childhood. When he got a job at a local theater making sure no one sneaked in without paying, he caught an older, white boy. When he got off work, the boy and his friends beat Gillespie. Even though outnumbered and smaller, Gillespie refused to back down, saying how past encounters with whites who wanted to beat him up made him tough. When the white boys called him nigger he "wouldn't take it. . . . I never considered myself inferior to white people. No one could make me feel inferior. I would always fight it. I always knew I was something special."[28]

Confrontations like these molded Gillespie's commitment to succeed, to prove his mettle, to display his equality. The same type of desire held true for Artie Shaw. In his childhood he had to deal with terms like *kike* or *sheeny* from his Protestant schoolmates. These words hurt the young musician, making him introverted, shy, and committed to proving himself. Being the outsider changed his whole life by the time he was eight: "[F]rom the moment I realized that my being Jewish was something to be jeered at for, called names for, or hated and excluded for—from that moment on I was no longer the same kid I had been before." This revelation put Shaw on the course to musical success, societal acceptance, and personal alienation.[29]

The alienation of being an outsider proved a great motivator. Garvin Bushell reasoned that one cause for the ethnic mixing that occurred in the 1930s was that many of the musicians came from backgrounds of oppression. Other groups had similar problems on "their side of the world." This unified them in a way that made them all equal. For many, this status led to isolation and introversion; and, with the class restrictions and economic situations of many of the swing musicians, creative outlets like music became their only comfort, the only expression of their situation. Sidney Bechet recalls that as a boy he had no toys and would have had no idea what to do with one had one been given to him. Because of this experience, later on Bechet started to write a song about a child who had no one or nothing to play with except a song. The boy sang and practiced this song "about being lonely, and as soon as he had the song, he wasn't lonely anymore. He was lucky. He was real well off; he had this thing he could trust, and so he could trust himself."[30]

It is nothing new to say that music and other creative endeavors were vital to the survival of outsiders in America. In antebellum days, slave consciousness was formed to some degree by the cultural ideas passed down through the generations through song, dance, and stories. After emancipation, the importance of music in the African American community was even more firmly entrenched; and, during the migration northward during the 1910s, those musical traditions entered the northern industrialized cities.[31]

Once in these urban areas, the African American encountered another group of outsiders who also held firm attachments to their musical lineage and who sought entrance into the American market. Many of the immigrants who migrated to the cities came from peasant backgrounds where the song and dance provided not only entertainment, but also information about their cultural heritage, heroes, and symbols. In the United States, music became the means by which Old World culture could be passed on to the young, hopefully holding off the forces that were chipping away the past. Music was particularly important. In the Jewish communities the cantor held special significance, as did the priests for the Eastern Orthodox Church, for their intonation and singing abilities. In the Catholic Church the ability to say high mass required certain vocal talents. On the social level most immigrant groups brought their traditional dances to this country: the polka, the hora, the tarantella, and a host of others. Music, as in the African American experience, was not simply for enjoyment, but was part of their ethnic heritage and changed in response to the new environment. *The Jazz Singer* details this exact experience. Al Jolson's character is born into a family where the cantor father expects the son to follow him into the synagogue. But the young boy likes ragtime and popular music, largely that of African Americans, and breaks from the family's ethnic past to become part of the American present and, mythically, the future. This transition takes on added flavor when one considers that in order for the ethnic Jolson to become American, he must utilize blackface caricature to achieve popular appeal. Jolson's attraction to the music of urban America was not unique, as many of those in the new cities of America found themselves attracted to the fast-paced and exciting sounds emanating from African American performers. Perhaps it traces back to the minstrel's sampling of cakewalk celebrations during the antebellum period; but certainly the popularity of ragtime and then jazz, a popularity which coincided with the emergence of the modernist ideals of capitalism, resonated with the urban audiences and brought the culture of African Americans to the mainstream marketplace. By the 1920s, the attraction of this urban music transcended race. Mary Lou Williams recalls that when she and Count Basie's band were in Kansas City in the early 1930s, they had "about 30 [white] pupils between" them who wanted to learn how to play jazz. Numerous whites were "always in the black district," and this sometimes caused trouble.[32]

Among both of these groups, musical ability held a level of prestige and respect. Music education for a child who showed promise was considered necessary, whether on the familial level or by hiring a tutor, which, given their class, was a great expense. In examining the musical training of the 227 swing musicians used to explore class in the last chapter, several interesting trends are revealed. All three groups—black, other ethnic, and native—received the bulk of their musical training through the family, and then through church, school, and, less often, formal private lessons. Regardless of ethnicity, over 60 percent in each group reported that their training came from these sources. But, when broken down to reveal where the working and lower classes received their training, the level of formal training or private lessons drops. As table 5.1 outlines, most of the musical training for those from the working class came from their schools.

While schools may have provided the basic rudiments of musical education, stories of family sacrifice for the sake of music are frequent among the swing musicians. Jonah Jones recalls getting his first instrument in depression-era Louisville, Kentucky, at the age of eleven. He had watched the Community Centre Band—which also bred Dicky Wells—and ran to his mother and grandmother crying for a trombone. Even though the grandmother thought the boy "crazy" for wanting a trombone when the family

	Working Class	Middle Class	Upper Class
FFS	27	18	5
CSF	10	5	0
FSP	6	1	0
FWS	47	14	0
LS	30	4	4
SSC	33	7	1

Note: Total N = 212. FFS stands for family, formal, and school training; CSF, for church, school, and family training; FSP, for family, school, and private lessons; FWS, for family and some school training; LS, for a little school training; SSC, for school and some church training.

Table 5.1. Musical Training

could not afford to "buy bread," the mother gave in and even contacted an expensive local teacher who told her that lessons were free at the center. Jones joined the Community Centre Band and took up the alto horn and later the trumpet.[33]

The reason that many families rewarded musical interest is that it was one of the few professional fields open to working- and lower-class ethnics and African Americans. Musical skill could often lead to good money, social acceptance, and prestige. Musical ability became a legitimate escape for many newly urban Americans. If they were lucky, it was even a way to become upwardly mobile economically. Sammy Cahn, the Tin Pan Alley lyricist, said the ghetto was the birthplace of America's great popular musicians because it provided daily reminders of the harshness of their contemporaries' lives. Immediate economic survival required the adoption of their American dream—to escape poverty one must work hard, prove ability, and adopt the ways of the dominant society.[34]

The American dream played a primary role in the swing generation's view of their musical production as an occupation. Many of the musicians who made it from these communities validated the dream for many of the young people still laboring to find a way out.[35] The fact that most of the stars of swing were ordinary Americans—ethnic minorities from the working class—proved that hard work and skill won the day. Regardless of their liabilities, namely, their class and ethnicity, they were accepted as an important part of the mainstream society. The elder Goodman used this type of reasoning in encouraging his boys to take seriously their musical talent, for while he enjoyed music aesthetically, he also saw in it the means by which his children could escape the poverty in which they lived.[36]

Part of this process involved recognizing and working with others, regardless of their ethnicity. Many of those who grew up to become swing musicians were exposed to many different ethnicities during their early years, so when they found they had to work with one another later on—to create music as an escape—they had some experience upon which to rely. Willie Smith converted to Judaism when a child due to the influence of his neighborhood, a local Newark rabbi, and his family. His other friends could not understand why he accepted the Hebrew faith when, being born black, he already had "one strike against" him. Smith reasoned that he had a "Jewish soul" and it seemed natural for him to be Jewish. His multiethnic situation extended beyond matters of faith, as his childhood gang, the Ramblers, contained whites and blacks, Jews and Gentiles. Mary Lou Williams went to school with little or no problem with Italians, Irish, and blacks. Maxine Sullivan's experience in Homestead, Pennsylvania, meant that she lived, worked, and studied alongside Hungarians, Slovaks, Poles, Italians, and many other ethnicities. Eddie London grew up with neighbors from almost all ethnic backgrounds, and his father defended the rights of blacks in his town outside Chicago. Down in New Orleans, Irving Fazola grew up Irish-Hungarian and by the fourth grade began mimicking the jazz styles of Louis Armstrong. Soon he befriended the black clarinet player Big Eye Nelson and began to hone his clarinet and saxophone skills by hanging around New Orleans' many dance halls. One of Jimmy Maxwell's earliest memories of his gambler father was when local authorities tried to run a black man out of town. Maxwell's dad knew the man was a gambler, and although his dad was white, he came to defense of the black man in trouble. The family had "to keep the house locked" up for several days after the rescue. As time passed the family became known for its pro-black attitude. When Maxwell was a teenager, neighbors would kid him by saying, " '[Y]ou're never going to be happy until you have a green suit and play with a nigger band.' . . . And [he] said, '[T]hat's right.' " Dicky Wells grew up in Tennessee and Kentucky and played with friends at the local swimming holes. Once, they found a hole with a sign posted saying, "No niggers allowed." Wells and his pals wrote "white" before "nigger," because in their "book, the word had no color." The owner of the farm where the hole was located took down the sign and put up another, opening the hole to all, regardless of color. Wells concluded that they "all had a ball and lived happily thereafter." If problems did develop, someone would simply fire "his shooting iron" in the air, and peace resumed.[37]

In many of the swing musicians' recollections, there are frequent stories of different ethnic groups befriending one another, or at least peacefully coexisting. Harry "Sweets" Edison recalled growing up in the 1920s in socially segregated Columbus, Ohio. Blacks were not allowed into the downtown theaters even if the performer was black, but the schools he attended were integrated and he had several white friends. "We all played together," he said, and did not grow up with a stigma "about being black or white." Eddie Sauter felt that all the people who came to America brought with them their musical heritage and, once here, "put it all together and made a mish-mosh of it." Russell Procope learned how to read music by trading his knowledge of jazz with a white musician he heard play at the Ginn Theater. He told the musician, Frank O'Bannon, that if "you teach me how to read good . . . [then] I'll teach you how to play jazz good." They traded musical cultures.[38]

This is not to suggest there were no racial or other ethnic tensions. Many swing musicians recall fights and harsh words. When some white kids called Andy Kirk and his friends "nigger," they went into an alley and fought it out, even if the offending person was their "best friend." Many confrontations had less to do with ethnicity or color than with neighborhood territory, girls, and bullies. When Garvin Bushell and his band decided to practice in a more ethnically diverse section of Harlem, he said, "Jewish and Italian boys tried to keep us out, and we had several bad fights." These encounters stemmed from Bushell and his mates going to the "ice cream parlor to try and pick up girls," which challenged the ethnic boys' sexual hegemony. While these stories reveal tensions, they also reveal that blacks, whites, and other ethnics did not always view each other within the confines of their generation, class, or family. They tried to view each other as people. Sir Charles Thompson realized that not "all white [people] hung black people" when he went into the army in the early 1930s and became company clerk. In this position he worked closely with the company commander, a white man. When local residents of Delta, Missouri, expressed disgust over having black troops in the area, the captain issued ammunition to the troops and said they weren't being run out of anywhere. To Thompson, this proved that "there was justice" in America, and not all people are like their stereotypes.[39]

The streets of the city and the swimming holes of the country exposed different races to one another, but it was the music that forged connections. Growing up white in New Orleans during the height of the jazz explosion and safely within his class pattern as a printers' assistant—a job he relished—Nappy Lamare turned his back on the job his father and grandfather had held to take up the guitar because one day he happened to see a musical parade led by Louis Armstrong and his all-black band. Andy Kirk saw few black bands come through Denver during his childhood and so took as his early musical influence the number of white bands that played the city. When in 1922 and 1923 his band shared a billing with Jack Teagarden and his seven-piece group, Kirk's group played "more white than Jack's band." Just the opposite was true of Jimmy Maxwell: "All of my favorite players were black. I never liked any of the white bands." Wingy Manone, also raised in New Orleans, recalls taking his traditional, white music teacher, Mrs. Green, up the river to Tobacco Road, where local blacks would gather to play the rudiments of what would become jazz. Manone informed his teacher that that was how he wanted to play. After admitting they had talent, she told the youth that if he wanted to play in that style she would "disown" him. Manone never went back to her: "Every chance I got, I went over there and listened to 'em. They didn't want no white folks around, but they let me come, as long as I stayed on the boundary line." Manone called this his "music school." Later, when he worked as a water boy on a grain elevator construction team, he received his finishing degree by listening to the black laborers "who toted the girders" sing on the job. Their call and response pattern "was great stuff for a kid who was nuts about music."[40]

In northern communities this cultural association was also being made. Max Kaminsky grew up in a Russian-Jewish household in the heart of the black section of Boston and was exposed to a variety of African American musics. He attended black churches to hear their gospel music and played in the streets full of black vendors singing the praises of their wares. Although the Kaminsky's moved from Roxbury to a more Jewish section later on, the influence of those streets remained.[41]

In the southwest similar situations took place. Guitarist Charlie Christian adopted a country-western swing style of playing while growing up in Oklahoma City. Playing with his father's band in the white sections of town, they adopted the style that best pleased their paying audience. The black church and gospel singing played a major role in Jack Teagarden's musical training. Growing up in Texas during the height of Jim Crow segregation the late 1910s, Teagarden was attracted to the musical sounds coming from local black churches and the occasional camp revival meetings. It was in listening to the hymns and shouts of the disaffected blacks that Teagarden was awakened to the importance of the beat: "It came to young Teagarden in the rhythmic hand claps, the laments and hosannas of half a hundred Negro voices. It came from a tawdry tent, gray and shapeless under the Texas stars. Long after he had gone to bed its swing pulse kept him throbbing all night."[42]

This type of exposure and even acceptance of other cultures had important ramifications. First of all, when these children grew older, the connection to multiethnicity remained part of their lifestyle. The practices and cultures of other ethnics were not feared, as they were among the more traditional white middle-class, but were absorbed, understood, and, in the case of music, utilized. The cultural exchange, which began in their youth as a result of their shared class, continued as they grew older. As a white musician interested in playing jazz, Bill Davison remembered Chicago jam sessions in the 1920s where white and black musicians played with "[n]o race problems." In fact, 1920s Chicago had a variety of mixed clubs. The interaction between the white and black musicians in these clubs helped account for the musical flowering of jazz in that city. Pee Wee Russell played with many of the popular white jazz and swing bands in and around New York City in the late 1920s and 1930s, and on evenings off, or after finishing a show, he and other white musicians headed uptown to the black clubs to hear and play music. One night he filled in for an ailing Coleman Hawkins in Fletcher Henderson's band and played much of the night with the band.[43]

During the swing generation these tendencies continued and the mixing of bands became more obvious. New York City, as Lewis Erenberg argues, "remained the realm of modern hopes of freedom," where black bands became "heroes" to their fans—black and white. Erenberg argues that their ability was seen as "living proof that blacks were eminently capable of

ROY ELDRIDGE...

★

HOTTEST OF THE HOT!

**Now with his own Swing Band ...
Sizzling on his Martin Trumpet
at Chicago's famous "3 Deuces"**

Formerly featured with Fletcher Henderson, Roy is unquestionably one of
the hottest, most sensational Trumpet
players this country has ever known.
It's a real treat to hear him play — hit
"C" above "High C" and go way on
up "out of sight". *And how easily he
does it on his Martin!*

The new Martin Trumpet and Cornet, along with the new Martin Saxophones, are recognized by outstanding
players everywhere as the finest instruments of all time. You'll find a
Martin will help you accomplish with
ease things that were difficult and even
impossible before and this, inevitably,
leads to increased recognition and
compensation. Arrange to try one
today. See your Martin dealer or drop
us a card. Interesting new folder FREE
upon request.

MARTIN BAND INSTRUMENT CO.
DEPARTMENT 1113   ELKHART, INDIANA

Fig. 5.1. *Metronome* 52 (November 1936): 38

achievements in those fields open to them," and through the forties they began to assert themselves more in the public sphere. Certainly this held true of the magazines which catered to the swing fan. A survey of advertisements in *Metronome* from 1936 to 1941 reveals that as swing became more integrated, black musicians were featured more often in ads hawking musical wares (see figs. 5.1 and 5.2). These ads seem to validate Erenberg's assertion that some black musicians became heroes, for the true gauge of status in the modern era was sales.[44]

But it was neither easy nor universally accepted that swing bands should integrate. When Art Hodes brought his band from Chicago to New York in 1940, he discovered that he could use a mixed band. Chicago's American Federation of Musicians (AFM) was still segregated, but the New York local had consolidated and mixed bands were fairly standard. Hodes also worked on occasion with Sidney Bechet, who got into trouble with some black musicians for hiring white musicians: "It didn't matter to Sidney what or who you were, [all] you had to be was a producer." Jimmy Maxwell was doing the *Mildred Bailey Show* on the radio in 1944 when the sponsor, Chesterfield Cigarettes, suggested they fire the black musicians in the band. As a south-

Fig. 5.2. *Metronome* 56 (January 1940): 21

ern company, they did not think it was a good idea to have a mixed band. When Maxwell—through Teddy Wilson—found out about Chesterfield's objective, he went to his AFM union representative, Willy Feiberg, who threatened to take every band off of CBS unless this situation was resolved.

Maxwell lost this job, and some friends thought he was "crazy" for making such a stand. He said, "I wasn't trying to fight a cause, it's just because it was my friends that they were hassling with." Artie Shaw "hired people for what they did," not for their color. While there were cases where musicians and fans were less than supportive, Lena Horne remembers that it was the "wonderful support" from the "boys in the band" that allowed her to endure.[45]

The effect of this racial and ethnic mixing was not lost to either the fans or musicians. When Goodman made Wilson and Hampton part of his show, "the public was so for the thing that not one negative voice in any audience did we get," said Teddy Wilson. The musicians themselves, white and black, "were all very much aware of what was going on," he continued, and, as musicians, "believed in what we were doing, socially and musically." Lionel Hampton said that Goodman's integration allowed for "Negroes to have their chance in baseball and other fields" later on. For Wilson, the inclusion of the black musician filled out the picture of the swing band, one made up of "Southerners . . . Jews and Christians and Lionel and [Wilson] represented the Negroes in the band." The situation made him feel that they "were like brothers, the whole outfit."[46]

There were factors, however, that prevented these "brothers" from truly being equal. America in the 1930s and 1940s was not as open as some of the above makes it appear. African Americans knew that while as musicians on the bandstand they might be equals and able to applaud each other's unique contribution to the swing sound, off the bandstand things were much different. For the white musicians, such as Benny Goodman or Artie Shaw, the ability to disguise their ethnic associations by changing their name or pattern of speech allowed them to become white. They could easily shed their ethnic association, like Shaw had, by simply dropping a letter from their last name or by shortening their ethnic first name to sound more American. For the black musicians this was not an option. Passing as white was difficult, both for pride and for complexion reasons, and many black musicians found that after the show their ability to mix was severely restricted.[47]

Touring in America reminded many of the black musicians that the equality of the stage did not transfer to social relations. Budd Johnson toured with Earl Hines in 1938 when events at a Fort Lauderdale, Florida, performance took a dangerous turn. They played their first set, ending with a wild version of "Honeysuckle Rose." As they were leaving the stage area, a white fan came up to Hines and asked if he could play "Honeysuckle Rose." Hines, confused, responded curtly that they had just finished playing that song. The man thought Hines was being arrogant and returned with a state trooper, who said, "Hey nigger, what's the matter with you that you can't play this white man's request?" Hines tried to explain to the trooper, but to no avail. A crowd had now formed around the band area, including some whites who wanted to invite Hines over for a drink. When the trooper heard this, he said he'd arrest the lot of them if he "would catch that nigger goin' over" to have a drink with white folks. Hines, sensing trouble, returned to the bus and hid. This left Johnson, as straw boss, responsible for the remainder of the show. It remained tense, and the members of the band saw right away that they were in a potentially dangerous situation. Most of the band had guns, as Johnson related, "I'm not just going to let him slap me on both cheeks and knock me down, drag me out and lynch me without a fight." No other event marred the performance though, and the band left Fort Lauderdale for their next show. Andrew Blakeney was playing with Fletcher Henderson's band in 1941 when he was arrested in Albany, Georgia. The reason for his arrest was unclear, but while incarcerated he was kicked and beaten about the head, resulting in a silver plate being put in his forehead. Milt Hinton was playing in Fort Lauderdale, Florida, and found it was hard to even "get off the stand for a drink of water unless [the band] had a police escort." In Lakeland, Florida, Andy Kirk's band allowed the son of the country club's white manager to sit in with the band. Later he learned the manager was fired because the patrons of the club did not like the idea of racial mixing. Doc Cheatham was playing with Cab Calloway's band in Memphis, Tennessee, when a white girl came to the bandstand for an autograph. When Cab's long hair fell and touched her, the crowd went wild. The fight saw chairs, bottles, and people fly through the air. The band members had to fight their way out of the hall and back to their Pullman railcar. Cheatham was rarely bothered by these activities, because he "was a southerner" and therefore used to such behavior. He simply never expected "to . . . walk into a restaurant, sit down and eat."[48]

Given these types of stories, why did the bands play the South? Andy Kirk echoes what many black leaders understood, "[W]e toured the south because that's where our records had sold the best." Even though harassed, beaten, and denied hotel and eating rights, Kirk saw his touring in the South as beneficial. Because they couldn't stay in white hotels or eat at white restaurants, they were oftentimes taken in by black residents and fed in their homes. This created long-term friendships and exposed the musicians directly to their fans and supporters. At the shows, most times whites and blacks enjoyed the music and danced, and for Kirk these experiences opened his eyes to other white southerners who did not want to "put their foot on [him]."[49]

But America's race consciousness did not stop at the Mason-Dixon line. As a *Downbeat* reporter reminded readers in 1938, it was white musicians who were initially the loudest complainers about Goodman's inclusion of Hampton and Wilson. As figure 5.3 reveals, readers still tended to view as humorous black musicians within the minstrel context. Furthermore, many northern American Federation of Musicians unions were, like their southern counterparts, segregated. Black locals in Boston, Chicago, San Francisco, Atlantic City, Bridgeport, and other northern cities meant that black musicians played for lower wages and were shut out of many venues which did not want to upset their clientele with a black band. Even in New York City, musical territories were defined as much by race as by location. The prominent hotels in midtown usually featured white, sweet dance music, although by the late 1930s many of the white leaders of swing—Goodman, Shaw, Norvo, Crosby, Berigan—played in these expensive clubs. Greenwich Village had few swing clubs and the small ones operated by featuring more experimental jazz as well as new faces on the scene. In the last two locations—Harlem and Fifty-second Street—white swing musicians would come down to watch, learn, and play with the black swing bands. While Harlem was the home of black jazz and many white musicians journeyed to jam with the greats there, Fifty-second Street became known as "Swing Street." It was here that most of the white and black mixing took place, not only among the musicians, but in the audiences as well. The best white musicians and black musicians played on Swing Street and audiences came from all over the city to hear the best of the best, but black musicians were rarely allowed the same privilege in the uptown spots.[50]

Even though many bandleaders integrated their groups, a system of exclusion continued to permeate the industry. Black musicians faced a number of very real roadblocks preventing their inclusion. For example, most times

Fig. 5.3. *Downbeat* 4 (December 1937): 12

African Americans were paid less under AFM union scales. Also, the handful of black players in the all-white bands oftentimes felt isolated and alienated within their bands. Roy Eldridge was the only black member of the Krupa band as they toured from the East to the West Coast. In town after town, hotels would not let Eldridge check in with the rest of the band and he would have to find other quarters. "It was a lonely life," he recalled. Finally in Hollywood, when he was told he could not sit with white patrons unless they were celebrities, he broke down and could not perform.[51]

This alienation in the midst of seeming acceptance helps one also to understand the role of women with the swing generation. Much like the other musicians who faced class, racial, and ethnic barriers while trying to "make it" in the American system, women faced these same obstacles, as well as social ones that held they should do "women's work." Their task was made even more complicated by a societal reluctance to allow women into the all-male popular music fold combined with the economic pressures of the depression, pressures which favored women leaving the workforce so that men could have their jobs. Even though they were not allowed to be equal members, women contributed to the sound and feel of the swing generation.

By the 1930s jazz seemed to be an all-male musical phenomenon. The members of bands saw themselves as part of a fraternity, an all-male ensemble, a group of guys traveling around having some fun. There seemed to be little room for women, who, the men thought, were too frail to endure the rigors of the road or not dedicated enough to suffer the oftentimes difficult musical schedule. Yet many women did contribute to the formation of swing in the 1930s and 1940s. Most were like Mary Lou Williams, who, despite her arranging and excellent piano playing for the Andy Kirk band in the early thirties, was never allowed to become a full-fledged member of the band. Vibraharpist Marjorie Hyams, who, despite being added to Woody Herman's band in 1944 and 1945, was forced to wear a dress rather than the band uniform worn by the male members: "There was more interest in what you were going to wear or how your hair was fixed," she said. More common was the experience of singer Anita O'Day, exemplified in figure 5.4. Regardless of talent, sexual innuendo sold better than musical skill.[52]

The role of women in swing is best understood when placed in the context of the effects of modernization on the role of women in American society. With the rise of industrial capitalism in the late nineteenth century and the corresponding growth of urban areas and immigration, women began to enter the workforce in more diverse occupations, but ones that continued to view them through the Victorian lens of domesticity. They took jobs as seamstresses, teachers, or mill operatives in the early phases of this industrial movement and accounted for nearly 15 percent of the labor force by 1870. As the country's industry changed, and with it the nature of capital, women's roles within the structure also changed. New clerical occupations in factories and stores and the continued feminization of teaching meant that fewer women worked as domestics. The number of women employed tripled by 1910, but since most were young and unmarried, it was assumed they would soon leave the workforce to marry and raise a family.[53]

Fig. 5.4. "She Scores with Chicago Musicians,"
Downbeat 6 (February 1939): 1

In the years leading to the swing generation, the country's women made great strides in the workplace and society. Certainly the Nineteenth Amendment helped in this process, as did the expanding economy of the 1920s. The shift from heavy industry to a more consumer-directed economy meant that advertisers were given larger roles not only in introducing items for sale, but also in creating demand for items. One group particularly targeted by these "apostles of modernity" was women. Using fear and alienation as the means to get their attention, advertisements encouraged women to consume products that would make their husbands stay at home or even help in getting a husband. But there were other more liberating themes in these ads. More than ever, women were seen as the primary consumer. This gave them power to negotiate which product to favor and why. Companies, recognizing this newfound power, attempted to cater to this market. As a result, women changed the nature of what Victorian society deemed as acceptable behavior and dress. The fashion revolution of the Chanel dress and the brassiere was stimulated by the same market demands that reinforced gender stereotypes. While the advertisers were encouraging them to buy the newest soap or the best canned soup, women used their newfound market power to demand changes that liberated them from the constrictive clothing and ideals of the Victorian era.[54]

The liberation in politics and fashion also affected the workplace. During the 1920s, women in professional occupations increased by 50 percent, and, for the first time, married women came to make up a significant portion of the workplace. Taken at face value these seem to signify advancement, but women workers found most male professions closed to them and were still "confined to 'women's professions,' and in the business world, to lower-level job categories." For example, the number of women employees at the Travelers Insurance Corporation increased during this period and was seen by the male executives as essential to the company. Yet the tasks they performed were designed "not to replace men"; women did the clerical work and made "the business more profitable." Working in an office as a clerk was considered respectable work for married women, and positions like these were highly sought after. Other women continued to labor in traditional female occupations such as seamstress, waitress, and laundress; and, while in decline, the largest single occupation remained domestic service. These married and single women labored not for the prestige or because they felt liberated by the times, but, as many women in the *Middletown* survey reported, because the family needed the money. This was particularly true for the growing numbers of African American women who migrated to the North during this period. While some had moved away from domestic work by the 1920s, three out of four still labored and lodged in people's homes.[55]

The limited advancements made in the 1920s withered during the hard times of the depression. Women were now encouraged to stay at home and adopt a more traditional view of their place in society. Jobs were reserved for family breadwinners, presumably male. Surveys taken during the era suggested that people believed that women in the workplace were taking jobs from men and thus making an already bad situation worse. Yet women were as hard hit by the crisis as the men. In January 1931 over two million women were out of work. Professional women saw their numbers decline in the midst of the crisis and saw many of the positions that were considered "women's work," such as librarians, social workers, and nurses, now open to male advance. Roosevelt's New Deal policies attempted to assist the unemployed women, especially with the Works Progress Administration (WPA), but the government programs fell far short of meeting the employment needs of the nation's women. This is not to suggest that women abandoned the workplace, for the need was great and the numbers of working women, single and married, increased to 30 percent of the workforce by 1940. But they often had to accept the lowest-paying clerical or light service jobs and found many of the professional occupations now closed to them.[56]

But there were other signs that suggested that the earlier advancements would not be lost. Roosevelt included many women in his top administrative posts, including Frances Perkins and Ellen Woodward, as well as opening up many mid-level administrative positions to women. One would be hard pressed to examine any of FDR's New Deal programs without seeing some role played by women administrators or employees. Leading this federal initiative was the First Lady, Eleanor Roosevelt, who used her position to exemplify the usefulness of a strong, intelligent, and caring woman for a society ravaged by depression. Her symbolic presence as well as her activism helped keep feminist ideology alive in a difficult era. The First Lady was not alone, as the lower marriage and birthrate stimulated by the economic crisis meant that more women made their own economic and social decisions. Because of the crash, the pressure to wed and stay at home and have babies lessened and allowed many young women the time to define themselves within their social world. Hollywood presented a variety of heroines, such as Joan Crawford, Bette Davis, Marlene Dietrich, or Carole Lombard, who were independent and strong, but who still operated within the male-controlled world. Perhaps the best known is the character played by Vivien Leigh in *Gone with the Wind*. On the surface and throughout the movie, one sees a woman flirting with the cult of domesticity her society places her within. Her desire is to have a man, children, and the comforts of home. But as her lifestyle and way of being crumble around her, including her marriage to Rhett Butler (Clark Gable), Scarlett emerges as a strong and intelligent woman who finds that finding a man does not solve her problems and that she must rebuild her life.[57]

The 1930s offered a contradiction for the place of women in American society. On one hand, economic factors made women's presence in the workplace a difficult one, where good jobs were hard to find and the threat of losing the position to a male breadwinner was a reality. On the other hand, women were being seen as powerful and equal in more areas of society, from the workplace to the unions, the voting booths, and government. These situations contributed to a change among women concerning their role in society, and while the era lacked cohesive feminist activity, a change in consciousness was taking place. This new way of being was not reserved for women; some men began to reevaluate the position and place of women in society. Popular culture played as much an active a role in this transformation as did political culture. In the early part of the twentieth century, largely as a result of making popular entertainment more open to the whole family, vaudeville sought to tame the "male audience" while at the same time providing the necessary space for women to poke fun at the restrictive Victorian culture. This opened the space up to women as individuals and provided men with the opportunity to see the humor inherent in the cult of domesticity.[58]

One particular area where this dichotomy held true was music. Traditionally, the role of women as teachers of music, particularly for the piano, meant that they occupied a significant segment of the musical field. Although their actual numbers would decline after the 1910 high of 84,478 teachers or performers of music, by the 1930s their numbers had increased and gone beyond the Victorian piano teacher model to include more diverse instruments and occupations. Yet these newer women musicians faced a job market that remained closed to them. Most conductors and symphony musicians, who were male, thought women lacked the necessary physical and intellectual abilities for the rigors of the orchestra. When *Etude* addressed the topic in "Women in Music" in 1929, it suggested that the greatest contribution made by women to music lay in their ability to cook, clean, sew, and take care of the male composer or musician.[59]

When the Great Depression forced philanthropic agencies and societies to lessen their subsidies to orchestras and opera houses, fewer and fewer jobs were available to the nation's women musicians. The American Federation of Musicians (AFM) did little to assist this group and, while nominally open to women, made little effort to include them in its fold. In fact, the union excluded music teachers, vocalists, and many types of pianists, most of whom were female. Women musicians made up nearly 47 percent of the total musical workforce, primarily as teachers of music, yet were not part of the AFM. In New York City, for example, while there were 17,000 men employed as performers, only 100 women held steady jobs as classical performers. When the WPA created the Federal Music Project (FMP) in August of 1935, one of the areas that administrator Harry Hopkins hoped to improve was the presence of women in orchestras. Although the FMP director, Nicolai Sokoloff, did not see eye to eye with Hopkins on this issue, Sokoloff's wife happened to be the former director of the National Federation of Music Clubs, and his immediate boss, Ellen Woodward, and later Florence Kerr, was very interested in using the arts projects to project positive images of women professionals. As a result, the FMP orchestras employed women in all aspects of the orchestra, from strings to brass to compositions to conductors. Yet little of this activity affected the attitudes and hiring practices of the major symphony orchestras. In the post-FMP era several women found employment: Mary Carr Moore, Antonia Brico, Marian Bauer, and Ruth Crawford. But the vast majority of women found the classical world closed to their skills.[60]

That few doors were open to professional women in the vernacular realm perhaps helps to explain their desire to enter the popular musical marketplace. And yet, their desire was oftentimes suffocated by the same prejudices held by those in the vernacular field. But, as popular music developed in the 1920s, stimulated by the radio and phonograph industries, women played an integral role. Mamie Smith's "Crazy Blues" (1920) sold over one hundred thousand records, and she became the model for other blues women who sang to the accompaniment of jazz greats like Louis Armstrong, Coleman Hawkins, Fletcher Henderson, and a slew of others. Jazz, early hillbilly, and much of Tin Pan Alley music owed a great debt to the women singers who helped popularize the commercial music, though, while it allowed for women to be seen as part of the bands, their role was usually reserved as the singer. When swing took hold in the mid-1930s, outside of Mary Lou Williams, Lil Hardin Armstrong, or a few others, few women participated in bands as musicians. Swing, like jazz and symphony music, was an all-boys club.[61]

Denied acceptance into this fraternity, women musicians found other ways to swing. Many all-women bands were formed, first during the jazz era, for example, Lil Hardin's Chicago group, and then later, led by the likes of Ina Ray Hutton and Her Melodears, Rita Rio's Orchestra, Phil Spitalny and His All-Girl Orchestra, and later the International Sweethearts of Rhythm. Hutton's band, initially formed in 1934 with her billed as the "Blonde Bombshell of Rhythm," was the first to be "accepted" into the swing circuit by 1936, largely as a result of her connection to Irving Mills's booking agency and the musical arrangements he supplied. The band played all the major venues, including the Paramount, and did a number of Hollywood films, including *The Big Broadcast of 1937*. The Melodears were popular and, while Hutton was not a musician and danced her way through leading the band, the women musicians who made up the orchestra, including pianist Betty Roudybush, guitarist Marian Gange, and trombonist Alyse Wills, were talented swing players. They wanted to "sound like Benny Goodman and Basie and everyone else." But booking agents, promoters, and other musicians saw them more as gimmicks. Rita Rio's group, formed in 1938, found itself in the same position. While the orchestra held many women who were able to play swing with the best of the boys, they were oftentimes reduced to a novelty act—come watch the girls try to swing.[62]

The all-women groups did have a positive effect. After an article questioning a woman's ability to play music appeared in *Downbeat* in February 1938, for example, both Rio and Peggy Gilbert wrote rebuttals outlining the difficulties women musicians faced in the male-controlled world. Both argued that men wanted to keep women in a position of subservience, and while they allowed them to play around with music, they stopped short of acceptance. Gilbert pointed out that men had traditionally not wanted to play music with women, thereby "not giving [women] the opportunity to prove their equality."[63]

Much akin to its time, this argument did much to raise the consciousness of the women, and some men, who read the magazine. More to the point, it revealed an activist stance that many of the women had adopted by this time period inside and outside of music. The idea that women were physically and intellectually inferior was crumbling under the sheer weight of its own limitations and was concurrent to the depression and World War II ideology that held that all people had something to contribute to America. Perhaps the days of sexual, class, and racial divisions were numbered.

There were other, more practical effects from the likes of Rio and Hutton. Namely, many women who had wanted to play in a band now saw it as a viable option. One such group was born out of the Piney Woods Orphanage in Mississippi in 1937, called the International Sweethearts of Rhythm. It was formed when the head of the school, Laurence Clifton Jones, saw Hutton's band in Chicago and heard Spitalny's band on the radio; Jones decided to create a dance band that would help to pay the cost of running the school. Fifteen of the best girls at the school were chosen and, after being taught how to play swing, began to play local performances. By 1940 the band was playing regionally throughout the South, and while the musicians' studies suffered, the school profited handsomely from the band. In 1941 several members complained of the low wages and the time spent on the road playing shows, making it hard for them to graduate. Fearing a strike, Jones fired the nonschool members of the band—Rae Lee Jones and Vivian Crawford—and ordered the seventeen other girls back to Mississippi. Instead, they went to Washington, D.C., and began working with promoter Dan Gary and arranger Eddie Durham, and by September they were playing the Apollo in New York City. From there the Sweethearts went on to become one of the most renowned all-women swing bands. With the likes of tenor saxophonist Vi Burnside and trumpet player Tiny Davis rounding out an excellent band, they continued to tour through 1947, when, like many male bands, the Sweethearts began to disband.[64]

The Sweethearts and many other all-women swing musicians were proof that women could contribute if given the chance. While these stories are uplifting, mainstream swing bands focused more on a woman's sexuality than on her musical ability. As a result, it was in being the girl singer, or the canary, that women made their most obvious contribution to the swing moment. Given that swing was part of a commercial enterprise that viewed profit as the bottom line, the image of a pretty girl singing to a group of high school and college-aged young men sold. Jo Jones recalled how in 1937 the Basie band, which already had singer Jimmy Rushing, wanted a female vocalist: "[W]e got tired of going out on the road with a bunch of men, so we got to have a vocalist. A girl, got to have some woman there, you know

Fig. 5.5. "For Musicians Only . . . ," *Downbeat* 5 (May 1938): 10

what I mean." For a band to make it in the highly competitive swing music field by the late 1930s, it was necessary to hire a pretty female vocalist. But they had to be more than the singer; they also had to appear attractive, sexual, and nonthreatening. They also had to provide for their own wardrobe and faced the constant judgment of the band and audiences alike on how their hair was fixed, how their dresses were pressed, and how their makeup was applied.[65]

The males who controlled the industry and the critics who were gatekeepers to the audiences took the image of the woman singer as mere sexual fluff as the accepted standard. As figure 5.5 suggests, women were judged not by what they could do, but by what the male gaze believed *they could do*. And as the *Downbeat* cover (see fig. 5.6) insinuated in 1940, talent mattered little with women members of the band: The potential vocalist has succumbed to the casting-couch method of securing employment. Naked and, by association, bereft of talent, she awaits the approval of the male "artist."

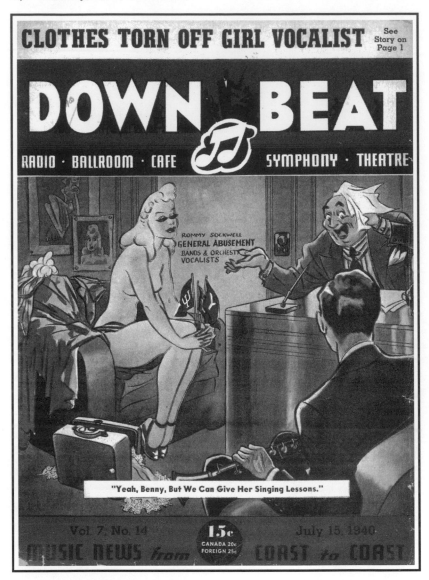

Fig. 5.6. *Downbeat* 7 (July 15, 1940): cover

In order to sell the sexual side of swing, while at the same time trying to deny its sexual nature, she holds in her hands the pennants of fraternities and colleges loyal to her beauty. Even the banner headline suggests sexual excitement, and readers no doubt associated the near-naked cartoon woman on the front with the real life singer whose "clothes were torn off." In actuality, Ella Fitzgerald had her gown ripped (not off) by autograph hounds after a New Orleans show. The fanzines that catered to the swing generation regularly played into this sexualized image of the female performer, running photos of the girl singers in provocative, yet safe, poses, or by running contests on the best-looking singer and reducing them musically to faces and bodies with little *real* talent.[66]

The focus on appearance many times overshadowed the real musical contributions that many of the woman singers made to the bands. Artie Shaw's band was made more powerful with the addition of Billie Holiday. Helen Ward contributed to Goodman's and James's outfits. The list of talented female vocalists—Doris Day, Lena Horne, Ella Fitzgerald, Rosemary Clooney, Helen O'Connell, Ivie Anderson, Helen Forrest, Jo Stafford, Kay Starr, Martha Tilton, Maxine Sullivan, Anita O'Day, Peggy Lee, and many others—belies the talentless, sexual image presented by the promoters and critics of the day.

But it was hard for these women to stop being judged outside their gender-defined roles as sexual object, girlfriend, or mother-cook. The gendered nature of popular music in both white and black cultures had dictated certain limitations as to how women were viewed and how women viewed the male musicians. Marge Singleton said, referring to the New Orleans jazz scene, that "the women loved musicians" and would do just about anything to get them and keep them. This, of course, led many of the male musicians to view women who were interested in jazz as sexual objects rather than peers. And when a woman was hired to sing with the band, it was presumed that she would become the girlfriend of someone in the group, most likely the leader. When Helen Humes joined the Basie band it was presumed she would be his girlfriend, but she sought to control the direction of the relationship: "He was just there. Sometimes we'd sleep together and sometimes we wouldn't." When Basie tried to stop her from going with her friends, she said, "I didn't stand all that."[67]

Humes's position in the band, while gendered and sexual, did not lack power. She and others like her recognized that they were artists and added vitality to the organization, and they sought to use their power to display their talents. Once, when Mary Lou Williams was jamming with Art Tatum, she played a difficult piano run that Tatum had been unable to play for several years, as had Count Basie. Both were thrilled to learn how to properly play this turn-around run. Yet, when the interviewer asked if they were jealous, meaning jealous of her musical skills, Williams assumed the question related to sexual issues and told several stories of women who were jealous of her close relationship to the male musicians. Even Humes found herself in the gendered role as caregiver and, willingly, cook. She had always liked to "cook for the musicians" and even opened a restaurant in Albany that catered to the traveling swing crowd. She enjoyed this role and never felt as though it were her responsibility. "I enjoyed doing some things [like cooking, and] I cooked all over the United States in all the big theatre dressing rooms, you know, cooking for the band." Other women in the bands walked this narrow line between empowerment and individual choice and the gendered role that society, and by extension the band, placed them in.[68]

In much the same way that the swing bands came to blend ethnicity, class, and race in their musical organization, many women found that once they had shown their musical chops, or skills, the gendered view of them as sex objects or canaries lessened. Those women who played instruments, such as Mary Lou Williams, Marjorie Hyams, or L'Ana Webster (who played saxophone with Mike Riley's band in 1937 and 1938), found that some musicians viewed them for their musical skills. As Sonny Greer said about Ivie Anderson, when the band wanted to go out partying, she would go too, the same as any other band member. But not all band members welcomed the female players, nor did audiences tend to see their position in the bands on an equal basis. Andrew Blakeney recalls that some men were worried that women pianists didn't have the strength or stamina, especially in their left hand, to give voice to the chords. Other musicians saw women as being too soft or feminine to withstand the rigors of performances and nights out on the road. And audiences tended to wait for women musicians to make a mistake or, if the band made one, to blame it on the female players. When it was an all-girl band, some fans waited for screwups, hoping to utter, as Gypsie Cooper, saxophonist for Phil Spitalny's band recalls hearing, "[T]hey're just a bunch of girls."[69]

With America's entrance into World War II and the subsequent drain of manpower for swing bands, one might assume that finally the day of equality came for the many women plying their musical craft. Certainly, the number of women in swing bands increased: Betty Sattley Leeds joined Louis Prima's band, Gracie Barrie replaced her husband as the lead for the Dick Stabile outfit, and the number of all-girl bands increased to fill war-related entertainment demands. Many of the women's band's performances were part of the United Services Organization (USO) or patriotic shows, and soldiers, promoters, and other males saw them as camp followers designed to please the war-weary soldier. While performers such as drummer Alice Whyte, saxophonist Peggy Gilbert, and reed player Deloros Reed found ample employment, some audiences found it difficult to accept them as musicians. As Ada Leonard told her musicians, "[B]ecause you're a girl, people look at you first, then listen to you second." This tendency encouraged the women to present their feminine qualities even more, and the drive to look glamorous while playing hot swing was added to their already difficult responsibilities. Joy Cayler, who played trumpet, recalled that her publicity photo made her look more like a stripper than a musician, "but that was the mode of the day."[70]

The women musicians and their bands faced other challenges. The AFM was concerned that their entrance into the wartime market would create too much competition for jobs after the war and so sought to limit their playing by forcing some clubs to hire a male band with the female group. In line with the general trend during the war, the nearly six million women in the workplace were paid less than their male counterparts. Women musicians averaged about one-third to one-half less pay than male players. And finally, the public's general perception held that these women were merely filling in for the men. When the war ended, it was assumed, they would go back to the home and kitchen where they belonged. After Jane Sager played a wartime music job, she asked the male bandleader for a job with the band on a full-time basis. While he was quick to credit her abilities, he told her that with the men coming home from the war, they had to support their families and so he couldn't use her. That the women were expected to return to the home after the war was not reserved for those in the swing bands, as society pressured all women to return to their prewar domestic roles. When that did not work, some companies just fired their women employees when the men returned.[71]

That the swing generation was filled with profound change yet continued to rely on old ideas is an accepted interpretation of those scholars who study the period. The rise of modernist capitalism, combined with the influx of migrants to new urban areas and the need for the federal government to assume greater powers to direct and control the economy of the country, meant that people had to change their understanding of one another. They could no longer be divided, as they had in the past, by their racial, economic, or gendered position, but had to begin viewing themselves as part of the whole America. Divisions between the people brought instability and, increasingly important, the prospect of revolution. Swing music played a prominent and early role in the redefinition of America, one that included all types of Americans regardless of their ethnic background, race, or gender. The glue that held this new vision of America together was money. Capitalism was held up as the most unique of American ideas and, combined with the New Deal's effort to rehabilitate capital's image in the public eye, became forever connected to the American identity. With this new vision of democracy, America was open to all, as the rewards of the marketplace went to those who were best able to capture the imagination and the dollars of the people. Capital was held up as the great equalizer, and the economy and the government were to be directed to meet this new goal. But this transition was not without problems, as this chapter outlines, mainly regarding America's continued racism and sexism. But the swing generation did much to begin to break down these barriers, and swing was among the first national, popular cultures to feature mixed bands on many levels: ethnic, gender, class. Swing's ability to navigate these new waters of acceptance was tempered by the gatekeepers but reflected the impulses of its generation and signaled the arrival of modern America.

Swing's Low

The Decline of Swing

S wing's popularity with the youth of America in 1935 had seemingly come out of nowhere; so, too, its decline appeared to happen overnight. In 1946, *Metronome* announced "The King is Dead" in reference to Goodman's declining commercial appeal. While his and other bands continued to perform, record sales indicated that swing was losing its ability to dominate the industry. The reasons for this decline were neither sudden nor surprising and, in fact, trace back to the evolution of swing's development and the ideologies that had helped it win the acceptance of the people.[1]

The Second World War usually takes the brunt of the blame for swing's demise. Certainly, military needs took many quality musicians out of the marketplace and replaced them with less skilled musicians, diluting the sound and quality of the music. Add to this the lack of quality younger players to reenergize the ranks of the swing movement, and the manpower drain became one of the key factors for the music's decline. Manpower issues were bad, but wartime rationing of gas and rubber also forced many bands to reduce their touring schedules or to cut costs by reducing the number of band members. As the war continued, a 20 percent amusement tax was imposed on entertainment venues; this tax, combined with the curfew, meant fewer people went out to the dance halls. This continued in the early postwar years, when inflation cut into profits and further reduced the schedules and bands.[2]

Yet to place the blame squarely on the shoulders of the war, the draft, and inflation ignores the fact that many musicians were able to avoid the draft and remain behind to perform. Other popular cultures, like movies and baseball, faced similar problems yet were able to rebound in the postwar era. As for the inflation and rationing explanation, during the height of the depression when many of these bands were formed, gas, oil, and tires were expensive relative to their earnings, yet the bands still toured and made do with less earnings for a larger band. And by the early 1940s most public schools had revived their music programs and more, not less, quality musicians were graduating and entering the marketplace. In fact, by the early forties, swing music became part of the accepted school band performance curricula.

While there is a certain amount of truth to the above claims, they only go so far in explaining why swing lost its preeminence with the listening audience. Its decline signals, as had its popularity, a period of transition. Swing's rise exemplified the depression ideal that asked that the people work together to build a sense of community in the midst of a social and economic depression that challenged the essence of the American dream. This communitarian spirit, tied closely to FDR's appeal to the American people to rebuild America via the New Deal, also encouraged the working people to join together in an age of the Congress of Industrial Organizations (CIO) spirit and further allowed for a general revival of Americanism in art, literature, composition, film, and music. The depression era, and right on its heels the call for unity that was World War II, gave swing its voice and was seen by its audience as the music that spoke both to and for them. Swing defined its era.

But by 1945 that epoch had begun to fade and a new one that was not entirely in synch with the new ideals was redefining Americans. There were several signposts pointing the way, and with the benefit of historical hindsight, these seem obvious. But to the many swing musicians within the historical moment, the reasons for their demise remained unclear and confusing.

One clear sign was the rise of bebop. Jazz historians view it as the next step in the evolution of jazz, which had in its structure (or lack of structure) a smaller band, more improvisation, less emphasis on dance rhythms, highly intricate melodies and chord transitions, and less commercial appeal. Eddie Barefield knew bop was just an extension of what had been occurring in jazz for some time, but because it "got too musically complicated for somebody . . . they cut it off." The *they* Barefield referred to was part of the many factors outside the music.[3]

The problems within swing during the forties, including the draft and the decrease in the number of bookings, helped to encourage bebop; but the reasons for its development occurred before the war exacerbated them. One of the most significant was the commercial popularity that big band swing enjoyed by the early 1940s. Its success had bred a certain homogenization and standardization in the music. Swing was integrated into part of the music industry by this time, driving the revival of record sales and jukebox usage. But this popularity had side effects, as alluded to in earlier chapters and by Barefield's *they*. The industry's reliance on swing meant a certain machine-bound standardization of the music in terms of timing, tone, and content. During the early period, from 1935 to 1940, the music was still marginal enough to allow for continued innovation; but by the early 1940s, radio programs, record companies, bandleaders, and even the musicians had come to expect a certain level of acceptance and pay. The war encouraged some of the more talented musicians and leaders to demand higher salaries and other perks because of the decline in the number of quality bands and players. For the musicians, this would lead to long-term labor strife (discussed below), while the bandleaders, now responsible for the musicians, the record companies, radio programmers, nightclubs, and their fans, began to shy away from innovation and give the people what they had come to expect. As Artie Shaw said later in the decade about the demise of the music, "[T]here are too many of the old guard trying to get by on their past reputations."[4]

Thus, by the early 1940s swing was defined not by what it was musically, but socially as a part of the American fabric. Within this, it was woven into the system as an important economic product within the growing culture industry. As swing's place in the entertainment industry was stabilized and secured, many leaders and musicians found themselves in a position where they had to sacrifice some artistic creativity in order to better maximize profit. Those unable to conform, regardless of talent, were let go or not hired. Many of these folks also happened to be African American. Swing music had made great strides by the early forties to integrate, but (in much the same manner in which the Negro Baseball Leagues would decline after Jackie Robinson's acceptance in the late forties) this meant that many of the best black players were brought into white-led bands. This, as well as the many wartime factors, encouraged a decline in the number of all-black bands, and many black musicians were left out of this integration. Others simply did not want to sacrifice their originality to conform to the sound of the accepted white bandleader. Earlier, there was still enough room in the elastic definition of jazz for these musicians to find work, but by the early forties the power of capital made it increasingly difficult to secure employ- ment. Mary Lou Williams, who had been around to define jazz in the late 1920s and contribute to the popularity of swing in the 1930s, saw bebop as an economic development stimulated by declining creative incentives: "All the bop musicians were jamming or playing there [in small clubs] every night because there was no work for them on 52nd Street . . . The whole idea was . . . our black people never get credit, receive credit for anything they do or create. So what they were doing, they created a new music . . . in order to get some kind of recognition for us. . . . Then everybody copied it; they lost again."[5]

Bebop, for these musicians, was as much a musical innovation as a call for independence. Amiri Baraka and others have viewed the bebop period as part of the emerging black nationalist movement. Tired of being con- trolled by white profiteers and critics, black musicians broke free of these constraints to create music outside the acceptable circle. Their choice of dissonance was as much a political statement as a musical one. Musicians such as Charlie Parker, Thelonious Monk, and Dizzy Gillespie saw their music as a subversion of the critically and commercially acceptable jazz— dance-oriented swing music—and as part of a larger struggle to liberate and promote black creativity. Jazz had once been the purview of African Ameri- can artistic creativity. The early years of jazz were dominated by African American performers who placed their musical production within the con- text of their experience, something Baraka called a "collection of attitudes." Bebop was a return to this attitude.[6]

Bebop was an artistic response to an increasingly competitive marketplace and a racially empowered cultural movement. Another factor concerned the growing division over what was "jazz" and what was commercialized popular music. At the heart of this canonical debate was the control of jazz. If it was cultivated or art music, and therefore a definitive expression of American music, how was it produced and by whom and what defined it? In the late 1930s and early 1940s, a group of musicians, record collectors, and critics began to revive what they considered to be true jazz in the face of the popular swing. These traditionalists argued that New Orleans–style, or Dixieland, was true to the meaning and function of jazz and that swing diluted this great sound by pandering to the mass audience. Swing's supporters responded in *Downbeat* and *Metronome* by suggesting that Dixieland was old-fashioned, "corny," and reflected a lack of growth in the jazz. They called the revivalists "Moldy Figs." As they continued to debate the merits of "real" jazz, bebop's adherents argued that if anyone was going to define jazz, they had to first take it out of the context of white America's acceptance and place it within the creativity and improvisation of African American culture. To this group, swing was the traditional, old-fashioned jazz music, and bebop was the modern music. The debates over the definition of jazz and who had the right to create each definition led the camps to label each other fakers. In the emerging postwar marketplace, with so many other factors contributing to swing's general decline, these canonical divisions helped split an already fragmenting audience and further reduced consumer appeal. If the musicians and critics were unable to agree on what they produced and called each other charlatans, what should the consumer consume?[7]

This division pointed to a larger problem among musicians, namely, increased competition for jobs and money. Between 1939 and 1946, as swing dominated record sales and radio time, the musicians and their union, the American Federation of Musicians (AFM), sought better royalty agreements and control over what they produced. The rise of these electronic media, so instrumental in swing's popularity, also sowed the seeds for its decline. The popularity of swing made the demand for records and radio programming increase, and the number of bands competing meant that others lost out. Radio stations, faced with public demand for swing music but with fewer "name" options, turned to recordings. Earlier union agreements paid the musicians a flat rate for their studio time, with the higher rate going to the more talented and popular sidemen, encouraging them to secure as many recording gigs as possible. These electronic transcriptions lacked control and protection by the musicians and could be played with few royalties going to the writer or performers.

Much has been made of James Petrillo's leadership of the AFM during these trying years. Like most of the musicians who were part of the swing generation, he was born into an immigrant and working-class family and left school after the fourth grade. He worked in a variety of bands in the Chicago area and by fourteen organized his own dance band. Soon after he also joined the local AFM. Moving quickly up the ranks, in 1919 he was elected vice president, and in 1922 he was the president of the Chicago local. From here he built a powerful machine which eventually helped get him elected president of the union in 1940. His platform that year was simple: to protect the increasingly mechanized and therefore displaced musician.[8]

The AFM recognized that the rise of mechanical reproduction of music would threaten their livelihood well before Petrillo became its leader. The rise of radio, phonograph, and, later, talking motion pictures displaced many musicians previous to 1930, but in the boom times of the 1920s they found other employment. The economic crisis of the early thirties hit the AFM hard, with unemployment rates running as high as 70 percent in some places, including Chicago. By 1935, when the swing phenomenon, the Federal Music Project, and radio renewed the public's interest in live music, the AFM realized it had to deal with the increased mechanization of music in order to provide its members with better job security. One such attempt occurred in 1937, when AFM president Joseph Weber successfully negotiated an agreement between the union and the radio networks. This agreement allowed stations to use recordings if they agreed to increase the number of live musical performances.[9]

This compromise did not last nor effectively deal with the encroachment of records and radio into the mainstream consciousness. Much of the success of swing came as a result of the records the musicians made. With the rise of four hundred thousand machines by 1941, jukeboxes accounted for nearly half of all record consumption. Combined with the inexpensive home phonograph, records became the means for both the band to make money and the consumer to hear the best and cleanest sound. Recording technology improved dramatically in the 1930s and 1940s, resulting in the creation of more high-quality records and the growing employment of studio musicians. For the bands, their ability to create a fan base and the success of their live performances depended on their recordings getting on jukeboxes and record stores' sale lists. For many of the name swing bands, the new technology meant increased work and wages; but for many smaller or less popular bands, the new technology meant fewer live performances and less money.[10]

Petrillo and the AFM sought to wean the popular musician from the influence of the technology and capital as soon as Petrillo took office in 1940 in two profound ways. First, the union announced that no bands could be formed with outside capital. Designed to prevent radio stations and record companies from forming bands and using them to break the power of the AFM, the ruling hurt the many younger musicians seeking to form bands. All the capital necessary to start a band—a considerable sum—would have to come from the musicians themselves. This made it unlikely for new bands to form on a level competitive with the big band giants. Many of the younger musicians began to regard the AFM as the protector of the established bands at their expense. This tension would lead to divisions amongst these players, divisions that would widen during the recording ban.[11]

The other action by the AFM was also motivated by the fear of technological displacement, but it, too, would result in the weakening of the union and swing music. With the 1937 agreement set to expire, many smaller radio stations wanted to end the mandatory live bands and buy more network remotes and use recorded music. The owners of these smaller radio stations argued that they could no longer afford to pay local musicians because of the appeal of network programming and that their audiences preferred their favorite bands, which could be played via records. Petrillo and the union found themselves facing a difficult situation. On the one hand, records allowed the people the freedom to choose what they wanted to hear. They could call up the radio station and ask to hear their favorite recording by Goodman or Basie, or they could search the dial for the remote of Shaw's Orchestra playing live from some far-off venue. To attack this choice now seemed to challenge the very basis of America—the right to choose— especially coming at a definitive time during the struggle with Nazism and the growing fear Soviet communism. On the other hand, the new technologies put many of the rank-and-file musicians in smaller venues out of work and weakened the union's power. After seeking the advice of the AFM delegates, Petrillo and the AFM announced that, beginning in August 1942, union musicians would no longer produce any form of mechanical music—recordings, radio, and film—until this situation could be rectified to the advantage of the union and its membership.[12]

The ban lasted from August 1942 until November 1944, and while the AFM would eventually "win," the victory was short-lived. One of the most devastating results of the ban came from the music industry's response. Record companies anticipated the AFM action and stockpiled recordings and overworked their studio musicians right up to the strike deadline. These musicians recorded stock instrumentals which the record companies later used to record vocalists. The companies also utilized nonunion musicians and vocalists, reissued "classic" records, many of which came from early jazz, and helped fuel the debate between the moldy fig, swing, and bebop fans.

Outside of the industry, the AFM also met some resistance. Despite the union solidarity that had grown during the 1930s, many consumers questioned the AFM's action for a variety of reasons. Some felt let down by the musicians and accused them of using the ban to make more money than they were already making. This was a situation similar to the Major League Baseball strike of 1994 and the National Basketball Association lockout of 1998, and the public saw the musicians as whiners seeking more when most people were being asked to accept less. The public did not understand Petrillo's actions and saw the strike as a power play in his bid to become "king" over their music. Even President Roosevelt, in the midst of World War II, appealed to Petrillo to end the strike for patriotic reasons. *Metronome* and *Downbeat* challenged the reasoning behind the strike, calling it futile to use a ban to stop the advance of technology. Their interests, obviously, were tied to the radio, recording, musical instrument, and phonograph industries—the principal advertisers in their magazines. With the public's lack of support for the ban, selling new subscriptions was difficult, which meant lower advertising revenues when the war had already cut into these magazine's profits. Even the musicians, while supporting the strike, were confused by the AFM's rationale. Coleman Hawkins remembers that as the ban was winding down, in 1943 or early 1944, he was summoned to Petrillo's office. Once there, the union boss told Hawkins that if he went to a recording session that RCA had set up for the musician, Petrillo would "throw [him] out of the union for the rest of [his] life." Hawkins agreed not to do the session, although he really didn't "know what it [the strike] was all about." All he knew was that until Petrillo gave him and other musicians his approval they better not work in the studios.[13]

Hawkins' confusion and fear reveals the dilemma many of those who were AFM members felt. The union was not as united as the name suggests, as divisions between cultivated and vernacular performers meant there was little real unity. As Jimmy Maxwell remembered, within the musical field there were far more divisions among the musicians, divisions that helped make the recording ban a paper strike. It also caused increased division among the AFM membership. In his recollection, there existed a musical hierarchy among professional musicians, both in terms of respect and pay. At the top were the symphony musicians, who were not paid very well but were well respected within society. Below them were the commercial and Broadway musicians, who were paid a decent salary, but got little respect. Next in line were the bands: "steady bands in the clubs, then the club date bands." The steady bands were those who were on record and radio and received the most popular support, while the club-date bands were those traveling bands trying to build a following. And below all these were individual musicians trying to break into the field by offering their services at lower rates or trying to form bands outside the control of the AFM. Maxwell's point in detailing this hierarchy was to point out the differences between all the groups covered under the AFM. It was the steady bands and to a lesser extent the symphony musicians who were the most affected by the ban. In fact the "club date musicians, the theater musicians were only too happy to go make those record dates." Even though there was a strike or ban, many saw this as their chance. When confronted, they responded by saying the strike "doesn't mean anything." And when other musicians reported these violations to the union, nothing was done. Maxwell and other musicians were convinced that "the [union] delegates were getting paid off."[14]

The end of the ban began in September 1943, when Decca Records agreed to a four-year deal with the AFM. The deal hinged on the fixed fee, in which record companies, in this case Decca, jukebox operators, and broadcasters, would pay the AFM compensation. The union would use the monies to encourage live performances. Once Decca signed, other record companies, fearful of Decca's advantage, followed suit. The fifty-plus companies who signed the agreement by January 1944 were not as important as the major companies—Columbia, RCA Victor, and the radio networks NBC and CBS. If these larger and more influential companies did not agree to the deal, then the ban and the early settlement meant little. It took several more months to iron out the details, but, finally, in November 1944 the majors agreed to the AFM's demands. Interestingly, the record ban coincided with the wartime difficulty in acquiring shellac, a necessary material for the recording process. In 1944 this raw material became more widely available. This suggests that the ban played more into the hands of the recording and radio industry. They would have had to pay higher costs for production. Only as the war was ending and the raw material became widely available and therefore cheap did these companies recognize they could once again produce and disseminate inexpensive records. Maybe this played into their decision-making process, but either way, by the end of November 1944 the ban was over.[15]

The union's victory provided little long-term job security for the AFM membership. The fixed-fee principle did not prevent the continued technological dislocation of the musicians, nor did it stop the drive for efficiency among the record and broadcast companies. In fact, the ban, combined with the draft, allowed for other popular music to grow its audience. The young consumer, faced with few new recordings by their swing favorites, turned to hillbilly, uptown rhythm and blues, or even the sounds of solo singers like Frank Sinatra. By the time the ban ended, the popular music marketplace was a much more competitive place, not only among the many different jazz and swing bands, but with a host of others who had developed a following during the ban years. Scott DeVeaux views the recording ban as a "convenient watershed in the history of jazz." Before it was swing and after came a "new age and a new sensibility."[16] Swing musicians came back from their labor ban to a much-changed cultural landscape, one in which they would never achieve the same level of acceptance as they had before the ban.

The ban came at a transitional time for union and worker solidarity in America. The 1930s witnessed the legitimation of the worker in America's consciousness, stimulated by the federal government and the creation of the CIO. The rise of industrial unions was seen as part of the economic cure for the imbalance that encouraged the collapse from 1929 to 1933. Taken in context, the age of the CIO was akin to the ideology of the American dream. Every person, the idea goes, has the right to try to succeed, and by working together all people in America could share in the rewards of the country's potential. This consensus of hope permeated the culture: It was seen in FDR's Fireside Chats, movies, radio broadcasts, literature, symphony halls, comic books, and, especially, advertising. All suggested that the dream was within reach, and, through hard work, integrity, and a general respect for those things valued American, one could succeed. The gauge of acceptance was the accumulation of the modern goods produced by America's great factories and workers. The dream allowed for Americans to celebrate America, and the hope suggested that the divisions of the past were forever banished.

It was this ideology which went to war in 1941. Coming face to face with a foreign enemy (and perhaps the Soviets), Americans changed, and the terms that defined America changed from this collective image to the sacrifices asked of every individual. But as the war continued and more sacrifices were asked of the American people—their sons and daughters, fathers and friends—and as the casualty rate increased, the hopefulness that permeated our early entrance soon turned to fear. Talk centered around how long the war would last, whether or not someone you knew or loved would be lost, and where, and how long would it be until the family was notified. The appearance of the gold stars in the windows of those people who had men and women abroad were both a symbol of nationalist pride and a constant reminder of the tremendous sacrifice Americans were making. These families balanced the faith that their children or husbands were involved in a noble struggle and the fear that one day they would hear the knock at the door and the news of a loved one's casualty that would forever alter their lives.

While the military spawned GI Joe and Rosie the Riveter, these were less symbols of collective identity and more conglomerates of individuals making sacrifices for freedom. The New Deal, so much a part of the mind-set of the 1930s and fuel for swing's acceptance, was among those things to be sacrificed. War stimulated production, and the programs to employ and uplift the under-employed and unemployed were eliminated, replaced by wartime councils controlling the production and consumption of goods. The war and its combatants came first, and American industries whirred with the sound of production at speeds never before imagined. As the war came to an end, many of the country's leaders wanted to ensure that these factories would continue to operate unabated by worker-inspired shutdowns or strikes.

To help secure this future, Congress revisited much of the "common man" legislation passed during the earlier decade. Oftentimes the Taft-Hartley Act of 1947 is viewed as the legislation that set the tone for the new era. It limited the ability of unions to use their memberships to win agreements. Among its provisions, it ended sympathy strikes and boycotts and allowed states to pass open-shop legislation. But Taft-Hartley was not the first law to place limitations on a union's ability to work for better wages and conditions. In 1946, largely as a result of the AFM's ban and Petrillo's seeming disregard for the American war effort, Congress passed the Lea Act. This law made the AFM's use of collective action a thing of the past. It forbade unions from threatening broadcasters with a ban or strike or from pressuring them into hiring more musicians. The law never specifically identified the AFM, but the Lea Act nullified the union's fixed-fee agreement by making it illegal to pay for services not performed. Many opposed this law, but its passage, combined with the Taft-Hartley Act, served to limit the AFM's and all unions' power.[17]

When the 1944 agreements expired in 1948, the networks and record companies refused the AFM's new offer. The union tried to issue a ban, but it lacked the power and intensity to make it work, and shortly thereafter an agreement was reached with few concessions to the union. Interestingly, the decline of the union's power came as membership in the union and the numbers of people entering the music industry were both increasing. The AFM's membership grew by 58 percent through 1948. But this increased number led to more competition for jobs and a decline in wages. In 1946, 2,433 staff musicians on 292 radio stations earned over $12 million; by 1950, 1,929 on 305 stations earned just over $10 million, and by 1957 the 98 radio stations remaining employed only 576 musicians for $3.5 million. The same trend held true for musicians hired by broadcasters: in 1946 musicians were hired for 337 shows for $8 million; by 1950, there were 194 shows at $4.7 million, and by 1957, 63 shows for just over $400,000. The AFM's ability to control the dissemination of mechanical music had failed.[18]

The union could not stop "progress," either technological or cultural, and swing became a major casualty of its time. Popular music was undergoing economic and generational changes during and after the war, changes that the AFM either ignored or did not understand. Earlier, in 1940, *Downbeat*'s Paul Eduard Miller wrote that swing would never die because "too much money [was] invested in swing—by booking offices, promoters, publishers, etc." But he also noted that without new ideas and innovation the music would lose its hold over the record-buying public. He was not alone in the fear that swing was running out of steam. "[T]here is no question that dance orchestras of standard instrumentation have reached their peak of efficiency," wrote critic Otto Cesana in 1942. Swing introduced fewer new bands because of high start-up costs, union interference, the draft, and the name-brand loyalty of the consuming public. By the time the war ended, since so few new bands had been formed, many of the older name bands restarted and dominated the music. The difference was that times had changed, and the revived bands found their costs higher and public demand lower, resulting in several leaders calling it quits. In 1945 alone, Les Brown, Gene Krupa, Jack Teagarden, Tommy and Jimmy Dorsey, Harry James, Woody Herman, and even the King, Benny Goodman, gave up their bands and retired. The death of swing was so complete that it became an albatross around the necks of those dance bands still trying to make a living. Tex Beneke tried to distance himself from the name swing in 1947, saying that the name was just a "romantic word" used by the kids to prove their hipness. The music was really just dance orchestra music, he said, more like that of Glenn Miller, who had died in the war. Beneke also said that the decline of swing had little to do with his sound, for he played dance music. By 1947 it seemed to many within the industry that the money invested in swing had moved to other popular musics, movies, and the new competitor, television.[19]

Clearly, this was part of a larger shift in national consciousness. When swing first became popular with its generation in the 1930s, magazines and newspapers attempted to define the musical phenomena in hopes of better understanding why it so appealed to the nation's young people. Musicians, critics, conductors, and ordinary fans were queried to try to determine the nature of swing and perhaps find its appeal. Oftentimes, as the first chapter makes clear, musicians, critics, and composers positioned their understanding within the musicological legacy of polyrhythmic scales, syncopation, blues notes, and other factors. When the people were asked, however, they spoke of the music in terms of generational social identification. One young woman, writing to the *New York Times* in 1939, offered her understanding of swing and perhaps best captured the meaning of the music: "Swing is the voice of youth striving to be heard in this fast-moving world of ours. Swing is the tempo of our time. Swing is real. Swing is alive. . . . The older folk may be more conservative and truly shocked at swing, but they should realize that our fast-moving world makes swing acceptable."[20] This was a consciousness she shared with many in her generation. Those who were fans of swing saw it as the music of their generation—"restless, tense." This ideology connected to the uncertainty and sacrifice of the depression era, the hope that one day things would improve through collective effort. But as the war ended, these same people were older and their consciousness had been changed by the crisis and loss of World War II. They came to be more protective and individualistic, focusing on their families, homes, and future. Tex Beneke said his audience was more conservative because they were "married now and [had] a couple of kids." Times had changed, and the fast-moving world of the depression-era youth moved beyond swing. Bob Crosby changed the style of his band's sound in 1946 to meet the changing demand. People no longer wanted to hear fast-paced dance numbers, but wanted slower and softer ballads, as they were more "interested in romancing than dancing." Another example of this change is a Capitol Records advertisement that featured the "history of Jazz" series in 1945. Of course, this was not the first time a record company had issued a history of the music, but what made this ad interesting was that it listed series entitled "Then Came Swing" and "This Modern Age" in its collection. The four-volume Capitol collection made it clear that swing's best days were behind it.[21]

This change of consciousness was accelerated by the war. While the New Deal sought to improve the economic condition of the country, by 1941 some 12 million workers were still without jobs. The war reversed this situation, as the unemployment rate dropped to as low as 3 percent. As business and industry profits rose, both the government and those in the private sector wanted this recovery to last when the war ended. Between 1945 and 1960 business and industry profits continued to skyrocket from $255 billion to $899 billion per year. The war provided the stimulus, but other factors aided in this process, chief among them were the low cost of electricity and oil and the direct involvement of government in stimulating the economy.

The Employment Act of 1946 clearly outlined the federal government's commitment to employment; and, coming with the rise of the Department of Defense and its huge government contracts, the top-down stimulation proved workable. The establishment of the military-industrial state reduced the uncertainty of profit and employment, and the newfound stability encouraged a revival in the spending habits of those employed. The war's end loosened pent-up consumer demands for automobiles, new homes, radios, and, increasingly, television. In 1948 there were only 172,000 televisions in American homes; by 1953 that number increased to 39 million, or 80 percent of all American homes. Television mirrored the network system introduced by radio, whose owners were quick to dominate this new entertainment and advertising medium. CBS and RCA were among the leaders who saw television as a much more direct and active delivery system to hawk the newest products to the largest numbers of people. The new technology allowed for the imagery of print ads to be combined with the pitch of radio, thereby increasing product identification to a greater number of potential consumers. Advertising dollars, once earmarked for radio, were now transferred to TV, and radio quickly became the secondary avenue for marketing dollars. Given the new wants of this postwar generation, the television offered the perfect medium to get the people the message of consumption.[22]

Many of these consumptive desires focused on the family and the home, preferably in the suburbs. The war unleashed a wholesale change in this area as well. More people were marrying and having children. After years of economic depression and four years of war, people not only wanted the new consumer items, but wanted children and homes. The baby boom, which meant 60 million babies born by 1961, resulted in a population increase from 139 million in 1945 to over 180 million by 1960. More and more of these children grew up in Federal Housing Administration–encouraged suburban areas. This population and demographic shift had positive effects on a variety of businesses, from automobiles to fast-food restaurants. The GI Bill of Rights also aided this transition, as it allowed many of the returning veterans to enter trade schools or universities. By 1949 nearly half of all those enrolled in the nation's colleges and universities were utilizing the GI Bill and graduating into more stable, higher paying careers.

These trends away from the cities, radio, and working-class ideology had a tremendous effect on the cultural consciousness of swing. The music had been born over the radio and had its greatest success in urban ballrooms and on soda shop jukeboxes. With television and the move to the suburbs, these venues became less influential. Record sales dipped by more than 20 percent after the war, resulting in a $50 million loss from 1947 to 1949. The industry tightened its belt and drove out smaller competitors. As control fell to a handful of companies, four companies—RCA Victor, Columbia, Decca, and Capitol—were responsible for 70 percent of all the hit records from 1948 to 1955. The record companies wanted to reduce the risk of failure and increase the likelihood of profit and so turned away from the innovative sounds of bebop or even new swing bands. Their domination meant fewer new acts were introduced as they featured bankable performers like Frank Sinatra, Bing Crosby, Frankie Laine, Vic Damone, Teresa Brewer, Dean Martin, Perry Como, Tony Bennett, Eddie Fisher, Dinah Shore, and a host of others. These singers, backed by studio orchestras, sang traditional songs of love and courtship, songs that were well received by the mainstream audiences radio now served. They alienated few listeners and reaffirmed the values of love, family, and the American dream. They were middle-class songs sung to the burgeoning middle class, and like their contemporary, the TV dinner, offered form without much substance.[23]

The history of the record industry from the birth of swing until its decline is in part the story of the industry's desire to bring modern factory techniques to the production of a consumer good. Much of this monograph concerns the modernist dilemma faced by the musicians caught up in this process. The new technology meant increased sales, exposure, and profits for a few of the top players, but the rank and file found themselves forced out by the same process. The 1942–1944 AFM record ban attempted to address this issue, but its failure signaled a victory for the industry. The development of magnetic tape (which allowed for multiple track recording), RCA's development of the 45 rpm single record, and Columbia's introduction of the long-playing 33 rpm album in 1948 only encouraged further alienation. When vinyl replaced the heavy shellac-based records of the earlier era in 1947, the limitations and costs of raw materials no longer determined the production of singles or albums produced by record companies. This meant more records (volume sales) and fewer bands (decreased risk).

The evolution of the record business into a more traditional industry left a considerable gap in the marketplace. Many consumers were uninterested by what they considered the stale and traditional sounds coming from the major record companies. This allowed for the growth in urban areas of small record companies catering to the needs of these consumers. The low cost of magnetic tape and vinyl allowed for record companies such as Los Angeles' Modern and Aladdin, Chicago's Chess, Cincinnati's King, and a host of others to target their releases to those groups not interested in the middle-of-the-road, suburban, and decreasingly working-class music issued by the major companies.

One of the groups targeted by these smaller companies was the many southern whites that had migrated to the North and West during the war. The decline of the sharecropper system in the South and the lure of good-paying jobs in the factories meant some eight to twelve million southerners migrated to urban areas between 1945 and 1960. They brought with them their cultural desires for food, clothing, automobiles, and music. Their influence did not go unnoticed, as hillbilly music, as *Billboard* and the industry called it, was making significant inroads into the marketplace. By 1941 *Time* opined that "the dominant popular music of the U.S. today is hillbilly." In cities like Detroit, Cleveland, and Pittsburgh jukebox operators began to notice as early as 1943 that people were choosing country music over all other musical choices. The selection chosen most frequently was Al Dexter's "Pistol-Packin' Mama."[24]

These instances aside, hillbilly music had been gaining market acceptance since the 1920s. When it first began, its homespun appeal was limited to southern rural areas, although it made inroads into larger markets through radio broadcasts over Chicago's WLS, Nashville's WSM, and Atlanta's WSB. In these early years, virtually all of the performers were from the South, and the music, musicians' appearances, and lyrics reinforced the rural and small-town nostalgia popular during the era. During the 1930s the emphasis on hillbilly decreased and the music found a new symbol to hang its hat on, the cowboy. The rise of cowboy Western B movie stars who were also singers, such as Gene Autry, Roy Rogers, and Tex Ritter, changed the costume of the hillbilly performers, whether they were westerners like the Sons of the Pioneers or Bob Wills or traditional southerners like Roy Acuff. The cowboy outfit, which symbolized that great and mythic hero of American individualism, resonated with movie, radio, and record audiences. The two thousand B movies produced between 1930 and 1954 gave momentum to country music's popularity. The plots of these films were formulaic—good guys win over bad guys—and the acting simplistic, but the audiences loved the openness, individualism, and freedom that the films celebrated. The 1941 ASCAP versus BMI licensing battle accelerated the proliferation of country music in America. Radio stations, goaded on by RCA-controlled NBC, tried to break ASCAP's control over radio programming by allowing their own licensing agent, BMI (made up largely of hillbilly and blues artists not represented by ASCAP), to represent artists on the air. ASCAP boycotted NBC affiliates, and this allowed BMI and the hillbilly and blues performers they represented to secure a place over the airwaves and, by extension, within the marketplace. When ASCAP and NBC settled the disagreement in 1944, the market had shifted significantly and the larger agent found itself scrambling to resecure its place as the more influential licensing and royalty agent. The breaking of ASCAP's monopoly coincided with the AFM record ban, as hillbilly and blues performers, rarely members of the union, continued to record and perform on radio and in film. These factors helped the music of the South make significant market gains—in 1947 there were over six hundred radio stations playing the music that *Billboard* now labeled country and western. During this postwar expansionist phase, when rural southerners found themselves more often in factories than on farms, a new country sound called honky-tonk made its appearance. Led by Hank Williams and his Drifting Cowboys, who sold over eleven million records from 1949 to 1953, these displaced workers sang of the days gone by and the fun of drinking, dancing, loving, and working. They used amplified instruments like the guitar and relied on complex background vocals to give lift to the main singer's voice. Performers such as Hank Snow, Ted Daffan, and Lefty Frizzel used the new technology to speak to and for those who felt alienated by the changes the last fifteen years had wrought. These were not conservative calls for a return to old times, but indicated confusion over how to navigate the modern ones.[25]

Blues music followed a similar pattern. African Americans left the South for much the same reasons their white brethren did, but they also fled the Jim Crow restrictions and lack of liberty that accompanied segregation. The great migration to the North began as the First World War was winding down, so that by the onset of the Great Depression nearly 1.5 million southern blacks had moved to places such as Chicago, Detroit, Cleveland, Pittsburgh, Oakland, and Los Angeles. They brought their specific needs and wants, and businesses in these regions learned to cater to the new migrant. Their rural music was one of the things they brought with them. One of the more influential styles of blues music, called the Delta blues, took root in Chicago and by the 1930s, as more southern blacks moved to the North, became popular with some of the transplanted. Many of those who performed for these migrants played in the country blues style with acoustic guitar, piano, and maybe a harmonica and sang songs reminiscent of the Delta and their past environment. The wartime stimulation of industry brought more migrants in search of work, averaging 160,000 per year during the 1940s. As they came, changes in the music were evident. Many of the migrants wanted the beat turned up and the moaning turned down. They wanted the music to jump and jive so that they could drink, dance, and party to the music. Performers such as Little Walter, Elmore James, Robert Nighthawk, Muddy Waters, Howling Wolf, and many others used amplified instruments and featured the drums to create a bigger sound for a cheaper cost. By 1947 these artists and others were building on some of the newer sounds that had come out of the swing era, most notably by Louis Jordan. As the war was declining, Jordan, a veteran of the big band era, changed his sound to one that absorbed some elements of the rising urban blues, called rhythm and blues, with the swing band arrangements. The result was a jump sound that almost forced listeners onto the dance floor. Because of the increased cost of travel and musicians' union scale, he featured a smaller band with amplified instruments and played a mixture of country-inspired songs ("Cho Cho Cho Boogie") and old-style Cab Calloway–like swing songs ("Caldonia"). These performers sang songs that spoke of their alienation and their desire for a good time regardless of cost. The tone of the tunes, like in honky tonk, was that one works hard, so one should play hard with no excuses. Rhythm and blues became a bona fide market in the postwar period, warranting its own *Billboard* chart. With songs like "When the Lights Go Out" (Jimmy Witherspoon), "Chains of Love" (Joe Turner), and "Hoochie Coochie Man" (Muddy Waters), they sold millions of records on small, local record labels, including Chess, Modern, and Specialty. The music was attractive to urban audiences as a source of racial pride. The music came from the streets of the African American communities and was sometimes played in the streets for the people. Unlike much of the big band swing sound that had been co-opted by white musicians and bandleaders and the difficult yet artistic sounds of Afrocentric bebop, rhythm and blues resonated a simplicity, ease, and joy that brought these diverse peoples of the same race together in America's cities.[26]

The changes in jazz, the rise of country and western, and the popularity of urban rhythm and blues help to describe part of the consciousness shift taking place in America. Much of American society distanced itself from the collective working-class identity so prevalent in the earlier era. The age of the CIO had passed as wartime and postwar wage increases made class divisions seemingly disappear. The wartime propaganda encouraged Americans to redefine themselves against their enemies and to see the war as a battle between individual choice and collective dictatorship. Those under the control of the tyrants Hitler and Mussolini were not bad, but they had allowed themselves to be led rather than choosing their own destiny. The American dream, so much a fantasy from the late 1930s, became the imagined reality during and after the war. The country redefined itself within the Hooveresque American individualist ideology, where each person was responsible for his or her own actions, successes, or failures. The accumulation of goods, so plentiful in the postwar era, became synonymous with this success. This increasingly consumer-driven narcissism did not forget the sacrifices of the many individuals to achieve this new paradise, and so was tempered by a call for unification. But this consensus, driven by the fear of past economic uncertainty and rising international cold war tensions, encouraged a conformity of individualism, where Americans loudly proclaimed their freedom of choice while systematically taking that freedom from others, or conforming to the marketplace, politics, family, and church.

The development of the cold war was part of this new individualism and the consensus of fear. The United States had long been uncomfortable with the USSR, and the periodic Red scares drove many of the fellow travelers from the country. In the late 1930s, Martin Dies and the House Committee on Un-American Activities (HUAC) began its long attack on the liberal policies of the New Deal, effectively destroying several projects and numerous careers. With American involvement in the Second World War came an unlikely ally, the Soviet Union, and the fear of the Reds subsided temporarily (although there remained a certain mistrust of the USSR and its leader Joseph Stalin). As the war ground to an end, the mistrust between the two sides grew and both exited convinced the other side was trying to destroy them. By 1946 an Iron Curtain, as Winston Churchill called it, had fallen over the areas liberated by the Soviets, and liberty and individual freedom were lost to the collective identity of totalitarianism. With the 1947 Truman Doctrine and the subsequent Marshall Plan, Berlin Airlift, and the formation of NATO and the Warsaw Block by 1949, it was clear that while no shots had been fired, America was involved in yet another war.

Yet this was a war of identity—what ideals defined the United States versus what ones defined the USSR. The state saw this as a life-and-death struggle and used all possible means to make sure American ideals— individualism based on consumer choice—were clearly known, promoted, and observed. In 1947 Truman issued Executive Order 9835, which institutionalized the loyalty oath and allowed for the federal investigation of 6.6 million government employees by 1952. City and states governments followed suit, and soon nearly every aspect of American society was on the lookout for Red sympathizers. Politicians including Richard Nixon and Joseph McCarthy made their political careers on the back of this Red scare, and no one in America was safe from either the devil of totalitarianism or the conformity of individualism.

The us (the people) versus them (those who had hunger, misery, and a lack of social justice) consensus of hope which drove the New Deal era was displaced by a consensus driven by fear between the larger us (United States) and them (USSR) and reduced the struggle to this: anyone not on America's team must certainly be on theirs. This simplistic explanation of the domestic ramifications of the international struggle between the United States and USSR only serves to detail the new ideology that replaced the machine-age ideology that defined the swing era. Each individual was now on his or her own, and, while individuals still worked together, a level of mistrust permeated the landscape. Even the development and popularity of the suburbs helps to explain this insulation from others. Each person had his or her own fenced-in plot of land and lived within the confines of their domicile. This internal containment was only broken by the television, which informed its viewers about the world outside their doors while promising domestic bliss with the products it advertised.

Popular music was caught up in this process. It is no surprise that, in the era after 1947, few groups topped the record sales lists. America had always favored individual performers, but with the swing era, these individuals merged themselves into the identity of their band—the Goodman, Shaw, Ellington, and Basie bands. Their identity was a result of the merging of identities of the band. One of the things, in fact, that defined swing was its reliance on arrangements which took away the individualistic need for improvisation. And, while most bands had great individual performers, they never separated themselves from the rest of the group; but when their solo came, they stood up from among the masses and then sat back down within the band. But after the war, the bands broke up, and popular music came to be identified by the individual—Hank Williams, Charlie Parker, Muddy Waters. Even among those who had made their name working for swing bands—singers Frank Sinatra, Dinah Shore, Doris Day, Eddie Fisher, Jo Stafford, and many more—their popularity and success overshadowed the bands they fronted. Perhaps encouraged by the recording ban of which they were not part, these new stars of American popular music were individuals who defined the new American consciousness.[27]

It would be a new musical phenomenon, which paralleled swing's rise and popularity, that would become the lodestone of this postwar ideology. Rock and roll music emerged in the early 1950s to become the music that captured the spirit of this new ideology, this new mood. When Charlie Barnet tried to reenter the popular music field in the early 1950s, he found that the landscape had changed dramatically and that the era of the big band was over. Smaller rock bands were in demand because, as Willie Randall recalled, "with all their amplification rock groups needed only five or six pieces."[28] Many people are credited with rock and roll music's rise and popularity, but one thing is certain—it was the natural culmination of swing, country and western, and rhythm and blues, and it took hold of the nation's youth by the middle of the 1950s and has yet to let go. The ideology that drove the music spoke for and to its generation—one bred in relative comfort and ease but haunted by a fear of conformity and nuclear death; one spurred on by the constant creation of new fads and consumer items but rebellious and critical of authority. The contradictory nature of the new music revealed the highest form of modernist ambivalence, where the divisions between creation and consumption, alienation and acceptance, success and failure were blurred. Most of the rock and rollers initially came from working-class backgrounds, for example, but when confronted with success, they either self-destructed or consumed so as to define themselves among the wealthy class. How else can one view Elvis Presley?

Rock and roll officially ended swing because swing was unable to adapt to the new ideology. Swing's whole being was focused on the group—the exact merging of sounds to create a unified sound. It spoke to and for a generation that had and expected little and so were enthralled by the escapism offered by the band's dance-oriented music. While swing bands had lyrics, they were secondary to the sound, the feel, the movement of the music. Besides, what could the words have said when everyone, it seemed, was in the same boat? Some of swing's pioneers continued to perform or stayed in the entertainment industry, but these positions were reserved for the bigger names—Dorsey, Goodman, Ellington, Herman, and others. Some of the better sidemen were able to find studio, television, or movie work. Some continued to play in small clubs on the jazz circuit, but Budd Johnson recalled how difficult it was to get gigs in this new era. The booking agencies eliminated the "co-operative business in bands" because they wanted to only deal with "one man."[29] But the vast majority left swing behind and took up jobs in the booming economy, raised a family, and became part of the new ideology. Andy Kirk, for example, went on to manage the Hotel Theresa in Harlem. His years in swing, like those of so many others, were reserved for fond memories recalling days gone by. Occasionally the old records would come out of storage and be played, but the technology had changed and the old and heavy records seemed antique and old-fashioned. In the ultra-modern world of the 1950s and 1960s, no one wanted to be seen as old, as it was clear that the newer the item the better it was—a trend that began with the swing generation. The swing era ended as it had come, slowly and over time and merging into the next era.

Notes

Introduction

1. Fletcher Henderson, introduction to *Down Beat's Yearbook of Swing*, by Paul Eduard Miller (1939; reprint, Westport, CT: Greenwood, 1978). The idea that swing was somehow less authentic than the jazz before it and the bebop that followed is one that was born with the rise of swing. Right from the start some critics worried that the popularity of swing would bring about jazz's demise, as the commercial demands would water down the artistic innovations of the music. Magazines like *Downbeat* and *Metronome* anointed themselves as guardians of the true sounds and used their pages to define *real* jazz and swing musicians from those it considered fakers, corn-ballers, or sweet players. See also Mark S. Harvey, "Jazz and Modernism: Changing Conceptions of Innovations and Traditions," in *Jazz in Mind: Essays on the History and Meaning of Jazz*, ed. Reginald T. Buckner and Steven Weiland (Detroit: Wayne State University Press, 1991), 128–47, in which the author locates swing as a "popular musical phenomenon not always identifiable with jazz but certainly a derivative from it to a greater or lesser extent" (135). Other works that echo this sentiment are numerous, but for an excellent discussion of the debate during the swing era regarding authenticity, see Bernard Gendron, " 'Moldy Figs' and Modernists: Jazz at War (1942–1946)," in *Jazz among the Discourses*, ed. Krin Gabbard (Durham: Duke University Press, 1995), 31–56.

2. Daniel Joseph Singal, "Towards a Definition of American Modernism," *American Quarterly* 39 (spring 1987): 7–26.

3. Henri Lefebvre, "These on Modernity," in *Modernism and Modernity*, ed. Benjamin H. D. Buchloh, Serge Guilbaut, and David Solkin (Nova Scotia: Press of Nova Scotia College of Art and Design, 1983), 3–6.

4. George T. Simon, *The Big Bands* (New York: Macmillan Company, 1967); George T. Simon, *Glenn Miller and His Orchestra* (New York: Thomas Y. Crowell Company, 1974); John Chilton, *Stomp Off, Let's Go: The Story of Bob Crosby's BobCats and Big Band* (London: Jazz Book Service, 1983); Gene Fernett, *Swing Out: Great Negro Dance Bands* (Midland, MI: Pendell Publishing, 1970); Gene Fernett, *A Thousand Golden Horns: The Exciting Age of America's Greatest Dance Bands* (Midland, MI: Pendell Publishing, 1966); Herb Sanford, *Tommy and Jimmy: The Dorsey Years* (New Rochelle, NY: Arlington House, 1972).

5. Count Basie, *Good Morning Blues: The Autobiography of Count Basie*, as told to Albert Murray (New York: Random House, 1985); Billie Holiday, *Autobiography* (1956; reprint, New York: Avon Books, 1976); Drew Page, *Drew's Blues: A Sideman's Life with the Big Bands* (Baton Rouge: Louisiana State University Press, 1980); Duke Ellington, *Music Is My Mistress* (Garden City: Doubleday, 1973); Barney Bigard, *With Louis and the Duke: The Autobiography of a Jazz Clarinetist*, ed. Barry Martin (London: MacMillan, 1985); Garvin Bushell, *Jazz from the Beginning*, as told to Mark Tucker (Ann Arbor: University of Michigan Press, 1988); Arthur Rollini, *Thirty Years with the Big Bands* (Urbana: University of Illinois Press, 1987); Helen Forrest with Bill Libby, *I Had the Craziest Dream* (New York: Coward, McGann & Georhegan, 1982); Kathy J. Ogren, "New Orleans Jazz Autobiographies: Legitimating Strategies Signifying on the Frontiers of Jazz" (paper presented at the American Studies Association annual meeting, New Orleans, LA, November 2, 1990); and Kathy Ogren, " 'Jazz Isn't Just Me': Jazz Autobiographies as Performance Personas," in *Jazz in Mind: Essays on the History and Meaning of Jazz*, ed. Reginald T. Buckner and Steven Weiland (Detroit: Wayne State University Press, 1991).

6. Martin T. Williams, *The Jazz Tradition* (New York: Oxford University Press, 1983); Andre Hodier, *Jazz: Its Evolution and Essence* (New York: DaCapo Press, 1980); Bob Yurochko, *A Short History of Jazz* (Chicago: Nelson-Hall, 1993); Gunther Schuller, *The Swing Era: The Development of Jazz, 1930–1945* (New York: Oxford University Press, 1989); Ted Gioia, *The History of Jazz* (New York: Oxford University Press, 1997); Mark Gridley, *Jazz Styles: History and Analysis*, 5th ed. (Englewood Cliffs: Prentice-Hall, 1994); Scott Deveaux, *The Birth of Bebop* (Berkeley: University of California Press, 1997); and for an excellent collection of scholarly essays, see Krin Gabbard, ed., *Jazz among the Discourses* (Durham: Duke University Press, 1995) and *Representing Jazz* (Durham: Duke University Press, 1995).

7. Neil Leonard, *Jazz and the White Americans: The Acceptance of a New Art Form* (Chicago: University of Chicago Press, 1962); Marshall Stearns, *The Story of Jazz* (New York: Oxford University Press, 1962); James Lincoln Collier, *Benny Goodman and the Swing Era* (New York: Oxford University Press, 1989); Burton Peretti, *The Creation of Jazz: Music, Race, and Culture in Urban America* (Urbana: University of Illinois Press, 1992); David Stowe, *Swing Changes: Big-Band Jazz in New Deal America* (Cambridge: Harvard University Press, 1994); Louis Erenberg, *Swingin' the Dream;*

Big Band Jazz and the Rebirth of American Culture (Chicago: University of Chicago Press, 1998).

8. Raymond Williams, "The Uses of Cultural Theory," in *The Politics of Modernism: Against the New Conformists*, ed. Tony Pinkney (London: Verso, 1989), 163–76. For recent works that apply Williams to their analysis, see Michael Denning, *The Cultural Front: The Laboring of American Culture in the Twentieth Century* (London: Verso Press,1999); and Suzanne E. Smith, *Dancing in the Street: Motown and the Cultural Politics of Detroit* (Cambridge, MA: Harvard University Press, 1999). For other methods that inform this theory, see George Lipsitz, "Listening to Learn and Learning to Listen: Popular Culture, Cultural Theory, and American Studies," *American Quarterly* 42 (December 1990): 615–36.

9. Ronald J. Grele, *Envelopes of Sound: The Art of Oral History* (New York: Praeger, 1985); Paul Thompson, *The Voice of the Past: Oral History*, 2nd ed. (New York: Oxford University Press, 1988); Michael Frisch, *A Shared Authority* (Albany: SUNY Press, 1990); Henry Louis Gates, *The Signifying Monkey: A Theory of Afro-American Literary Criticism* (New York: Oxford University Press, 1986); Norman K. Denzin, *Interpretive Ethnography: Ethnography Practices for the Twenty-First Century* (Thousand Oaks, CA: Sage Publications, 1997); and, specifically in regards to jazz and the collections at both Rutgers and Tulane Universities, see Burton Peretti, "Oral Histories of Jazz Musicians: The NEA Transcripts as Texts in Context," in *Jazz among the Discourses*, ed. Gabbard, 117–31; and Douglas Henry Daniels, "Oral History, Masks, and Protocol in the Jazz Community," *Oral History Review* 15 (spring 1987): 146–83.

Chapter 1

1. Marshall Stearns, *The Story of Jazz* (New York: Mentor, 1958), 149–50; W. Royal Stokes, *The Jazz Scene: An Informal History from New Orleans to 1990* (New York: Oxford University Press, 1991), 69–70; James Lincoln Collier, *Benny Goodman and the Swing Era* (New York: Oxford University Press, 1989), points out that the shows previous to the Palomar breakthrough were not all that unsuccessful (see pages 163–69). Even Teddy Wilson, who was invited to go to Chicago to play in jam sessions, conforms to the story of swing's birth. See Teddy Wilson transcript, Jazz Oral History Project, Rutgers University, New Brunswick, NJ (hereafter cited as JOHP), 14–15.

2. Collier, *Benny Goodman* , 178–79; Stokes, *Jazz Scene*, 71.

3. Mel Torme, *Traps, the Drum Wonder: The Life of Buddy Rich* (New York: Oxford University Press, 1991), 29.

4. Collier, *Benny Goodman* , 191, 205–7; Nat Shapiro and Nat Hentoff, *Hear Me Talkin' To Ya: The Story of Jazz as Told by the Men Who Made It* (New York: Dover Publications, 1955), 315–16.

5. For the best discussion on the role and development of the popular music

industry, see Russell Sanjek, *American Popular Music and Its Business: The First Four Hundred Years*, vol. 3 (New York: Oxford University Press, 1988); for details on the early twentieth century, see especially 68–146; Collier, *Benny Goodman*, 257; *Variety*, August 1939, as quoted in *Glenn Miller and His Orchestra*, by George Simon (New York: Crowell Company, 1974), 13–14; *Newsweek* (June 3, 1940), 48; Andy Kirk, *Twenty Years on Wheels* (Ann Arbor: University of Michigan Press, 1989), 86–87.

6. The definitions were taken from Irving Kolodin, "Number One Swing Man," *Harper's* 79 (September 1939): 433; Gama Gilbert, "Swing: What Is It?" *New York Times*, September 5, 1937, 5:1; Otto Cesana, "Swing Is—Well It's Here," *Metronome* 52 (June, 1936): 14; and "Swing It," *International Musician* (December 1936), 12; Doron K. Antrim, "More Than the King Have Abdicated," *Metronome* 53 (January 1937): 15; "400,000 U.S. Musicians Get Jobs in 1937," *Downbeat* 5 (January 1938): 6. The AFM also played a part in this revival of live bookings in 1934, when it was able to work out with bands and booking agents a compromise which lowered the 30 percent tax against traveling bands to 10 percent, making it more feasible for popular radio and recording bands to travel to promote their business. See Robert D. Leiter, *The Musicians and Petrillo* (New York: Bookman Associates, 1953), 64–65.

7. Collier, *Benny Goodman* , 149–51. For a more complete examination of the role and use of women, see chapter 5; "Deke Says: How Long Will Swing Last?" *Metronome* 54 (March 1938): 9; David W. Stowe, *Swing Changes: Big-Band Jazz in New Deal America* (Harvard University Press: Cambridge, 1994).

8. Arthur Rollini recounts the Goodman band's time on the Let's Dance program in his *Thirty Years with the Big Bands* (Urbana: University of Illinois Press, 1987), 46–63.

9. Collier, *Benny Goodman*, 193; Beth Bailey, *From Front Porch to Backseat: Courtship in Twentieth-Century America* (Baltimore: Johns Hopkins University Press, 1988), 6–12; Paula Fass, *The Damned and the Beautiful: American Youth in the 1920s* (New York: Oxford University Press, 1977), especially 10–51.

10. "Swing Still up in the Air," *Metronome* 52 (March 1936): 16; Stearns, Story of Jazz, 148–49; George Engles, "Radio-Friend or Enemy to the Music Profession," *Musician* 35 (September 1930): 7; Collier, *Benny Goodman* , 193–94; D. Duane Braun, *The Sociology and History of American Music and Dance, 1920–1968* (Ann Arbor: Ann Arbor Publishers, 1969), 24–53; Grace Palladino, *Teenagers: An American History* (New York: Basic Books, 1996), 4–9, 36–56; Warren S. Thompson and P. K. Whelpton, "The Population of the Nation," in *Recent Social Trends in the United States: Report on the President's Research Committee on Social Trends, with a Foreword by Herbert Hoover* (New York: McGraw-Hill, 1933), 25–28; See also Richard A. Reiman, *The New Deal and American Youth: Ideas and Ideals in a Depression Decade* (Athens: University of Georgia Press, 1992), which, although dealing with the creation and operation of the National Youth Administration, provides insight into the generation. There was also much fear about the course that youth might take, re-

flected in works such as *American Youth: An Enforced Reconnaissance*, Thacher Winslow and Frank P. Davidson, eds. (Cambridge: Harvard University Press, 1940), see especially the foreword by Eleanor Roosevelt, and George S. Pettee's "The Appeal of Totalitarianism," 107–24; and Dorothy Dunbar Bromley and Florence Haxton Britten, *Youth and Sex: A Study of 1,300 College Students* (New York: Harper and Brothers, 1938), especially 7–25 and 272–86. For work on subcultures and the models for their determination, see Dick Hebdige, *Subculture: The Meaning of Style* (London: Routledge, 1979), particularly 80–120; and Mike Brake, *Comparative Youth Culture: The Sociology of Youth Cultures and Youth Subcultures in America, Britian, and Canada* (London, Routledge, 1985).

11. "Mail-Bag Excerpts," letter from Lillian Breslau, *New York Times*, February 26, 1939, E9; "Name Bands," *International Musician* (August 1939), 8.

12. Bob Blumenthal, "First-Person Memories of Swing," *Downbeat* 61 (July 1994): 18; Don Albert digest, Hogan Jazz Archive, Tulane University, New Orleans, LA, reel 2, pg. 1; Harry "Sweets" Edison transcript, JOHP, 15.

13. "Swing Secrets Taught in High School," *Metronome* 55 (March 1939): 12; Lilla Belle Pitts, "Music and Modern Youth," *Music Educators Journal* 26 (October 1939): 19, 68.

14. Dr. Thomas Tapper, "Has To-Day's Music a Place in the Teaching Repertoire?" *Etude* 60 (April 1942): 243, 276; Stowe, *Swing Changes*, 28.

15. "Swing Is Art and Is Becoming Great Art," *Science News Letter* (December 14, 1940), 377; Alvin Levin, "Swing Glories in Its Humble Origin," *Musician* 44 (April 1939): 66.

16. Advertisement, Robbins Music Corporation, "The Right Road to Stardom!" *Metronome* 56 (September 1940): 40.

17. Wilder Hobson, "Swing High," *Vogue* 87 (March 15, 1936): 90–91; "Swing Viewed as Musical Hitlerism: Professor Sees Fans Ripe for Dictator," *New York Times*, November 2, 1938, 25:3; "They're Killing Our Swing," *Metronome* 54 (September 1938): 11, 40. This type of criticism against swing in the 1930s is similar to the protests over Jazz in the 1920s. For an excellent discussion see Kathy J. Ogren, *The Jazz Revolution: Twenties America and the Meaning of Jazz* (New York: Oxford University Press, 1989).

18. "Let Freedom 'Swing,'" *New York Times* November 6, 1938, 12:3; Virgil Thomson, "Swing Again," *Modern Music* 15 (March/April 1938): 160–66.

19. For a discussion on the debate between cultivated and vernacular music in the twentieth century, see H. Wiley Hitchcock, *Music in the United States: A Historical Introduction*, 2nd ed. (Englewood Cliffs, NJ: Prentice-Hall, 1974), chapters 3–6; Kenneth J. Bindas, *All of This Music Belongs to the Nation: The WPA's Federal Music Project and American Society, 1935–1939* (Knoxville: University of Tennessee Press, 1995), 1–15.

20. Alvin Levin, "Swing Marches On," *Musician* 44 (December 1939): 219; Irving Kolodin, "What about Swing," *Parents' Magazine* 14 (August 1939): 18–19.

21. "Swing, Swing, Oh Beautiful Swing!" *Metronome* 52 (February 1936): 19, 33.

22. Gary Tomlinson, "Cultural Dialogics and Jazz: A White Historian Signifies," in *Disciplining Music: Musicology and Its Canons*, ed. Katherine Bergeron and Philip V. Bohlman (Chicago: University of Chicago Press, 1992), 64–94, quotes from pgs. 76 and 78.

23. "Jazz versus Swing: Despite Alteration It's Still Syncopation," *Metronome* 60 (April 1944): 23.

24. See Leroy Ostransky, *Jazz City: The Impact of Our Cities on the Development of Jazz* (Englewood Cliffs, NJ: Prentice-Hall, 1978).

25. Ethan A. Secor, "Just What Really Is Swing Music?" *Etude* 58 (April 1940): 240.

26. Larry Clinton, "Swing Grows Up: A Prophecy for Days to Come," *Good Housekeeping* 107 (October 1938): 13, 92; James W. Poling, "Music after Midnight," *Esquire* 5 (June 1936): 92; B. S. Rogers, "Swing Is from the Heart," *Esquire* 11 (April 1939): 43; Sam Rowland, "Debunking Swing," *Esquire* 6 (August 1936): 79, 111.

27. Elliott Carter, "Forecast and Review," *Modern Music* 16 (January/February 1939), 99–100; "FCC Dodges 'Swing' Issue But Urges Care in Its Use," *New York Times*, November 3, 1938, 25:6; B. S. Rogers, "Swing Is from the Heart," *Esquire* 11 (April 1939): 43; Joseph V. Rubba, "Much Ado about Swinging," *Metronome* 52 (August 1936): 9; William F. Ludwig, "Why the Public Likes Swing," *Metronome* 52 (October 1936): 18; and Scotty Lawrence, "Swing Is Here to Stay," *Metronome* 53 (August 1937): 13.

28. Raymond Wheelock, "Did Swing Come from The Indians?" *Educational Music Magazine* 23 (November 1943): 20–21, 50.

29. Marvin W. Strate, "Swing: What Is It? The Jazz Prodigal's Return," *Musical America* 56 (May 25, 1936): 6–7. The illustrations which appear with the article are by George Hager. Marshall Stearns, in *The Story of Jazz* (New York: Oxford University Press, 1956), points out that "the distinction between these colored bands [Webb, Hines, Ellington, Lunceford, Redman, Moten, etc.] and the Goodman band . . . [was that] Goodman stressed precision and the accurate pitch essential to European harmony" (see 143–44); Krin Gabbard, *Jammin' at the Margins: Jazz and the American Cinema* (Chicago: University of Chicago Press, 1996), 2.

30. William Howland Kenney, *Recorded Music in American Life: The Phonograph and Popular Memory, 1890–1945* (New York: Oxford University Press, 1999), 26–40. Influential contemporary music historians and critics still label swing as a connection to traditional jazz. Gunther Schuller's second volume of the history of jazz, *The Swing Era*, argues that swing was a continuation of jazz and that its musicians were dominated by great jazz performers. James Lincoln Collier, in his *Benny Goodman and the Swing Era*, takes great pains to convince readers that Goodman was no mere popular musician, but a jazz great. In describing what made swing, most of these and other contemporary analyses point out that all the musical elements that made up

swing existed in jazz music before 1935, namely, the tempo, rhythm, interpretation, and the organization of the orchestra. See for example, Ted Gioia, *The History of Jazz* (New York: Oxford University Press, 1997), who views swing as the apex of the modern sound of jazz and as the pathway to more innovative sounds after 1945; Gunther Schuller, *The Swing Era* (New York: Oxford University Press, 1989), especially 20–24, 198–229; Collier, *Benny Goodman*, 36–37, 152–53; Joseph Levey, *The Jazz Experience: A Guide to Appreciation* (Englewood Cliffs, NJ: Prentice-Hall, 1983), 55–71; Bob Yurochko, *A Short History of Jazz* (Chicago: Nelson-Hall, 1993), 69–70; Albert McCarthy, *Dance Band Era: The Dancing Decades from Ragtime to Swing, 1910–1950* (New York: Spring Books, 1971), 123–26; Herb Sanford, *Tommy and Jimmy: The Dorsey Years* (New Rochelle, NY: Arlington House, 1972), 224–25; and David W. Stowe, "Jazz in the West: Cultural Frontier and Region during the Swing Era," *Western Historical Quarterly* 23 (February 1992): 53–73.

31. Eric Hobsbawn, *The Jazz Scene* (New York: Pantheon, 1989), xliv–79; originally published under the name Francis Newton (London: MacGibbon and Kee, 1959).

32. Editorial, "Who's Got the Button," *Musician* 44 (March 1939): 54; transcript of interview with Mario Bauza, JOHP, pg. 24.

33. Gabbard, *Jammin' at the Margins*, 24–25.

Chapter 2

1. In his *The Story of Jazz* (New York: Oxford University Press, 1956), Marshall Stearns retells the story of the supposed naming of swing by the British Broadcasting System when, afraid that the hot jazz had too much of an immoral and perhaps racial connotation, it suggested their announcers call the music "Swing" (140). William Howland Kenney, in his discussion on the growth and popularity of black Chicago jazz in white neighborhoods in the 1920s, points out that many white civic leaders did not like the racial connotation of jazz and together with some dance club owners and musicians held a contest to rename it. The winning choice was "SyncoPep." Kenney, *Chicago Jazz: A Cultural History, 1904–1930* (New York: Oxford University Press, 1993), 78–80.

2. Cecilia Tichi, *Shifting Gears: Technology, Literature, Culture* (Chapel Hill: University of North Carolina Press, 1987), especially 15–96; David A. Hollinger, "The Knower and the Artificer," *American Quarterly* 39(spring 1987): 37.

3. The Watson quote comes from another excellent overview of the machine age, *The Machine Age in America, 1918–1941*, by Richard Guy Wilson, Dianne H. Pilgrim, and Dickran Tashjian (New York: Brooklyn Museum in association with Harry M. Abrams, 1986), 25. For contemporary assessments, see Staurt Chase, *Men and Machines* (New York: Macmillan Company, 1929); Henry Ford, "Machinery: The New Messiah," *Forum* (March 1928), 359–64; and Michael Pupin, *Romance of the Machine* (New York: Charles Scribner's Sons, 1930). There is an extensive

amount of literature from this period describing the hope and future of technological and human advancement; those selected here serve only as an example.

4. Daniel Joseph Singal, "Towards a Definition of American Modernism," *American Quarterly* (spring 1987), 7–26; Chase, *Men and Machines*, 335. See also Benjamin H. D. Buchloh, Serge Guilbaut, and David Solkin, eds., *Modernism and Modernity*, the Vancouver Conference Papers (Nova Scotia: Press of the Nova Scotia College of Art and Design, 1983), especially Guilbaut's "The Relevance of Modernism" and Henri LeFebrve's "Modernity and Modernism." For an excellent overview of modernism and mass culture, see James Naremore and Patrick Brantlinger, eds., *Modernity and Mass Culture* (Bloomington: Indiana University Press, 1991), 1–23.

5. George Gershwin, "The Composer in the Machine Age," in *Revolt in the Arts*, ed. Oliver M. Sayler (New York: Brentano's, 1930), 265, 268.

6. Walter Benjamin, "The Work of Art in the Age of Mechanical Reproduction," in *Illuminations*, ed. Hannah Arendt (New York: Harcourt, Brace, & World, 1968), 226, 228; Lawrence W. Levine, *Highbrow/Lowbrow: The Emergence of Cultural Hierarchy in America* (Cambridge, MA: Harvard University Press, 1988), especially 167–95; Joan Shelley Rubin, *The Making of Middle-Brow Culture* (Chapel Hill: University of North Carolina Press, 1991), xi–33; Russell Lynes, *The Lively Audience: A Social History of the Visual and Performing Arts in America, 1890–1950* (New York: Harper & Row, 1985), 1–26, 393–440.

7. Peter Wollen, "Cinema/Americanism/the Robot," in *Modernity and Mass Culture*, Naremore and Brantlinger, 54.

8. Alice G. Marquis, *Hopes and Ashes: The Birth of Modern Times, 1929–1939* (New York: Free Press, 1986), 10–12; Terry Smith, *Making the Modern: Industry, Art, and Design in America* (Chicago: University of Chicago Press, 1993), 1–11, 15–56.

9. Alan I. Marcus and Howard P. Segal, *Technology in America: A Brief History* (New York: Harcourt, Brace, Jovanovich, 1989), 133–34.

10. David Nye, *Electrifying America: Social Meanings of a New Technology, 1880–1940* (Cambridge, MA: MIT Press, 1991), 22, 156; Ronald C. Tobey, *Technology as Freedom: The New Deal and the Electrical Modernization of the American Home* (Berkeley: University of California Press, 1997), which provides an excellent overview of the effects of the New Deal on this modernization process.

11. Kenney, *Chicago Jazz*, 51.

12. Raymond Grew, "Modernization and Its Discontents," *American Behavioral Scientist* 21 (November/December 1977): 289–312.

13. W. Royal Stokes, *The Jazz Scene: An Informal History from New Orleans to 1990* (New York: Oxford University Press, 1991), 158–59; interview with Tiny Grimes, Jazz Oral History Project, Rutgers University, New Brunswick, NJ (hereafter cited as JOHP), handwritten typescript, 2; Erskine Hawkins, JOHP, transcript, 11.

14. Jimmy Maxwell, JOHP, transcript, 7, 13; interview with "Sir" Charles Thompson, JOHP, transcript, 140; Joe Williams, Hogan Jazz Archive, Tulane University, New Orleans, LA, interview excerpts, 1.

15. J. Fred MacDonald, *Don't Touch That Dial: Radio Programming in American Life from 1920–1960* (Chicago: Nelson-Hall, 1979), 10, 25–62; Marquis, *Hopes and Ashes*, 21, 27; Robert S. Lynd and Helen Merrell Lynd, *Middletown in Transition: A Study of Cultural Conflicts* (New York: Harcourt Brace & Co., 1937), 263; Lizabeth Cohen, *Making a New Deal: Industrial Workers in Chicago, 1991–1939* (New York: Cambridge University Press, 1990), 134.

16. For an interesting discussion of the debate concerning which musical culture should be featured over the airwaves in the 1920s, see Frank Biocca, "Media and Perceptual Shifts: Early Radio and the Clash of Musical Cultures," *Journal of Popular Culture* 24 (spring 1990): 1–15, which compares to Kathy J. Ogren's discussion concerning the debate over jazz during the same decade in *The Jazz Revolution: Twenties America and the Meaning of Jazz* (New York: Oxford University Press, 1989).

17. Dr. Thomas Tapper, "Has To-Day's Popular Music a Place in the Teaching Repertoire?" *Etude* 60 (April 1942): 243.

18. For an excellent overview of the rise of radio as a business medium, see Susan Smulyan, *Selling Radio: The Commercialization of American Broadcasting, 1920–1934* (Washington, DC: Smithsonian Institution Press, 1994), especially 93–124 (quote from 119).

19. Interview with Charlie Barnet, JOHP, transcript, 4–5. For an excellent overview of the factors that shaped the development and creation of jazz from the early twentieth century into the 1930s, see Burton W. Peretti, *The Creation of Jazz: Music, Race, and Culture in Urban America* (Urbana: University of Illinois Press, 1992), 155–56; James P. Kraft, *Stage to Studio: Musicians and the Sound Revolution, 1890–1950* (Baltimore: Johns Hopkins University Press, 1996), 73–74 (quotes from 128); David W. Stowe, *Swing Changes: Big-Band Jazz in New Deal America* (Harvard University Press: Cambridge, 1994), 108.

20. Eddie Sauter, JOHP, transcript, 178.

21. Smulyan, *Selling Radio*, 85–86; Artie Shaw, *The Trouble with Cinderella: An Outline of Identity* (New York: Farrar, Straus, and Young, 1952), 232–36; Sauter quote from Peretti, *Creation of Jazz*, 192.

22. Columbia University's Office of Radio Research, "Making a Hit," *Modern Music* 8 (January/February 1941): 90–97.

23. Columbia University's Office of Radio Research, "Making A Hit," 90, 97; advertisement, "Victor and Bluebird Record Artists Sweep *Metronome* Poll," *Metronome* 55 (July 1939): 15; Trummy Young, JOHP, transcript, tape no. 4, 8; Stowe, *Swing Changes*, 112–13.

24. Arnold Shaw, *The Jazz Age: Popular Music in the 1920s* (New York: Oxford University Press, 1987), 31–33; Stokes, *Jazz Scene*, 24–25.

25. Interview with Woody Herman, JOHP, transcript, 5–6.

26. Advertisement, "You Are the Soloist with Acompo Records," *Metronome* 54 (September 1938): 46.

27. Interview with Russell Procope, JOHP, transcript, 20; interview with Albert

"Budd" Johnson, JOHP, transcript, 14; interview with Buddy Tate, JOHP, transcript, 12–13; Edie Barefeild, JOHP, transcript, 7.

28. Gene Krupa, "Krupa Urges Study of Drum Rudiments," *Metronome* 54 (January 1938): 56.

29. Bill Crow, *Jazz Anecdotes* (New York: Oxford University Press, 1990), 107–8.

30. Interview, Eddie Sauter, JOHP, transcript, 33–34.

31. Kraft, *Stage to Studio*, 32, 59.

32. George Lewis, Hogan Jazz Archive, digest with excerpts, 25.

33. Stowe, *Swing Changes*, 114; William Howland Kenney, *Recorded Music in American Life: The Phonograph and Popular Memory, 1890–1945* (New York: Oxford University Press, 1999), 340–45.

34. Charlie Barnet, JOHP, transcript, cassette 1, 27; Bob Crosby, Hogan Jazz Archive, transcript, 7–8.

35. "America's Jukebox Craze: Coin Phonographs Reap Harvest of Hot Tunes and Nickels," *Newsweek* 23 (June 3, 1940): 49–50; Kraft, *Stage to Studio*, 78 (Dorsey quote from 78).

36. Miles Orvell, *The Real Thing: Imitation and Authenticity in American Culture, 1880–1940* (Chapel Hill: University of North Carolina Press, 1989), xv–xxii, 141–46, 154–58.

37. Eric Hobsbawn, *The Jazz Scene* (New York: Pantheon, 1989), 154–60; interview with Eddie Sauter, JOHP, transcript, 109. See Gunther Schuller's *The Swing Era* (New York: Oxford University Press, 1989) for a good introduction to the swing styles. Interview with Eddie Barefield, JOHP, transcript, 50.

38. John A. Kouwenhoven, *The Arts in Modern Civilization* (New York: Norton, 1948), 197–224. Kouwenhoven goes so far as to include a quote from Frederick Taylor's *Principles of Scientific Management* as proof on page 221; Martin William, *The Jazz Tradition* (New York: Oxford University Press, 1970), 11; Bud Freeman as quoted in *Hear Me Talkin' To Ya: The Story of Jazz as Told by the Men Who Made It*, by Nat Shapiro and Nat Hentoff (New York: Dover Publications, 1955), 323–24.

39. Lawrence W. Levine, "The Folklore of Industrial Society: Popular Culture and Its Audiences," *American Historical Review* 97 (December 1992): 1369–99. Paul Whiteman called jazz the folk music of the machine age in 1927, but others had given the music the label before this. Whiteman, "Folk Music of the Machine Age," *Literary Digest* 92 (March 26, 1927): 27. Gene Fernett, *Swing Out: Great Negro Dance Bands* (Midland, MI: Pendell Publishing Company, 1970), 11. Tichi argues that the bigness and functionalism of objects like the skyscraper helped define modernist America. Tichi, *Shifting Gears*, 289–90.

40. Horace M. Kallen, *Art and Freedom: A Historical and Biographical Interpretation of the Relations between the Ideas of Beauty, Use, and Freedom in Western Civilization from the Greeks to the Present Day*, vol. 2 (New York: Duell, Sloan, and Pearce, 1942), 832–34.

41. George Lipsitz, *Time Passages: Collective Memory and Collective Culture* (Minneapolis: University of Minnesota Press, 1990), 6–12.

42. Interview with Jimmy Maxwell, JOHP, transcript, 48–49.

43. Teddy Wilson, JOHP, transcript, 21.

44. Shapiro and Hentoff, *Hear Me Talkin' To Ya*, 313.

Chapter 3

1. Mario Bauza, Jazz Oral History Project, Rutgers University, New Brunswick, NJ (hereafter cited as JOHP), transcript, 19.

2. Terry Smith, *Making the Modern: Industry, Art, and Design in America* (Chicago: University of Chicago Press, 1993), 353–55.

3. Charles McGovern, "Consumption and Citizenship in the United States, 1900–1940," in *Getting and Spending: European and American Consumer Societies in the Twentieth Century*, ed. Susan Strasser, Charles McGovern, and Matthias Judt (New York: Cambridge University Press, 1998), 37–58, quote from 48.

4. Rita Barnard, *The Great Depression and the Culture of Abundance: Kenneth Fearing, Nathanael West, and the Mass Culture in the 1930s* (New York: Cambridge University Press, 1995), 3–11 (quote from 9); Robert S. Lynd, "The People as Consumers," in *Recent Social Trends in the United States: Report of the President's Research Committee on Social Trends* (New York: McGraw-Hill, 1933).

5. Susan Strasser, *Satisfaction Guaranteed: The Making of the American Mass Market* (New York: Pantheon Books, 1989), 5–19, 28–39, 95, 161.

6. Bernard Gendron, " 'Moldy Figs' and Modernists: Jazz at War (1942–1946)," in *Jazz among the Discourses*, ed. Gabbard (Durham: Duke University Press, 1995), 16–17.

7. Roland Marchand, *Advertising the American Dream: Making Way for Modernity, 1920–1940* (Berkeley: University of California Press, 1885), 117–234; Strasser, *Satisfaction Guaranteed*, especially 124–62, 285–88; Stuart Ewen, *Captains of Consciousness: Advertising and the Social Roots of the Consumer Culture* (New York: McGraw-Hill, 1976), 3–19, 81–102; Stuart Ewen and Elizabeth Ewen, *Channels of Desire: Mass Images and the Shaping of American Consciousness* (New York: McGraw-Hill, 1982), 169–225; Stuart Ewen, *All Consuming Images: The Politics of Style in Contemporary Culture* (New York: Basic Books, 1988), 57–85; Peter Wollen, "Cinema/Americanism/the Robot," in *Modernity and Mass Culture*, ed. Naremore and Brantlinger (Bloomington, IN, 1991), 61–63; Jackson Lears, *Fables of Abundance: A Cultural History of American Advertising* (BasicBooks: New York, 1994), introduction, 196–200, 225, 247–48.

8. Robert S. Lynd, "The People as Consumers," in *Recent Social Trends in the United States: Report on the President's Research Committee on Social Trends, with a Foreword by Herbert Hoover* (New York: McGraw-Hill, 1933), 2: 242.

9. Paul Alan Bro, "The Development of the American-Made Saxophone: A

Study of Saxophones Made by Buescher, Conn, Holton, Martin, and H. N. White" (Ph.D. diss., Northwestern University, 1992), 16–40.

10. Robert Cantwell, "The Magazines," in *American Now*, ed. Harold E. Stearns (New York: Scribner's, 1938), 350–55.

11. Ron Welburn, "Jazz Magazines of the 1930s: An Overview of Their Provocative Journalism," *American Music* 5 (fall 1987): 255–70; Robert Draper, *Rolling Stone Magazine: The Uncensored History* (New York: Doubleday, 1990).

12. Lears, *Fables of Abundance*, 334.

13. "Swingmaster," *Metronome* 53 (April 1937): 43; "Try the Benny Goodman Clarinet Mouthpiece," *Metronome* 53 (January 1937): 57; "Play the Trumpet Harry James Plays," *Downbeat* 9 (January 1, 1942): 5; "Benny Goodman Stars," *Metronome* 53 (April 1937): 8; "Get in the Swing, Play a King," *Metronome* 52 (June 1936): 10; "It's Tommy Dorsey Swinging with His King," *Metronome* 53 (October 1937): 12; "Buddy Rich, the New Sensation," *Metronome* 54 (June 1938): 41; "The King of the Drums," *Metronome* 55 (April 1939): 9; "Biggest News of the Year," *Metronome* 56 (January 1940): 3; "Babe Ruskin . . . uses Conn," *Metronome* 56 (March 1940): 28; Lears, *Fables of Abundance*, 322–24.

14. All advertisements from *Metronome*: "There Goes the Conn you wanted Doing PT Duty," 59 (January 1943): 2; "Johnny's Got A New Tune," 60 (May 1944): 28.

15. Lears, *Fables of Abundance*, 238–39

16. "New Triumphs for Benny Goodman," *Metronome* 54 (February 1938): 35; "Selmer Users Have the Advantage Even Before they Start to Play," *Metronome* 53 (June 1937): 43; "Yes! Buescher Players Are Definitely in the Money," *Metronome* 54 (March 1938): 38; "A Tremendous Hit in Both Swing and Sweet bands," *Metronome* 53 (February 1937): 9, "He Got His Start from a Music Dealer," *Downbeat* 8 (February 1, 1941): 4; "Why Can't I Get A Break," *Metronome* 56 (May 1940): 3; "Micro Products Pay Big Dividends," *Metronome* 54 (October 1938): back cover.

17. Lears, *Fables of Abundance*, 330–31; "Joe Doaks . . . He Knows Everything," *Metronome* 53 (September 1937): back cover; "Roth Band Instruments presents Johnny McGee," *Metronome* 57 (February 1941): 38; "5 out of 7 all star band WINNERS Play Selmer," *Metronome* 55 (January 1939): inside front cover; "Freddie Goes to Town," *Downbeat* 5 (February 1938): 27; You'll be 'Out Of This World' Playing the New Buescher True Tone 400," *Metronome* 58 (February 1942): inside front cover.

18. "The Tomorrow We Are Fighting For Today," *Downbeat* 11 (November 1, 1944): 7; "$25 After-The-War Purchase Bond," *Metronome* 59 (September 1943): 3; "Be Ready for that post-war Music Boom," *Metronome* 59 (December 1943): 3; "The Sax of the Future," *Metronome* 60 (February 1944): 35; "His Post War Planning is Built Around Martins," *Metronome* 61 (August 1945): 2; "One of These Days," *Metronome* 61 (February 1945): 3; "The Big Day Draws Closer," *Metronome* 61 (September 1945): 30. The expansion of the advertising industry during the war is an

interesting study unto itself. Jackson Lears points out how the Office of War Information was made ineffective and unnecessary by the success and ability of the War Advertising Council, which also helped usher in an age of unprecedented consumerism and advertising and the merging of business, sales, and entertainment. See Lears, *Fables of Abundance*, 249.

19. "As Modern As Tomorrow," *Downbeat* 3 (July 1936): 9.

20. Lears, *Fables of Abundance*, 314–17; Miles Orvell, *The Real Thing: Imitation and Authenticity in American Culture, 1880–1940* (Chapel Hill: University of North Carolina Press, 1989), 181–85; Roland Marchand, "Customer Research as Public Relations: General Motors in the 1930s," in *Getting and Spending: European and American Consumer Societies in the Twentieth Century*, ed. Susan Strasser, Charles McGovern, and Matthias Judt (New York: Cambridge University Press, 1998), 85–107, quote from 96.

21. Bro, "The Development of the American-Made Saxophone," 48–50, 153–156.

22. All advertisements from *Metronome*: "Uncle Harry Wasn't Afraid to Change," 60 (June 1944): 26; "It Was A Real McCoy in 1911," 53 (July 1937): back front cover; "Twenty-Three Skidoo," 53 (November 1937): 5.

23. T. Smith, *Making the Modern*, 159–62, 178–80, 384; "New Designs, New Features," *Downbeat* 6 (October 1, 1939): 8; "New Models on the Horizon," *Downbeat* 6 (August 1939): 15; "New Super '400' Saxophones," *Metronome* 58 (April 1942): 2; "The Sax of the Future," *Metronome* 60 (November 1944): 35; "Maccaferri's "Futurity'," *Metronome* 59 (March 1943): 2; "Soft Sweet Solid Unlimited Response," *Metronome* 60 (January 1944): 29; "Ciccone Symmetricut Reeds," *Metronome* 59 (January 1943): 3; Edmund Hall, Hogan Jazz Archive, Tulane University, New Orleans, LA, transcript, reel 1, track 1, 1.

24. T. Smith, *Making the Modern*, 375–78; "Maccaferri's 'Futurity,' " *Metronome* 60 (April 1944): 29; "The Buescher 400 Gives You a New Perfection in Brass," *Downbeat* 6 (September 1, 1939): 33; "Modern as a Streamliner," *Metronome* 8 (June 15, 1941): 7.

25. "Science Triumphs," *Metronome* 56 (April 1940): 4; "Precision means Perfection," *Metronome* 62 (July 1946): 2; *Downbeat* 5 (November 1938): 11.

26. All advertisements from *Metronome*: "A Micro Triumph," 51 (October 1935): 60; "Featherweight," 55 (August 1939): 11; "The Saxophone, Sensation of ALL Time," 61 (December 1945): 3; "Post-war plans for you . . . ," 61 (January 1945): 3; "Conn," 61 (October 1945): 2; "For An Age of Better Things," 62 (March 1946): 7.

27. Don Albert, Hogan Jazz Archive, digest, reel 2, 2; Doron K. Antrim, "The Deke Says More Than the King Have Abdicated," *Metronome* 53 (January 1937): 15; *New York Tribune*, October 12, 1938; Bro, "The Development of American-Made Instruments," serial number statistics, 62. What these numbers reveal is a tendency for sales growth as manifest by the changes in serial numbers from year to year.

However, this is not to suggest sales, for a number of factors skew the data: during the heyday period, no numbers were included for 1918 and 1919, and the sales during the 1920s came during a period of tremendous expansion of school musical education programs; the numbers from 1935 must take into account the abandonment of these programs and the economic crisis in general, and from 1942 to 1945 there was the change over to war production while still maintaining some sales. The numbers also do not reflect the expansion of musical sales of all instruments, the addition of new instruments, or the increased competition in the tight market of thirties. For the years 1916 to 1930, the serial numbers change from #35, 000 in 1916 to #237,800 in 1930, while 1935 begins with #263,500 and runs to #320,000 in 1947.

28. Andrew Bergman, *We're in the Money: Depression America and Its Films* (New York: New York University Press, 1971), outlines the formula films used during the thirties; Lawrence W. Levine, "Hollywood's Washington: Film Images of National Politics during the Great Depression," in *The Unpredictable Past: Explorations in American Cultural History*, by Levine (New York: Oxford University Press, 1983), 231–55; Lary May and Stephen Lasonde, "Making the American Way: Moderne Theatres, Audiences, and the Film Industry, 1929–1945," *Prospects* 12 (1987): 89–124; Lizabeth Cohen, *Making a New Deal: Industrial Workers in Chicago, 1991–1939* (New York: Cambridge University Press, 1990), tables 8 and 9 outline the existence of theaters in working-class Chicago.

29. Doron K. Antrim, "Here's How to Talk Their Lingo," *Metronome* 53 (April 1937): 13.

30. "Should Weber Withdraw All Musicians from Hollywood?" *Downbeat* 6 (January 1939): 10; James P. Kraft, *Stage to Studio: Musicians and the Sound Revolution, 1890–1950* (Baltimore: Johns Hopkins University Press, 1996), 88–97.

31. For a comprehensive listing of jazz in film, consult Leonard Maltin, *Leonard Maltin's Movie and Video Guide* (New York: Signet, 1994); David Meeker, *Jazz in the Movies* (New York: Da Capo Press, 1981); Krin Gabbard, *Jammin' at the Margins: Jazz and the American Cinema* (Chicago: University of Chicago Press, 1996),19–27, quotes from 22 and 26.

32. Robert P. Crease, "Divine Frivolity: Hollywood Representations of the Lindy Hop, 1937–1942," in *Representing Jazz*, ed. Krin Gabbard (Durham: Duke University Press, 1995), 207–28, quote from 209; D. Duane Braun, *The Sociology and History of American Music and Dance, 1920–1968* (Ann Arbor: Ann Arbor Publishers, 1969), 39–66; Neil Leonard, *Jazz: Myth and Religion* (New York: Oxford University Press, 1987), 167–73.

33. Paul M. Hirsh, "Processing Fads and Fashions: An Organization-Set Analysis of Cultural Industry Systems," in *Rethinking Popular Culture: Contemporary Perspectives in Cultural Studies*, ed. Chandra Mukerji and Michael Schudson (Berkeley: University of California Press, 1991), 313–33; Andreas Huyssien, *After the Great Divide:*

Modernism, Mass Culture, and Postmodernism (Bloomington: Indiana University Press, 1986), 21–26, 141–44.

34. John Tomlinson, *Cultural Imperialism: A Critical Introduction* (Baltimore: John Hopkins University Press, 1991), 126–31.

35. Geoffrey Nowell-Smith, "The Kanawa, Garland, and the Culture Industry, in *Modernity and Mass Culture*, Naremore and Brantlinger, 76–79; Michael Denning, *The Cultural Front: The Laboring of American Culture in the Twentieth Century* (New York: Verso, 1996).

36. For an introduction to Gramsci, see Roger Simon, *Gramsci's Political Thought* (London: Lawrence and Wishart, 1982). Richard Butsch, "Leisure and Hegemony in America," in *For Fun and Profit: The Transformation of Leisure into Consumption*, edited by Richard Butsch (Philadelphia: Temple University Press, 1990), 3–27, quote from 8; T. J. Jackson Lears, "The Concept of Cultural Hegemony: Problems and Possibilities," *American Historical Review* 90 (June 1985): 567–93; Walter L. Adamson, *Hegemony and Revolution: A Study of Antonio Gramsci's Political and Cultural Theory* (Berkeley: University of California Press, 1980), 174, although the whole book is an excellent overview of Gramsci's view of culture.

37. David Riesman, "Listening to Popular Music," *American Quarterly* 2 (1950): 359–71.

38. Interview with Teddy Wilson, JOHP, transcript, 22.

39. Alvin Frederick Levin, "Swing Marches On," *Musician* 44 (December 1939): 219.

Chapter 4

1. Lawrence Glickman, "Inventing the 'American Standard of Living': Race and Working-Class Identity, 1880–1925," *Labor History* 34 (spring/summer 1993): 221–35, quotes from 235; John Bodnar, Roger Simon, and Michael P. Weber, *Lives of Their Own: Blacks, Italians, and Poles in Pittsburgh, 1900–1960* (Urbana: University of Illinois Press, 1982), 115 outlines the basic nature of their study to determine how this process operated; James R. Barrett, "Americanizing from the Bottom Up: Immigration and the Remaking of the Working Class in the United States, 1880–1930," *Journal of American History* (December 1992), 998–1000.

2. Lizabeth Cohen, *Making a New Deal: Industrial Workers in Chicago, 1991–1939* (New York: Cambridge University Press, 1990), 1–10. 99–158; Lizabeth Cohen, "The Class Experience of Mass Consumption: Workers as Consumers in Interwar America," in *The Power of Culture: Critical Essays in American History*, ed. Richard Wrightman Fox and T. J. Jackson Lears (Chicago: University of Chicago Press, 1993), 135–62, quote from 152.

3. Michael Denning, *The Cultural Front: The Laboring of American Culture in the Twentieth Century* (New York: Verso Press, 1996), especially parts 1 and 2, 1–114.

4. Reeve Vanneman and Lynn Weber Cannon, *The American Perception of Class* (Philadelphia: Temple University Press, 1987), 3–15, 39–49.

5. Robert H. Zieger, *American Workers, American Unions, 1920–1985* (Baltimore: Johns Hopkins University Press, 1986), 3–20, quote from 10.

6. Richard Polenberg, *One Nation Divisible: Class, Race, and Ethnicity in the United States since 1938* (New York: Viking Press, 1980), 8, 16–18.

7. Robert S. Lynd and Helen Merrell Lynd, *Middletown: A Study in Modern American Culture* (New York: Harcourt, Brace & World, 1929), quotes from 59, 67, 72, 76, and 245; Bodnar, Simon, and Weber, *Lives of Their Own*, 117–19; Cohen, *Making a New Deal*, 184–201.

8. Robert S. Lynd, "The People as Consumers," in *Recent Social Trends in the United States: Report of the President's Research Committee on Social Trends* (New York: McGraw-Hill, 1933; reprint, Westport, CT: Greenwood Press, 1970), 814–20; Frank Stricker, "Affluence for Whom? Another Look at Prosperity and the Working Classes in the 1920s," *Labor History* 24 (winter 1983): 5–33; Irving Bernstein, *The Lean Years: A History of the American Worker* (Boston: Houghton Mifflin Company, 1960), 54–70; Allan H. Spear, *Black Chicago: The Making of a Negro Ghetto, 1890–1920* (Chicago: University of Chicago Press, 1967), reminds us that wages for black workers were far below these norms and, carrying through the 1920s, blacks remained underpaid and the last hired and first fired. See also St. Clair Drake and Horace R. Cayton, *Black Metropolis: A Study of Negro Life in a Northern City*, vols. 1 and 2 (1945; reprint, New York: Harcourt, Brace & World, 1962).

9. Robert S. Lynd and Helen Merrell Lynd, *Middletown in Transition: A Study of Cultural Conflicts* (New York: Harcourt Brace & Co., 1937), 7–75; Judith E. Smith, *Family Connections: A History of Italian and Jewish Immigrant Lives in Providence, Rhode Island, 1900–1940* (Albany: State University of New York Press, 1985). Smith argues that workers in the 1930s recognized that their work was changing and that technology was making their labor less necessary; this they also equated with the rise of chain stores and institutionalized culture.

10. Gil Evans, Jazz Oral History Project, Rutgers University, New Brunswick, NJ (hereafter cited as JOHP), transcript, 5–7; Gene Ramey, JOHP, transcript, 1–6; Reeve Vanneman and Lynn Weber Cannon, *The American Perception of Class* (Philadelphia: Temple University Press, 1987), 130–35, quote from 134.

11. Throughout much of the book these sources have been identified.

12. Count Basie, *Good Morning Blues: The Autobiography of Count Basie*, as told to Albert Murray (New York: Random House, 1985), 25–26; Jay McShann, JOHP, transcript, 2–4; Jess Stacy information in *American Musicians: Fifty-Six Portraits in Jazz*, by Whitney Balliett (New York: Oxford University Press, 1986), 156; Benny Goodman with Irving Kolodin, *The Kingdom of Swing* (New York: F. Ungar, 1939), 15–28.

13. Billie Holiday, *Autobiography* (1956; reprint, New York: Avon Books, 1976), 1.

14. George T. Simon, *Glenn Miller and His Orchestra* (New York: Thomas Y. Crowell Company, 1974), 20–26; Benny Carter, JOHP, 10; William Lee, *Stan Kenton: Artistry in Motion* (Los Angeles: Creative Press, 1980), 1–5; J. Smith, *Family Connections*, 71.

15. Lynd and Lynd, *Middletown*, 48–51; Vic Dickenson in *American Musicians*, by Balliett, 168.

16. Sam Wooding, JOHP, transcript, 1–20, 25–33, quote from 33; Doc Cheatham, JOHP, transcript, 1–20.

17. Nappy Lamare in *Stomp Off, Let's Go: The Story of Bob Crosby's Bobcats and Big Band*, by John Chilton (London: Jazz Book Service, 1983), 201; Willie the Lion Smith with George Hoefer, *Music on My Mind: The Memoirs of an American Pianist* (Garden City, NY: Doubleday, 1964), 12–13; Cozy Cole in *The World of Swing*, ed. Stanley Dance (New York: Scribners, 1974), 183.

18. Harry James in *Strike up the Band! Bandleaders of Today*, by Alberta Powell Graham (New York: Nelson, 1949), 84–85; Mel Torme, *Traps, the Drum Wonder: The Life of Buddy Rich* (New York: Oxford University Press, 1991), 9–16; Drew Page, *Drew's Blues: A Sideman's Life with the Big Bands* (Baton Rouge: Louisiana State University Press, 1980), 7.

19. Lynd and Lynd, *Middletown in Transition*, 56–58; Susan Ware, *Holding Their Own: American Women in the 1930s* (Boston: Twayne, 1982), 17, 142–52; Winifred Wandersee, "A New Deal for Women: Government Programs, 1933–1940," in *The Roosevelt New Deal*, ed. Wilbur J. Cohen (Austin: LBJ Library, 1986), 185–90; Alice Kessler-Harris, *Out to Work: A History of Wage-Earning Women in the United States* (New York: Oxford University Press, 1982), 250–72; Janet M. Hooks, *Women's Occupations through Seven Decades* (Washington: GPO, 1947), 27–167; Kenneth J. Bindas, *All of This Music Belongs to the Nation: The WPA's Federal Music Project and American Society, 1935–1939* (Knoxville: University of Tennessee Press, 1996), 86–95; Elaine Tyler May, *Homeward Bound: American Families in the Cold War Era* (New York: Basic Books, 1988), 37–57.

20. Viola Jefferson in *The Autobiography of Black Jazz*, ed. Dempsey J. Travis (Chicago: Urban Research Institute, 1983), 401–2; Holiday, *Autobiography*, 14, 20–31.

21. Clark Terry in *The Autobiography of Black Jazz*, ed. Travis, 457–58; Quentin Jackson, Sir Charles Thompson, and Willie Smith in *The World of Count Basie*, ed. Stanley Dance (New York: Scribners, 1980), 293–94, 336–37, 93–94; Andy Kirk, *Twenty Years on Wheels* (Ann Arbor: University of Michigan Press, 1989), 27–28; Carter, JOHP, 16.

22. Buck Clayton, JOHP, transcript, 2–24; Jay McShann, JOHP, transcript, 34–36.

23. John Simmons, JOHP, transcript, 34–41, quotes from 40–41.

24. W. Lloyd Warner and Paul S. Hunt, *The Social Life of a Modern Community* (New Haven: Yale University Press, 1941), 372–77; Artie Shaw, *The Trouble with Cinderella: An Outline of Identity* (New York: Collier Books, 1952), 53–54; Goodman

with Kolodin, *The Kingdom of Swing*, 31; Art Hodes in *American Musicians*, by Balliett, 381; W. Smith, *Music on My Mind*, 16–17. The connection to crime did not end in childhood for many in the swing world. As they came to be part of the jazz and then swing musical scene, most recall the control of the venues they performed in, especially in the early 1930s and in specific areas such as Kansas City, as being controlled by the mob or underworld. Many, including Eddie Durham, Irene Kitchens, and a host of artists in *Hear Me Talkin' To Ya: The Story of Jazz as Told by the Men Who Made It*, by Nat Shapiro and Nat Hentoff (New York: Dover Publications, 1955), recall with fondness their underworld employers, labeling them fair and loyal. For an excellent examination of the role the underworld played in the popularity and spread of jazz and swing, see Ronald L. Morris, *Wait until Dark: Jazz and the Underworld, 1880–1940* (Bowling Green, OH: Popular Press, 1980).

25. Duke Ellington, *Music Is My Mistress* (Garden City: Doubleday, 1973), 9; Sy Oliver in *The World of Swing*, by Dance, 130; Eddie Barefield in *The World of Count Basie*, by Dance, 312–13; Budd Johnson in *The World of Earl Hines*, ed. Stanley Dance (New York: Scribner's, 1977), 203.

26. Barney Bigard, *With Louis and the Duke: The Autobiography of a Jazz Clarinetist*, ed. Barry Martin (London: MacMillan, 1985), 8–9; Hoagy Carmichael, *The Stardust Road* (New York: Rinehart, 1946), 17; Cab Calloway and Bryant Rollins, *Of Minnie the Moocher and Me* (New York: Crowell, 1976), 16–17.

27. Eddie Miller in *Stomp Off, Let's Go*, by Chilton, 162–63; Jimmy Rushing in *The World of Count Basie*, by Dance, 18–19; Garvin Bushell as told to Mark Tucker, *Jazz from the Beginning* (Ann Arbor: University of Michigan Press, 1988),10–17; "Big T," in *American Musicians*, by Balliett, 162; Stuff Smith in *The World of Swing*, by Dance, 176; Goodman with Kolodin, *The Kingdom of Swing*, 3–17; James Lincoln Collier, *Benny Goodman and the Swing Era* (New York: Oxford University Press, 1989), 6–24; Arthur Rollini, *Thirty Years with the Big Bands* (Urbana: University of Illinois Press, 1987), 12.

28. Lynd and Lynd, *Middletown in Transition*, 47–50; Johnny Board in *The Autobiography of Black Jazz*, ed. Travis, 206.

29. Page, *Drew's Blues*, 5; : Dizzy Gillespie with Al Fraser, *To BE, or not . . . to BOP: Memoirs* (New York: Da Capo Press, 1985), 16; Vic Dickenson, in *American Musicians*, by Balliett, 168; Kirk, *Twenty Years on Wheels*, 4–7; Sammy Price, *What Do They Want? A Jazz Autobiography* (Urbana: University of Illinois Press, 1990), 14–15.

30. Lawrence O. Koch, *Yardbird Suite: A Compendium of the Music and Life of Charlie Parker* (Bowling Green, OH: Popular Press, 1988), 9–11; Holiday, *Autobiography*, 5–31; Carol Chilton in *The Autobiography of Black Jazz*, ed. Travis, 251–53.

31. Dickie Wells, *The World of Earl Hines*, by Dance, 2–3; Sandy Williams in *The World of Swing*, by Dance, 64–66; Cat Anderson in *The World of Duke Ellington*, by Stanley Dance (New York: Scribner's Sons, 1970), 144–49.

32. Jack Teagarden in *American Musicians*, by Balliett, 162.

33. Lee Collins, as told to Mary Collins, *Oh, Didn't He Ramble: The Life Story of Lee Collins* (Urbana: University of Illinois Press, 1989), 5–11; Ed Kirkeby, *Ain't Misbehavin': The Story of Fats Waller* (New York: Dodd, Mead, and Company, 1966).

34. Martin Williams, *The Jazz Tradition* (New York: Oxford University Press, 1970), 15; Elmer Snowden in *The World of Swing*, by Dance, 45–46.

35. William Howland Kenney, *Chicago Jazz: A Cultural History, 1904–1930* (New York: Oxford University Press, 1993), 37–38; Eddie "Lockjaw" Davis in *Jazz Anecdotes*, by Bill Crow (New York: Oxford University Press, 1990), 25.

36. Lee Collins, as told to Mary Collins, *Oh, Didn't He Ramble: The Life Story of Lee Collins* (Urbana: University of Illinois Press, 1989), 5–11; Ed Kirkeby, *Ain't Misbehavin': The Story of Fats Waller* (New York: Dodd, Mead, and Company, 1966).

37. Jimmy McPartland in *Voices of the Jazz Age: Profiles of Eight Vintage Jazzmen*, by Chip Deffaa (Urbana: University of Illinois Press, 1990), 150–52; Stan Kenton in *Stan Kenton*, by Lee, 8–13; Mark Tucker, *Ellington: The Early Years* (Urbana: University of Illinois Press, 1991), 46.

38. Kirk, *Twenty Years on Wheels*, 38–43.

39. Vanneman and Cannon, *The American Perception of Class*, 257; Rita Barnard, *The Great Depression and the Culture of Abundance* (New York: Cambridge University Press, 1993), 22–23;

40. Denning, *The Cultural Front*, 4–10; quote from 9.

41. Richard Sennett and Jonathan Cobb, *The Hidden Injuries of Class* (New York: Knopf, 1972), 75–100.

42. On aspects of the 1930s, the works that discuss the variety of Americanism are extensive and include Warren Susman, *Culture as History: The Transformation of American Society in the Twentieth Century* (New York: Pantheon, 1984); Alfred Kazin, *On Native Grounds* (New York: Reynal and Hitchcock, 1942); Charles Alexander, *Nationalism in American Thought, 1930–1942* (Chicago: Rand McNally, 1969); Lawrence W. Levine, "American Culture and the Great Depression," in *The Unpredictable Past: Explanations in American History*, by Levine (New York: Oxford University Press, 1993), 206–30; and Bill C. Malone, *Country Music USA: A Fifty Year History* (Austin: University of Texas Press, 1968).

43. Andrew Bergman, *We're in the Money: Depression America and Its Films* (New York: Praeger, 1974); Nancy L. Grant, *TVA and Black Americans* (Philadelphia: Temple University Press, 1989); Rhonda F. Levine, *Class Struggle and the New Deal: Industrial Labor, Industrial Capital, and the State* (Lawrence: University of Kansas Press, 1988); Alan Howard Levy, *Musical Nationalism: American Composers' Search for Identity* (Westport, CT: Greenwood Press, 1984); Francis V. O'Connor, *Art for the Millions: Essays from the 1930s by Artists and Administrators of the WPA Federal Art Project* (New York: New York Graphic Society, 1973); Richard Pells, *Radical Visions and American Dreams* (Middletown, CT: Wesleyan Press, 1974); Studs Terkel, *Hard Times* (New York: Pantheon Press, 1986).

44. James P. Kraft, *Stage to Studio: Musicians and the Sound Revolution, 1890–1950* (Baltimore: Johns Hopkins University Press, 1996), 114–35, quote from 114.

45. Lawrence Brown, JOHP, transcript, 13–14.

Chapter 5

1. Artie Shaw, *The Trouble with Cinderella: An Outline of Identity* (New York: Collier Books, 1952), 22–27; Maxine Sullivan, Jazz Oral History Project, Rutgers University, New Brunswick, NJ (hereafter cited as JOHP), transcript, tape 7, side B, 506; Trummy Young, JOHP, transcript, tape 1, 2–6.

2. Alan Kraut, *The Huddled Masses: The Immigrant in American Society, 1880–1921* (Arlington Heights, IL: Harlan Davidson, 1986), 115–16; Stephen Steinberg, *The Ethnic Myth: Race, Ethnicity, and Class in America* (Athenaeum, 1981), ii–x; James R. Barrett, "Americanization from the Bottom Up: Immigration and the Re-making of the Working Class in the United States, 1880–1930," *Journal of American History* (December 1992), 996–1020, details this renegotiation process.

3. Immigration statistics from Kraut, *The Huddled Masses*, chart, 76–77; Richard Polenberg, *One Nation Divisible: Class, Race, and Ethnicity in the United States since 1938* (New York: Viking, 1980), 18–19,34–39; *Recent Social Trends*, 1930, 22; John Bodnar, Roger Simon, and Michael P. Weber, *Lives of Their Own: Blacks, Italians, and Poles in Pittsburgh, 1900–1960* (Urbana: University of Illinois Press, 1982), table 2, 30; Drake and Cayton, *Black Metropolis: A Study of Negro Life in a Northern City* (New York: Harcourt, Brace & Co., 1945), fig. 2, 10, and table 3, 11.

4. *The Melting Pot* was used in 1909 as the title of a highly assimilationist play by Israel Zangwill. Robert Park, *Race and Culture* (Glencoe, IL: Free Press, 1950); Steinberg, *The Ethnic Myth*, 46–49; Stephen Meyer, *The Five Dollar Day: Labor Management and Social Control in the Ford Motor Company, 1908–1921* (Albany: University of New York Press, 1981).

5. Oscar Handlin, *The Uprooted: The Epic Story of the Great Migrations That Made the American People* (Boston: Little, Brown, 1951). For an excellent overview of the evolution of the historical assimilationist arguments, see Gary Gerstle, "Liberty, Coercion, and the Making of Americans," *Journal of American History* 84 (September 1997): 524–58, for the section on the Melting Pot theorists, see 529–32; Steinberg, *The Ethnic Myth*; Richard Gambino, *Blood of My Blood: The Dilemma of the Italian-Americans* (Garden City, NY: Doubleday, 1974); Nathan Glazer and Daniel Patrick Moynihan, *Beyond the Melting Pot* (Cambridge: MIT Press, 1970); Michael Novak, *The Rise of the Unmeltable Ethnics* (Macmillan, 1971); John Higham, *Send These to Me: Jews and Other Immigrants to Urban America* (Baltimore: John Hopkins University, 1975), 195–202; Gary Gerstle, *Working-Class Americanism: The Politics of Labor in a Textile City, 1914–1960* (New York: Cambridge University Press, 1989), 31–60; 331–35; Roger Daniels, *Coming to America: A History of Immigration and Ethnicity in American Life* (New York: Harper Collins, 1990).

6. Gerstle, *Working-Class Americanism*, 534–43. The historiography is voluminous: For a brief survey see Herbert Gutman, *Work, Culture, and Society in Industrializing America* (New York: Knopf, 1976); Lawrence Fuchs, *The American Kaleidoscope: Race, Ethnicity, and the Civic Culture* (Middletown, CT: Wesleyan University Press, 1990);Virginia Yans-McLaughlin, *Family and Community: Italian Immigrants in Buffalo, 1880–1930* (Ithaca: New York University Press, 1982); John Bodnar, *The Transplanted: A History of Immigrants to Urban America* (Bloomington: Indiana University Press, 1985); Thomas Kessner, *The Golden Door: Italian and Jewish Immigrant Mobility in New York City, 1880–1915* (New York: Oxford University Press, 1977); Werner Sollors, *Beyond Ethnicity: Consent and Descent in American Culture* (New York: Oxford University Press, 1986); and Kathleen Neils Conzen et al., "The Invention of Ethnicity: A Perspective from the U.S.A.," *Journal of American Ethnic History* 12 (fall 1992): 3–41.

7. Migration statistics from U.S. Bureau of the Census, *The Social and Economic Status of the Black Population in the United States: An Historical Overview, 1790–1978*, Current Populations Reports, no. 80 (Washington, DC: Government Printing Office, n.d.), table 52; Earl Lewis, "Expectations, Economic Opportunities, and Life in the Industrial Age, Black Migration to Norfolk, Virginia, 1910–1945," in *The Great Migration in Historical Perspective: New Dimensions of Race, Class, and Gender*, ed. Joe William Trotter (Bloomington: Indiana University Press, 1991), 22–27; R. D. McKenzie, "The Rise of Metropolitan Communities," in *Recent Social Trends*, 1930, table 10, 470, and table 5, 567; Drake and Cayton, *Black Metropolis*, vol. 1, tables 1 and 2, 8–9; Stanley Coben, *Rebellion against Victorianism: The Impetus for Cultural Change in 1920s America* (New York: Oxford University Press, 1991), 70–71; Ronald Takaki, *A Different Mirror: A History of Multi-Cultural America* (Boston: Little, Brown & Company, 1993), 240–52. There were, of course, a larger number of white southerners emigrating to the North and West during this period. While their numbers and stories are important, they are not necessarily part of the swing story, as many of their numbers would be more attracted to what was called hillbilly music until 1948. See Bill C. Malone, *Singing Cowboys and Musical Mountaineers: Southern Culture and the Roots of Country Music* (Athens: University of Georgia Press, 1993).

8. Jay R. Mandle, *Not Slave, Not Free: The African American Economic Experience since the Civil War* (Durham: Duke University Press, 1992), especially 44–57; T. J. Woofter Jr., "The Status of Racial and Ethnic Groups," in *Recent Social Trends*, 1930, 566; Washington quote from Takaki, *A Different Mirror*, 345; Charles Thompson, JOHP, transcript, 110–11; William H. Harris, *The Harder We Run: Black Workers since the Civil War* (New York: Oxford University Press, 1982), especially 51–76.

9. Joe William Trotter Jr., "Black Migration in Historical Perspective," in *The Great Migration in Historical Perspective*, ed. Trotter, 1–19; Bodnar, Simon, and Weber, *Lives of Their Own*, 4–5.

10. There are a number of studies; some of the best include Peter Gottlieb, *Making Their Own Way: Southern Blacks' Migration to Pittsburgh, 1916–1930* (Urbana:

University of Illinois Press, 1987); Joe William Trotter, *Black Milwaukee: The Making of an Industrial Proletariat, 1915–45* (Urbana: University of Illinois Press, 1985); David Levering Lewis, *When Harlem Was in Vogue* (New York: Oxford University Press, 1979); Jervis Anderson, *This Was Harlem: A Cultural Portrait, 1900–1950* (New York: Farrar Straus Giroux, 1981); James R. Grossman, *Land of Hope: Chicago, Black Southerners, and the Great Migration* (Chicago: University of Chicago Press, 1989); Allan H. Spear, *Black Chicago: The Making of a Negro Ghetto, 1890–1920* (Chicago: University of Chicago Press, 1967); Kenneth L. Kusmer, *A Ghetto Takes Shape: Black Cleveland, 1870–1930* (Urbana: University of Illinois Press, 1976); Russell Procope, JOHP, transcript, tape 1, 4; Garvin Bushell, *Jazz from the Beginning*, as told to Mark Tucker (Ann Arbor: University of Michigan Press, 1988), 15–16; John Chilton, *Who's Who of Jazz: Storyville to Swing Street* (Philadelphia, Chilton Book Co., 1972), 19; Burton Peretti, *The Creation of Jazz: Music, Race, and Culture in Urban America* (Urbana: University of Illinois Press, 1992), 39–75.

11. W. Lloyd Warner, J. O. Low, Paul S. Lunt, and Leo Strole, *Yankee City*, vol. 1, abridged edition, ed. W. Lloyd Warner (New Haven: Yale University Press, 1963), 43.

12. W. Lloyd Warner, *American Life: Dream and Reality* (Chicago: University of Chicago Press, 1953), 190–97; W. Lloyd Warner and Paul S. Lunt, *The Social Life of a Modern Community* (New Haven: Yale University Press, 1941), 222–23; Bodnar, Simon, and Weber, *Lives of Their Own*, table 17, 145.

13. For example, see Roy Rosenzweig, *Eight Hours for What We Will: Workers and Leisure in an Industrial City, 1870–1920* (New York: Cambridge University Press, 1983); Lewis A. Erenberg, *Steppin' Out: New York Nightlife and the Transformation of American Culture, 1890–1930* (Westport, CT: Greenwood Press, 1981); Elizabeth Ewen, *Immigrant Women in the Land of Dollars: Life and Culture on the Lower East Side, 1890–1925* (New York: Monthly Review Press, 1985); David Nasaw, *Children of the City: At Work and Play* (New York: Anchor Press, 1985); Robert W. Snyder, *The Voice of the City: Vaudeville and Popular Culture in New York* (New York: Oxford University Press, 1989); William H. Kenney Jr., *Chicago Jazz: A Cultural History, 1904–1930* (New York: Oxford University Press, 1995); Michael Denning, *The Cultural Front* (New York: Verso Press, 1998); Kathy Lee Peiss, *Cheap Amusements: Working Women and Leisure in Turn of the Century New York* (Philadelphia: Temple University Press, 1986), for an excellent overview on the affect and effect of migratory populations on early twentieth-century American society.

14. Kraut, *The Huddled Masses*, 116–17; Lisabeth Cohen, *Making a New Deal*, 11–50, tables from 18–20; Bodnar, Simon, and Weber, *Lives of Their Own*, 68; Gottlieb, *Making Their Own Way*, 208–12; Spear, *Black Chicago*, 228–29; Lynd and Lynd, *Middletown*, 463.

15. Kraut, *The Huddled Masses*, 118–20; William H. Kenney, in his Recorded Music in American Life (New York: Oxford University Press, 1999) discusses the rise and fall of these ethnic recording mini-empires; see 127–60. See also Ruth

Glasser's *My Music Is My Flag: Puerto Rican Musicians and Their New York Communities, 1917–1944* (Berkeley: University of California Press, 1995), 129–68; Cohen, *Making a New Deal*, 53–98; David Gerard Hogan, *Selling 'Em by the Sack: White Castle and the Creation of American Food* (New York: New York University Press, 1997), 38–46.

16. Kraut, *The Huddled Masses*, 114–15; Cohen, *Making a New Deal*, 50–58; Drake and Cayton, *Black Metropolis*, quote from 443; Michael Rogin, *Blackface, White Noise: Jewish Immigrants in the Hollywood Melting Pot* (Berkeley: University of California Press, 1996), especially 100, 121–56; Nicholas Tawa, *A Sound of Strangers: Musical Culture, Acculturation, and the Post–Civil War Ethnic American* (Metuchen, NJ: Scarecrow, 1982), 20–28; Kenney, *Chicago Jazz*, 88–95; Coben, *Rebellion against Victorianism*, 34–35, 57–59.

17. Susan Curtis, *Dancing to a Black Man's Tune: A Life of Scott Joplin* (Columbia: University of Missouri Press, 1994), 98–128; David Joyner, "The Ragtime Controversy," in *America's Musical Pulse: Popular Music in Twentieth-Century Society*, ed. Kenneth J. Bindas (Westport, CT: Greenwood Press, 1992), 239–48; Edward Pessen, "The Great Songwriters of Tin Pan Alley's Golden Age: A Social, Occupational, and Aesthetic Inquiry" *American Music* 3 (summer 1985): 180–97; Lawrence Levine, *Highbrow/Lowbrow: The Emergence of Cultural Hierarchy in America* (Cambridge: Harvard University Press, 1988), 169–242; Robert W. Synder, *The Voice of the City: Vaudeville and Popular Culture in New York* (New York: Oxford University Press, 1989); Neal Gabler, *An Empire of Their Own: How the Jews Invented Hollywood* (New York: Crown Publishers, 1988); Steinberg, *The Ethnic Myth*, 52–53.

18. James Lincoln Collier, *Benny Goodman and the Swing Era* (New York: Oxford University Press, 1989), 174 75; Teddy Wilson, JOHP, transcript, 44–47; Denning, *The Cultural Front*, 336–37; W. Royal Stokes, *The Jazz Scene: An Informal History from New Orleans to 1990* (New York: Oxford University Press, 1991), 887–89; Jimmy Maxwell, JOHP, transcript, 40–41.

19. Jimmy Maxwell, JOHP, transcript, 40–41; Teddy Wilson, JOHP, transcript, 8–9; Benny Goodman, in *Hear Me Talkin' To Ya: The Story of Jazz as Told by the Men Who Made It*, ed. Nat Shapiro and Nat Hentoff (New York: Dover Publications, 1955), 318–19.

20. Collier, *Benny Goodman*, 174; Cliff Leeman, JOHP, transcript, 52–54; Bob Blumenthal, "First-Person Memories of Swing," *Downbeat* 61 (July 1994): 18–20.

21. Shaw, *The Trouble with Cinderella*, 22–27.

22. Thomas F. Gossett, *Race: The History of an Idea in America* (Dallas: SMU Press, 1963): 253–408, quotes are from 286 and 407; Jimmy Maxwell, JOHP, transcript, 23–24.

23. John Simmons, JOHP, transcript, 37–39; Buck Clayton, JOHP, transcript, 25–28.

24. Lynd and Lynd, *Middletown*, 481–84; Warner et al., *Yankee City*, 415–23.

25. Steinberg, *The Ethnic Myth*, 256.

26. Collier, *Benny Goodman*, 295–303; Shaw, *The Trouble with Cinderella*, 90–91. Rogin's *Blackface, White Noise* provides an excellent explanation for this masking of ethnic identity and its role and influence within the Jewish cultural community; see 1–18, 73–120.

27. Steinberg, *The Ethnic Myth*, 52.

28. Gillespie, *To Be, or Not . . . to Bop: Memoirs* (Garden City: Doubleday, 1979), 16–17.

29. Shaw, *The Trouble with Cinderella*, 25.

30. Sidney Bechet, *Treat It Gentle: An Autobiography* (New York: DaCapo Press, 1978), 5; Garvin Bushell, Hogan Jazz Archive, Tulane University, New Orleans, LA, transcript, 45.

31. Lawrence W. Levine, *Black Culture and Consciousness: Afro-American Folk Thought from Slavery to Freedom* (New York: Oxford University Press, 1977).

32. Tawa, *A Sound of Strangers*, 1–125, quote from 25; Rogin, *Blackface, White Noise*, 73–120; Mary Lou Williams, JOHP, transcript, 87.

33. Jonah Jones, in *The World of Swing*, ed. Stanley Dance, (New York: Scribners, 1974), 161.

34. Sammy Cahn, in *A Sound of Strangers*, by Tawa, 162; Steinberg, *The Ethnic Myth*, 53–55.

35. Richard Pells, *Radical Visions and American Dreams: Culture and Social Thought in the Depression Years* (Middletown, CT: Wesleyan Press, 1973); June S. Sochen, *The Unbridgeable Gap: Blacks and Their Quest for the American Dream, 1900–1930* (Chicago: Rand McNally, 1972).

36. Goodman, *The Kingdom of Swing* (New York: Stackpole Sons, 1939), 15–23.

37. W. Smith, *Music on My Mind*, 10–22; Mary Lou William, JOHP, transcript, 109; Maxine Sullivan, JOHP, transcript, 494; Eddie Condon, *We Called It Music: A Generation of Jazz* (New York: H. Holt, 1947), 49–50; Fazola, in *Stomp Off, Let's Go: The Story of Bob Crosby's BobCats and Big Band*, by John Chilton (London: Jazz Book Servoce, 1983), 227–30; Jimmy Maxwell, JOHP, transcript, 25–27; Dickie Wells, *The Night People: Reminiscenes of a Jazzman* (Boston: Crescendo Press, 1971), 2.

38. Harry "Sweets" Edison, in *The World of Count Basie*, ed. Stanley Dance (New York: Scribner's Sons, 1980), 98; Eddie Sauter, JOHP, transcript, 51–65; Russell Procope, JOHP, transcript, 13–15.

39. Andy Kirk, *Twenty Years on Wheels* (Ann Arbor: University of Michigan Press, 1989), 14–15; Bushell, *Jazz from the Beginning*, 17; Charles Thompson, JOHP, transcript, 114–24.

40. Nappy Lamare, in *Stomp Off, Let's Go: The Story of Bob Crosby's BobCats and Big Band*, by John Chilton (London: Jazz Book Service, 1983), 201; Kirk, *Twenty Years on Wheels*, 46, 57; Jimmy Maxwell, JOHP, transcript, 28; Wingy Manone, *Trumpet on the Wing* (Garden City, NY: Doubleday, 1948), 12–13, 24.

41. May Kaminsky, *My Life in Jazz* (New York: Harper & Row, 1963), 2–3.

42. Gunther Schuller, *The Swing Era: The Development of Jazz, 1930–1945* (New

York: Oxford University Press, 1989), 564; Jack Teagarden, in *Jack Teagarden: The Story of a Jazz Maverick*, by Jay D. Smith and Len Guttridge (London: Jazz Book Club, 1960), 18–19.

43. Peretti, *The Creation of Jazz*, 76–99; Bill Davison in *The Jazz Scene*, by Stokes 18–19; Pee Wee Russell, "Even His Feet Look Sad," in *American Musicians: Fifty Six Portraits in Jazz*, by Whitney Balliett (New York: Oxford University Press, 1986), 132–33.

44. Lewis Erenberg, "News from the Great Wide World: Duke Ellington, Count Basie, and Black Popular Music, 1927–1943," *Prospects* 18 (1993): 483–84, 500–501; advertisements all from *Metronome*: "Roy Eldridge . . . Hottest of the Hot," 52 (November 1936): 38; "Benny Carter . . . ," 56 (January 1940): 21; "How Famous Drummers Set Up Their Outfits," 56 (August 1940): 5; "Sonny Greer . . . ," 56 (December 1940): 20; "Joe Jones . . . ," 56 (October 1940): 27.

45. Art Hodes, *Hot Man: The Life of Art Hodes* (Urbana: University of Illinois Press, 1992), 53–65; Jimmy Maxwell, JOHP, transcript, 30–34; Shaw, in *The Jazz Scene*, by Stokes, 94; Lena Horne, in *Hear Me Talkin' to Ya*, ed. Shapiro and Hentoff, 330.

46. Collier, *Benny Goodman*, 175–75; Teddy Wilson, JOHP, transcript, 5–7.

47. Gerstle, "Liberty, Coercion, and the Making of Americans," 552–53, details the this whitening process in the general terms of American history.

48. Budd Johnson, JOHP, transcript, tape 5, 2–7; Andrew Blakeney, in *Jazz Masters of the Fifties*, JOHP, 47; Milt Hinton, in *Hear Me Talkin' To Ya*, ed. Shapiro and Hentoff, 326–27; Kirk, *Twenty Years on Wheels*, 92; Doc Cheatham, JOHP, transcript, 125–29.

49. Kirk, *Twenty Years on Wheels*, 89; Benny Goodman in *Hear Me Talkin' to Ya*, ed. Shapiro and Hentoff, 318–19.

50. Frank Marshall Davis, "No Secret—Best White Bands Copy Negroes," *Downbeat* 5 (June 1938): 5; cartoon "For Musicians Only. . . by Danny," *Downbeat* (December 1937), 12; George Setzer, *Music Matters: The Performer and the American Federation of Musicians* (Metuchen, NJ: Scarecrow, 1989), 108–18; Donald Spivey, ed., *Union and the Black Musician: The Narrative of William Everett Samuels of Chicago Local 208* (Lantham, MD: University Press of America, 1984), 10–15, 30–49, 52–58; Edward Pessen, "The Kingdom of Swing: New York City in the Late 1930s," *New York History* 70 (July 1989): 277–308.

51. Roy Eldridge, in *Hear Me Talkin' To Ya*, ed. Shapiro and Hentoff, 328–29.

52. The idea of the maleness of jazz is something that has existed in the trades since the 1930s. For the best understanding of its role and meaning, see Neil Leonard, *Jazz: Myth and Religion* (New York: Oxford University Press, 1987), chapter 2; Peretti, *The Creation of Jazz*, 123; Linda Dahl, *Stormy Weather: The Music and Lives of a Century of Jazzwomen* (New York: Pantheon Press, 1984), 121; "She Scores with Chicago Musicians," *Downbeat* 6 (February 1939): 1.

53. For an excellent overview, see Nancy Woloch, *Women and the American Ex-*

perience, 2nd ed. (New York: McGraw-Hill, 1994), 220–80; S. P. Breckenridge, "The Activities of Women outside the Home," in *Recent Social Trends*, 1: 715–30.

54. William Leach, *Land of Desire: Merchants, Power, and the Rise of a New American Culture* (New York: Pantheon, 1993), 91–110; 298–315; Susan Strasser, *Satisfaction Guaranteed: The Making of the American Mass Market* (New York: Pantheon Books, 1989), 89–123; Woloch, *Women and the American Experience*, 382–410.

55. Woloch, *Women and the American Experience*, 384–93, quote from 389; Tracey M. Wilson, "Success and the Travelers Insurance Woman, 1920–1950," in *Work, Recreation, and Culture: Essays in American Labor History*, ed. Martin Henry Blatt and Martha K. Norkunas (New York: Garland Publishing, 1996), 3–16, quote from 5; *Middletown in Transition* records a number of occupations considered outside the woman's purview, see 183–86; Breckenridge, "The Activities of Women," in *Recent Social Trends*, 1: 717–29; Lynd and Lynd, *Middletown*, 73–89; Darlene Clark Hine, "Black Migration to the Urban Midwest: The Gender Dimension, 1915–1945," in *The Great Migration in Historical Perspective*, ed. Joe William Trotter Jr. (Bloomington: Indiana University Press, 1991), 127–46.

56. Susan Ware, *Holding Their Own: American Women in the 1930s* (Boston: Twayne, 1982), 12–35; Lois Scharf, *To Work and to Wed: Female Employment, Feminism, and the Great Depression* (Westport, CT: Greenwood Press, 1980), 86–109; Alice Kessler-Harris, *Out to Work: A History of Wage-Earning Women in the United States* (New York: Oxford University Press, 1982), 250–75.

57. One of the best overviews of the social role of women during the depression era and afterward is Elaine Tyler May's *Homeward Bound: American Families in the Cold War Era* (New York: Basic Books, 1988), 37–50.

58. Kathy Peiss, "Commercial Leisure and the 'Woman Question,'" in *For Fun and Profit: The Transformation of Leisure into Consumption*, ed. Richard Butsch (Philadelphia: Temple University Press, 1990), 105–17, quote from 111.

59. Kenneth J. Bindas, *All of This Music Belongs to the Nation: The WPA's Federal Music Project and American Society, 1935–1939* (Knoxville: University of Tennessee Press, 1995), 86–89; Carl Engel, "What Great Music Owes to Women," *Etude* 48 (November 1929): 797.

60. Bindas, *All of This Music*, 90–95. See also Susan McClary, *Feminine Endings: Music, Gender, and Sexuality* (Minneapolis: University of Minnesota Press, 1991), chapter 3; John Sheperd, "Music and the Male Hegemony," in *Music and Society: The Politics of Composition, Performance, and Reception*, ed. Richard Leppert and Susan McClary (Cambridge: Cambridge University Press, 1987), 151–63; and Christine Ammer, *Unsung: A History of Women in American Music* (Westport, CT: Greenwood Press, 1980).

61. The best sources for the role of women in jazz are Linda Dahl, *Stormy Weather: The Music and Lives of a Century of Jazzwomen* (New York: Pantheon Books, 1984); Sally Placksin, *American Women in Jazz: 1900 to the Present, Their Words,*

Lives, and Music (New York: Seaview Books, 1982); and D. Antoinette Handy, *Black Women in American Bands and Orchestras* (Metuchen,NJ: Scarecrow Press, 1981).

62. Both Dahl and Placksin provide excellent description of these and other all-women bands during the period. See Dahl, *Stormy Weather*, 45–135; and Placksin, *American Women in Jazz*, 86–99.

63. Quote taken from Placksin, *American Women in Jazz*, 89; *Downbeat* 5 (February 1938): 8.

64. Handy, *Black Women in American Bands*, 46–53; Rosetta Reitz, liner notes, *International Sweethearts of Rhythm*, Rosetta Records, RR 1312.

65. Dahl, *Stormy Weather*, 121–35; Jo Jones, JOHP, transcript, 182.

66. B. Jones, "For Musicians Only . . . ," *Downbeat* 5 (May 1938): 10; *Downbeat* 7 (July 15, 1940): cover, accompanied article "Ella Fitzgerald Mobbed by Crowd; Clothes Ripped Off," 1. George T. Simon's 1967 book, *The Big Bands* (New York: Macmillan Company, 1967), does little to dispute this idea that, while occasionally talented and part of the band, the women singers tended to be showpieces rather than musicians; see 33–39.

67. Mrs. Singleton, JOHP, transcript, 66–70; Helen Humes, JOHP, transcript, 68–69.

68. Mary Lou Williams, JOHP, transcript, 112–13; Helen Humes, JOHP, transcript, 44–45. See also Helen Forrest with Bill Libby, *I Had the Craziest Dream* (New York: Coward, McGann & Georhegan, 1982); Anita O'Day and George Eells, *High Times, Hard Times* (New York: Putnam, 1981); Peggy Lee, *Miss Peggy Lee: An Autobiography* (New York: D. Fine, 1989); and Robert O'Meally, *Lady Day: The Many Faces of Billie Holiday* (New York: Arcade Publishers, 1991).

69. Dahl, *Stormy Weather*, 79–96; Handy, *Black Women in American Bands*, 294–97; Sonny Greer, JOHP, transcript, 60; Andrew Blakeney, JOHP, transcript, 43–44; Gypsie Cooper, "Can Women Swing?" *Metronome* 5 (September 1936): 30. It is interesting to note that Cooper's invited article begins with her recognition that *Metronome* is a "man's magazine."

70. Placksin, *American Women in Jazz*, 127–33; Sherrie Tucker, "Working the Swing Shift: Women Musicians during World War II," *Labor's Heritage* 8 (summer 1996): 46–66, quotes from 48 and 57.

71. Tucker, "Working the Swing Shift," 48–58; Placksin, *American Women in Jazz*, 106–7; May, *Homeward Bound*, 58–91.

Chapter 6

1. "Bands Busting up Big," *Metronome* (January 1947), 58.

2. Marshall Stearns, *The Story of Jazz* (New York: Oxford University Press, 1956), 155–72; Gunther Shuller, *The Swing Era: The Development of Jazz, 1930–1945* (New York: Oxford University Press, 1998), 844–49; James Lincoln Collier, *Benny Good-*

man and the Swing Era (New York: Oxford University Press, 1989), 304–21; George T. Simon, *The Big Bands* (New York: Macmillan & Co., 1967), 31.

3. Bob Yurochko, *A Short History of Jazz* (Chicago: Nelson-Hall, 1993), 101–15; Eddie Barefield, Jazz Oral History Project, Rutgers University, New Brunswick, NJ (hereafter cited as JOHP), transcript, 48.

4. Ira Gitler, *Swing to Bop: An Oral History of the Transition in Jazz in the 1940s* (New York: Oxford University Press, 1985), 219–90; G. Simon, *The Big Bands*, 31, 316; Artie Shaw, quoted in "Shaw through with Dance Bands: To Play Longhair," *Downbeat* 16 (February 25, 1949): 1.

5. Mary Lou Williams, JOHP, transcript, 97.

6. Imiri Baraka, *Blues People: Negro Music for White People* (New York: Morrow, 1963), 13–18; Steven B. Elworth, "Jazz in Crisis: Ideology and Presentation," in *Jazz among the Discourses*, ed. Krin Gabbard (Durham: Duke University Press, 1995), 58–61; Gary Tomlinson, "Cultural Dialogics and Jazz: A White Historian Signifies," in *Disciplining Music: Musicology and Its Canons*, ed. Katherine Bergeron and Philip V. Bohlman (Chicago: University of Chicago Press, 1992), 64–79.

7. The best discussion of this debate comes from Bernard Gendron, " 'Moldy Figs' and Modernists: Jazz at War (1942–1946)," in *Jazz among the Discourses*, ed. Gabbard, 31–56. See also Krin Gabbard, *Jammin' at the Margins: Jazz and the American Cinema* (Chicago: University of Chicago Press, 1996), 103–23. An interesting side note to this debate comes from Paul Chevigny's study of New York City's cabaret laws, which governed how many musicians were allowed to perform in a specific venue. He argues that within New York City the ability of clubs to get permits for larger jazz bands became increasingly difficult after 1944, encouraging the development of sextets, quartets, and other smaller combos, out of which developed bebop. See Paul Chevigny, *Gigs: Jazz and the Cabaret Laws in New York City* (New York: Routeledge, 1991).

8. Robert D. Leiter's *The Musicians and Petrillo* (New York: Bookman Associates, 1953) is an excellent source for much of the Petrillo years, although the work is not a very balanced examination. Two more recent works, James P. Kraft's *Stage to Studio: Musicians and the Sound Revolution, 1890–1950* (Baltimore: Johns Hopkins University Press, 1996) and George Seltzer's *Music Matters: The Performer and the American Federation of Musicians* (Metuchen, NJ: Scarecrow, 1989), place the AFM's struggle within the context of worker-class struggles in this modern period and, while not specifically about Petrillo, place his leadership into a much more focused context.

9. Kraft, *Stage to Studio*, 111–16.

10. Barry Ulanov, "The Jukes Take Over Swing," *American Mercury* 51 (October 1940): 172–77.

11. "Any More Bands Today?" editorial, *Metronome* 58 (March 1942): 42.

12. Kraft, *Stage to Studio*, 130–36; Leiter, *The Musicians and Petrillo*, 120–31.

13. "Just Like Jack the Bear," editorial, *Downbeat* (August 1, 1942), 10; "Please: Government by request—not by Law," editorial cartoon (which portrays business

and Roosevelt prostrate to the king Petrillo), *New York Sun*, October 6, 1944; Kraft, *Stage to Studio*, 150–52; Coleman Hawkins, JOHP, transcript, 275–76.

14. Jimmy Maxwell, JOHP, transcript, 29–30.

15. "Decca First to Sign, Rest Set to Follow Suit," *Downbeat* 10 (October 1, 1943): 1;. Kraft, *Stage to Studio*, 152–58. See also Leiter, *The Musicians and Petrillo*, 132–42.

16. Scott Deveaux, *The Birth of Bebop* (Berkeley: University of California Press, 1997), 296.

17. Leiter, *The Musicians and Petrillo*, 149–59, 166–68; Kraft, *Stage to Studio*, 174–90.

18. Employment numbers from Kraft, *Stage to Studio*, 198–99.

19. Paul Eduard Miller, "Money Invested in Swing Music Will Keep It Alive, Says Miller," *Downbeat* 7 (April 15, 1940): 6; Otto Cesana, "Have Dance Orchestras Reached Their Peak?" *Downbeat* 9 (March 1, 1942): 9; Collier, *Benny Goodman*, 315–25; Tex Beneke, "Swing Was Never King!" *Metronome* 63 (February 1947): 20–21, 37.

20. Lillian Breslau, letter to the editor, *New York Times*, February 26, 1939, 4, 9:7.

21. Larry Clinton, "Swing Grows Up: A Prophecy for Things to Come," *Good Housekeeping* 107 (October 1938): 13; Beneke, "Swing Was Never King!" 21; Crosby quote from G. Simon, *The Big Bands*, 138; "The History of Jazz," advertisement for Capitol Records in *Metronome* 61 (December 1945): 2.

22. George Lipsitz's "Consumer Spending as a State Project: Yesterday's Solutions and Today's Problems," in *Getting and Spending: European and American Consumer Societies in the Twentieth Century*, ed. Susan Strasser, Charles McGovern, and Matthias Judt (New York: Cambridge University Press, 1998), 127–47, argues that the United States' federal policies after 1950 "favored a vision of consumptive practices aimed at eliminating the sites and social relations conducive to the emergence of social movements" (131).

23. Russell Sanjek, *American Popular Music and Its Business: The First Four Hundred Years* (New York: Oxford University Press, 1988), 3: 215–330; Patrick R. Parsons, "The Business of Popular Music: A Short History," in *America's Musical Pulse: Popular Music in Twentieth-Century Society*, ed. Kenneth J. Bindas (Westport. CT: Greenwood Press, 1992), 139–47; Steven B. Elworth, "Jazz in Crisis, 1948–1958," in *Jazz among the Discourses*, ed. Gabbard, 57–75; Lynn Spigel, "Installing the Television Set: Popular Discourses on Television and Domestic Space, 1948–1955," *Camera Obscura* 16 (1988): 18–22.

24. "Songs from Texas," *Time* (March 24, 1941), 36; George Lipsitz, *Rainbow at Midnight: Labor and Culture in the 1940s* (Urbana: University of Illinois Press, 1994), 204–6.

25. Still the best overview of the history of the music is Bill C. Malone's *Country Music U.S.A.*, rev. ed. (Austin: University of Texas Press, 1985); Bill C. Malone,

Southern Music, American Music (Lexington: University of Kentucky Press, 1979), 89–94; Kenneth J. Bindas, "Cool Water, Rye Whiskey, and Cowboys: Images of the West in Country Music," in *Wanted Dead or Alive: The American West in Popular Culture*, ed. Richard Aquila (Urbana: University of Illinois Press, 1996), 216–39; Kenneth J. Bindas, "Western Mystic: Bob Nolan and His Songs," *Western Historical Quarterly* 17 (October 1986): 439–56; Ray White, "The Good Guys Wore White Hats: The B Western in American Culture," in *Wanted Dead or Alive*, ed. Aquila, 135–59; James E. Akenson, "Social and Geographic Characteristics of Country Music," in Bindas, *America's Musical Pulse*, 45–52; Lipsitz, *Rainbow at Midnight*, 208–10.

26. Some of the best studies of the blues and its transition into rhythm and blues include William Ferris, *Blues from the Delta* (London: Studio Press, 1970); Charlie Gillett, *The Sound of the City* (New York: Pantheon, 1983); Michael Haralambos, *Right On* (New York: Drake, 1975); Robert Palmer, *Deep Blues* (New York: Penguin, 1981); Mike Rowe, *Chicago Breakdown* (New York: Drake, 1975); Helen Oakly Dance, *Stormy Monday: The T-Bone Walker Story* (Baton Rouge: Louisiana State University Press, 1987); Arnold Shaw, *Honkers and Shouters: The Golden Age of Rhythm and Blues* (New York: MacMillan, 1978); and Jon Michael Spencer, *Blues and Evil* (Knoxville: University of Tennessee Press, 1993).

27. George Lipsitz's *Rainbow at Midnight* does a good job of describing this process; Collier, *Benny Goodman*, 320; Charlie Barnet, *Those Swinging Years: The Autobiography of Charlie Barnet* (Baton Rouge: Louisiana State University Press, 1984), 138–39.

28. Barnet, *Those Swinging Years*, 151; Willie Randall, in *The World of Earl Hines*, ed. Stanley Dance (New York: Scribner's, 1977), 234.

29. Budd Johnson, in *The World of Earl Hines*, ed. Dance, 218–21.

Index